The Campus History Series

New York City College of Technology

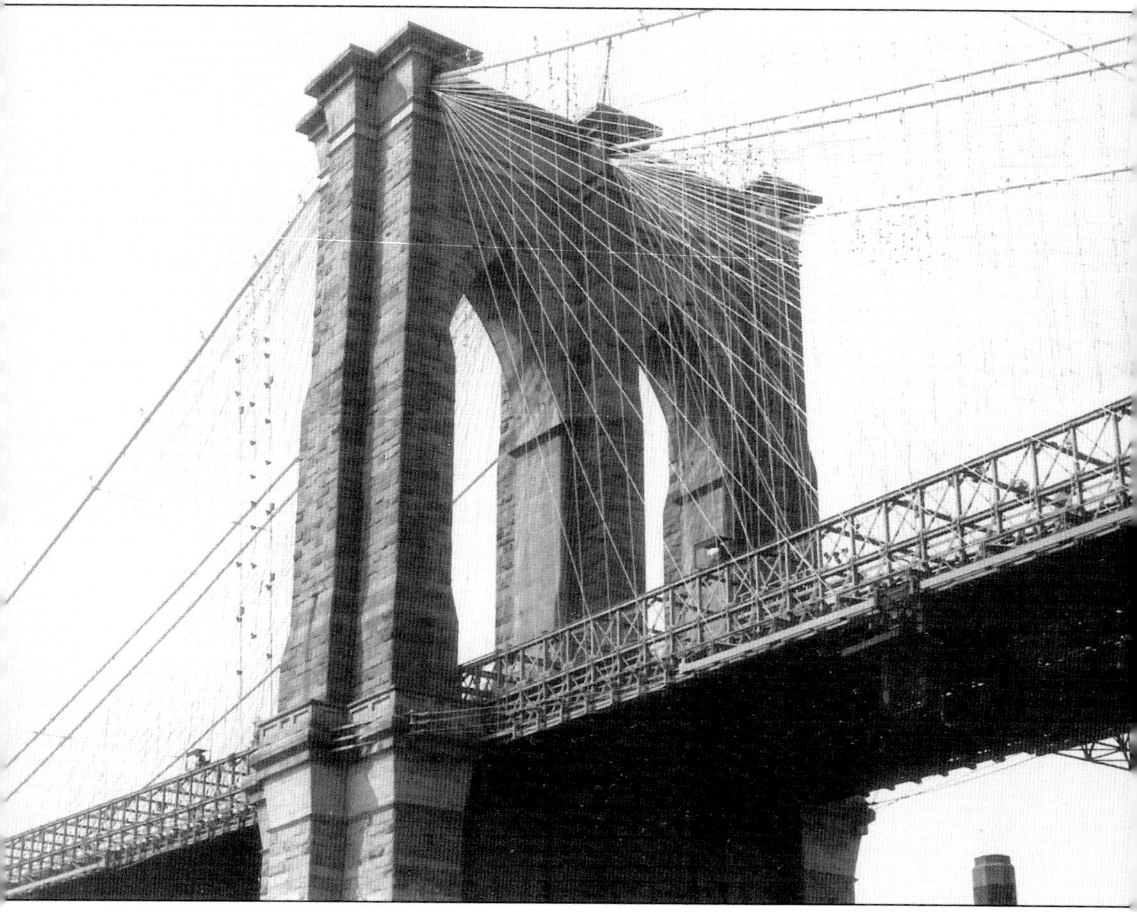

The New York City College of Technology is located at the foot of the Brooklyn Bridge on the Brooklyn side. A few years ago, the college was contemplating renaming itself Roebling College, named after Washington Roebling who was the builder of the Brooklyn Bridge. In the end, it was decided to change the name from New York City Technical College to New York City College of Technology.

On the cover: In the years following the World War II, returning GIs and others needed to be trained in the technologies to fill positions in the post-war economy. It was a critical mission and one for which a special type of college was needed. The New York State Institute of Applied Arts and Science was created with exactly this mission in mind. (Courtesy of the New York City College of Technology.)

The Campus History Series

NEW YORK CITY COLLEGE OF TECHNOLOGY

DR. MARTIN GARFINKLE AND DR. STEPHEN M. SOIFFER

ARCADIA PUBLISHING

ISBN 978-0-7385-4975-0

Published by Arcadia Publishing
Charleston SC, Chicago IL, Portsmouth NH, San Francisco CA

Printed in the United States of America

Library of Congress Catalog Card Number: 2006937592

For all general information contact Arcadia Publishing at:
Telephone 843-853-2070
Fax 843-853-0044
E-mail sales@arcadiapublishing.com
For customer service and orders:
Toll-Free 1-888-313-2665

Visit us on the Internet at www.arcadiapublishing.com

Dedicated to the 78,000 alumni who demonstrate every day the excellence and the value of a City Tech education. Steve Soiffer would like to dedicate this book to Pamela Ferner. If she wonders why, it's because every part of his life that she touches is the better for it. Martin Garfinkle would like to dedicate the book to Caryn Garfinkle and will simply repeat Steve Soiffer's eloquent words.

CONTENTS

ACKNOWLEDGMENTS

This book could not have happened without the efforts and hard work of Limor Garfinkle, who is a student at the New York City College of Technology and the daughter-in-law of Martin Garfinkle. Limor worked tirelessly to make the pictures we chose appropriate for this book, using the skills that she has learned in the Advertising Design and Graphic Arts Program. She did the layout of the book. In total, the hours she put into this book exceeded the amount of time she would have spent in class.

We also want to thank all of these individuals who contributed to and donated pictures to this book, Professors Nick Manos, Leonard Friedman, Julia Jordan, Albert Sherman, Pam Beck, Carmen Negron, Van Ford, and Justine Pawlukewicz. Prof. Robin Michals was extremely helpful in capturing digital images from aging photographs. A special thank you goes to Keith Muchowski, New York City College of Technology archivist, who went above and beyond in making the archives of the college accessible to us. Without him, we could not have accomplished what we did. Quite a few of the current photographs were taken by Alberto Vargas of the College Office of Image and Visual Communication ,and others were from the photograph archives maintained by Dale Tarnowieski of the Communications Office. Their help was very much appreciated. Special thanks to our editor Erin Vosgien and our proofreader Sara Desharnais from Arcadia Publishing. We are grateful for the assistance of Julie May, photo archivist of the Brooklyn Historical Society.

FOREWORD

It is a pleasure to provide the introduction to this photographic history of New York City College of Technology on the occasion of its 60th anniversary.

The Namm family's association with this remarkable school dates back to its founding in 1946 as the New York State Institute of Applied Arts and Sciences. I first learned of the new institute from my late father, Maj. Benjamin H. Namm, around the family dinner table shortly after my discharge from the U.S. Navy. Few topics enjoyed as much conversation, except perhaps how the Brooklyn Dodgers were doing that season and the impending doubling of the New York City transit fare from a nickel to a dime.

My father owned and operated a major department store on Brooklyn's busy Fulton Street and also served as president of the National Retail Merchants Association. A veteran of World War I, he longed to do something to help the young men and women who would be returning to civilian life from active duty in World War II. The wartime effort was producing a host of new inventions, industrial processes, manufacturing and other technologies that would characterize the post-war economy and the millions of new jobs it would create. But these jobs would demand specialized skills lacked by many returning service personnel.

My father had the notion that New York State should offer them a college-level general education and comprehensive training in the new and emerging technologies of the era under the GI Bill. He took the idea to Gov. Thomas E. Dewey, who liked it a lot and set in motion a process that led to the establishment of the institute in an empty warehouse on downtown Brooklyn's Pearl Street and at other borough locations. Of course, dad got more than he asked for, when Governor Dewey requested that he serve as first chairman of the institute's board of trustees, a position he held until 1964.

On the first day of classes in February 1947, nearly 240 veterans and other students were enrolled in the 20 classes offered by the institute's four Departments of Chemical, Electrical, Mechanical, and Structural Technology. I soon went off to school out of state, but spoke with my parents regularly. The conversations with dad always included talk about his work at the institute. He relied on me to provide him with my perspective on the stresses and special needs confronting college students. I must have done a fairly decent job, because he incorporated some of my suggestions into his work with the school. My father died in 1969, but lived to see Mayor Robert F. Wagner break ground in 1964 for a new, 11-story academic building bearing dad's name and the opening of the new Jay Street facility shortly before his death.

My first active involvement with the New York City College of Technology began with a phone call in 1980 from then Pres. Ursula C. Schwerin, who asked me to join a group she was putting together to create a foundation to benefit students. I wasn't looking for more activities, but Schwerin was insistent and effectively countered every obstacle I put up. She added that she also wanted me to serve as the foundation's first chairman, a job I didn't seek or expect. While Schwerin also prevailed in that request, I did step down as chairman when she retired in the late 1980s, but remain an active member of the board as chairman emeritus.

Now 27 years after my board service began, I am pleased with what the New York City College of Technology has achieved and see a college with enormous potential for the future. Nearly three years ago, Dr. Russell K. Hotzler was named president by the City University of New York's (CUNY) Board of Trustees. This was a terrific break for the college, because he brought to the job nearly 30 years of administrative and academic experience at CUNY. The work that he is doing to expand and further strengthen the New York City College of Technology's academic programs, enlarge and support its talented faculty, fully integrate 21st century instructional technology into its classrooms and labs, and modernize its physical plant deserves the highest commendation. And with notable skill, he is shepherding plans for the construction of a new state-of-the-art academic building in CUNY's first public-private partnership with a world-class developer.

A few years ago, I had the pleasure of lunching on campus with Thomas E. Dewey Jr. We talked about our fathers and the roles they played in the founding and early nurturing of this remarkable school. At the conclusion of our luncheon and tour of the New York City College of Technology facilities, we agreed that our dads would be proud of what their efforts had helped produce and that we were very proud of them for what they had done.

In addition to helping coordinate a scholarship program funded by the Namm and Doran Families, I recently recommended a student to the college after he told me that the New York City College of Technology was just what he needed to prepare for his career of choice. He asked me how he could thank me for my help. I asked him never to forget what the New York City College of Technology was doing for him and to give back to his alma mater in every possible way following graduation.

Andrew I. Namm
Chairman Emeritus
New York City College of Technology Foundation

INTRODUCTION

The evolution of the New York City College of Technology, also known as City Tech, over the past 60 years correlates closely with the phenomenal transformation and economic growth experienced by the great city it serves. As you will learn from the pages of this book, the college was founded in 1946, under the name "New York State Institute of Applied Arts and Sciences," the urgent mission at the time was to provide technical and clinical training to GIs returning from the World War II and to provide New York with the proficient workforce it would need to thrive in the emerging post-war economy.

No one could have predicted the transformation that the college has experienced. From its beginnings as an institute, to being chartered as a community college, and subsequently transitioning to senior college status, it has grown from serving 234 students in the class of 1947, to a population today of over 13,300 students—4,000 in baccalaureate degree programs. The college's mission, however, has not changed—it is still urgent and it is still focused on developing a technically proficient workforce and well-educated citizens who can prosper in a world that has become flat, fast, and unforgiving to those who are not educationally prepared.

While technologies have changed and professions have been transformed, what is at the heart of the New York City College of Technology remains constant: our basic educational approach. The New York City College of Technology is a place where dedicated faculty, many joining us after successful professional careers in their chosen fields, work side-by-side with students in classroom and laboratory settings. The college was founded as a beacon of opportunity available to those who might not otherwise have access to higher education, and it still performs this function today. And just as was true on the chilly morning in February when the college opened its doors, we strive to have one foot in the present and one in the future—preparing our students for careers and opportunities we cannot yet imagine.

Russell K. Hotzler
President

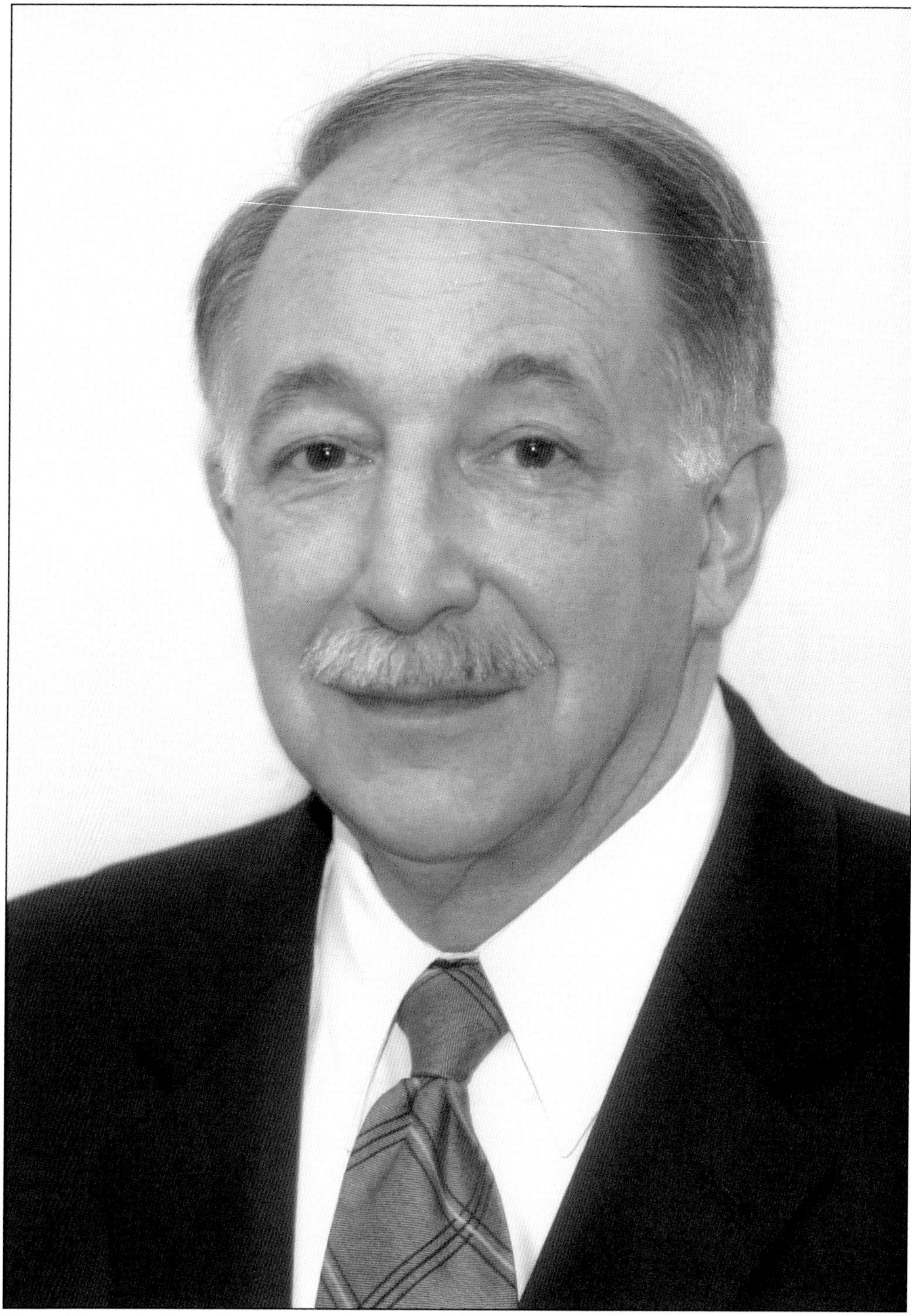

Since his arrival at the New York City College of Technology in 2004, Pres. Russell Hotzler has led a remarkable period of development, expansion, and recognition. President Hotzler's administration has already added considerable luster to the image of the college.

One

The Trade School Movement and the Voorhees Institute of Technology 1880–1970

This is the story of New York City College of Technology, the senior college of technology of The City University of New York, popularly known as City Tech. It is a distinctive college with an altogether unique history. As will be seen in the next chapter, the college was started as the New York State Institute of Applied Arts and Sciences. Its first class, in 1947, had 234 students. In the fall of 2006, the college had 13,370 students, including about 4,000 in the upper two years of their bachelor's degree programs. It is recognized today as among the foremost engines of high-tech workforce development for the largest city in the country. It has come a long way.

In 2006–2007, the college celebrates its 60th anniversary. Yet the college has also acquired a heritage that stretches much further into the past. In 1971, the college merged with the formerly independent Voorhees Institute of Technology, which had a much longer history, from its founding in 1880. Thus the college has acquired, by marriage as it were, a history that begins in the 19th century, at a pivotal point in American history. And it is with this earlier history that the story begins.

The Voorhees Institute of Technology had a unique history, starting as the tiny Technical Schools of the Metropolitan Museum, in a back room of the Metropolitan Museum of Art. It soon became the Trade School of New York, in a separate building of its own and with a mission much more extensive than serving the technical needs of the museum.

The year of its founding is important, since it represents the start of one of the most active periods of immigration into the United States. From 1880 until the racist reactions to Asian and other immigrants in the period before World War I, the United States provided a haven for the millions of immigrants—the large majority from western and southern Europe—who flocked to these shores in search of a better future than a seemingly worn-out Europe offered. These new immigrants were largely the clientele of the trade schools that sprang up in every major city to which they were attracted.

The trade school movement was the joint effort of union leaders such as the legendary Samuel Gompers, founder of the American Federation of Labor, and major philanthropists like J. P. Morgan, who endowed what was then a large sum on the new Trade School of New York. Philanthropists saw the trade schools as a way to integrate new immigrants into the U.S. industrial economy and worked together with civic reformers like the members of the Women's Christian Temperance Union to "civilize" the new immigrants, teaching them the Protestant-based work ethic, temperance, respect for time clocks, and, above all, how to be productive workers. The interests of the wealthy, the civic reformers, and the labor movement all came together in the trade schools, and what was later to become the Voorhees Institute of Technology was a perfect example.

The Trade School of New York prepared its students for the types of employment that were made important by the full-blown industrial revolution that reached maturity in the period after the Civil War. Some of these pictures show students learning to become electrical engineers, in precisely the era when Thomas A. Edison opened a commercial electric station in New York City with approximately 85 customers. Sign painters were much in demand as factories and retail establishments expanded. Mechanics were needed for the trolleys, the subways, and later the automobiles that moved people in the bustling urban center. The construction trades absorbed thousands of trained men as housing was built for the waves of new immigrants, remaking the urban landscape.

One should note in the pictures that follow that almost all of the students shown in this section are men and almost all are white. While the trade school movement was inclusionary, designed to integrate new immigrants into the economy, it was not universal. The Voorhees Institute of Technology, the name adopted by the Trade School of New York in 1961 to honor Enders M. Voorhees, a prominent industrialist, did not admit its first women until 1965, less than a decade before its demise.

The trade school movement was important in its time, but it was also bound by that time. As the vision of universal education swept American culture, the trade schools were institutions that had outlived their mission. The New York City College of Technology is proud that it can incorporate this important piece of American history into its own. The pictures in this chapter will present the flavor of the trade school, and allow one to see how far education for the technical professions, still a part of the mission of the New York City College of Technology, has come.

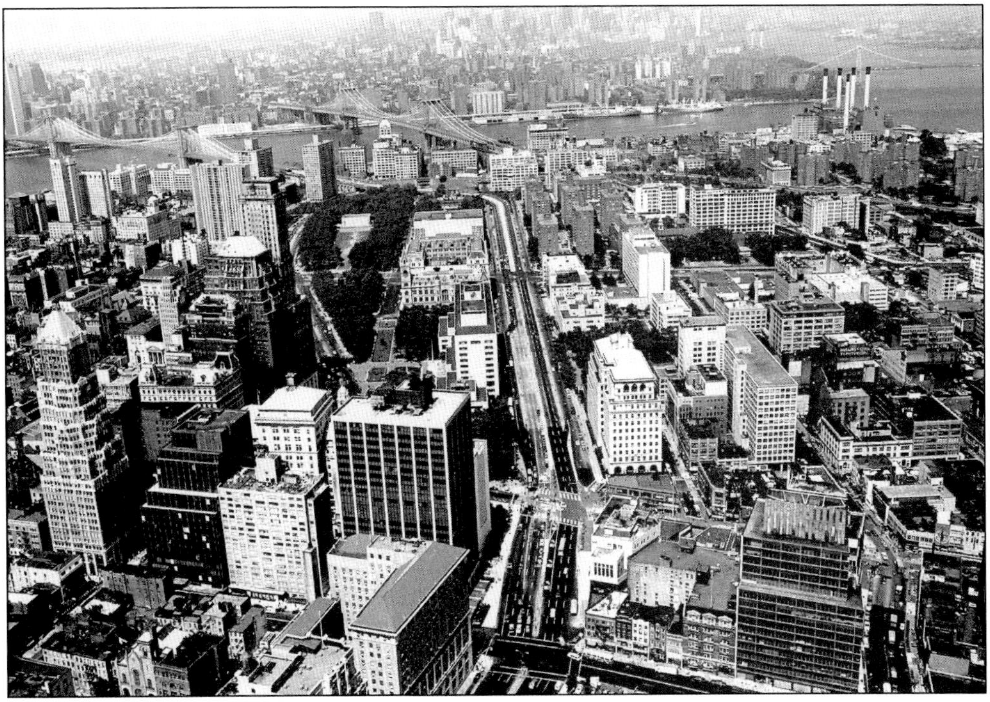

This picture depicts downtown Brooklyn today, showing both the Brooklyn and Manhattan Bridge to the west. The New York City College of Technology is located conveniently between both of these bridges. This scene is vastly different from the Brooklyn of earlier times.

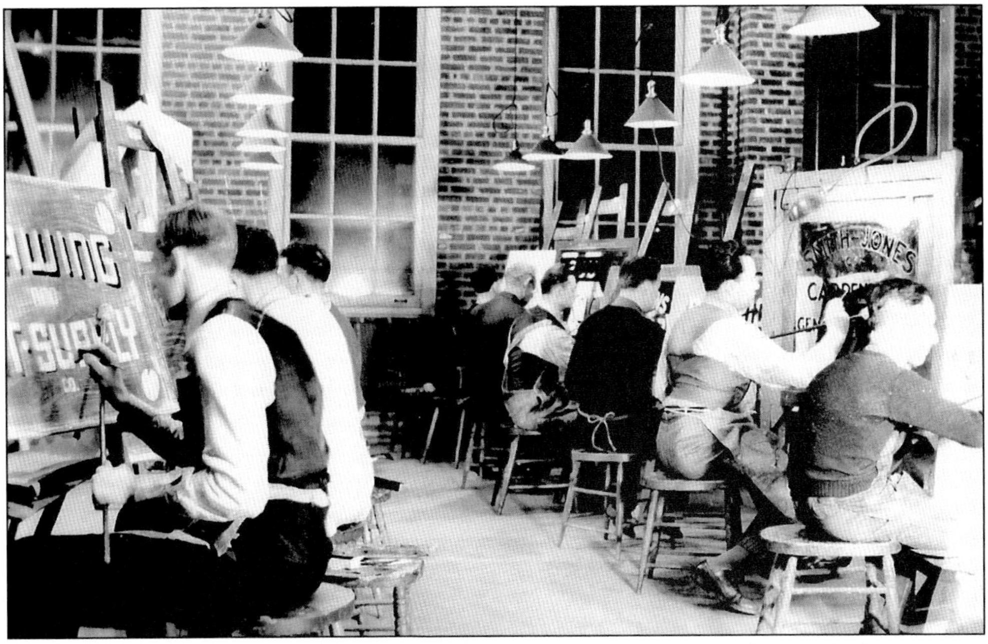

This picture from the 1890s shows men learning sign painting. Sign painting was an important trade during the late 18th century since computers and mass production did not exist then. Notice that some of the men were wearing vests, which was quite common during this era.

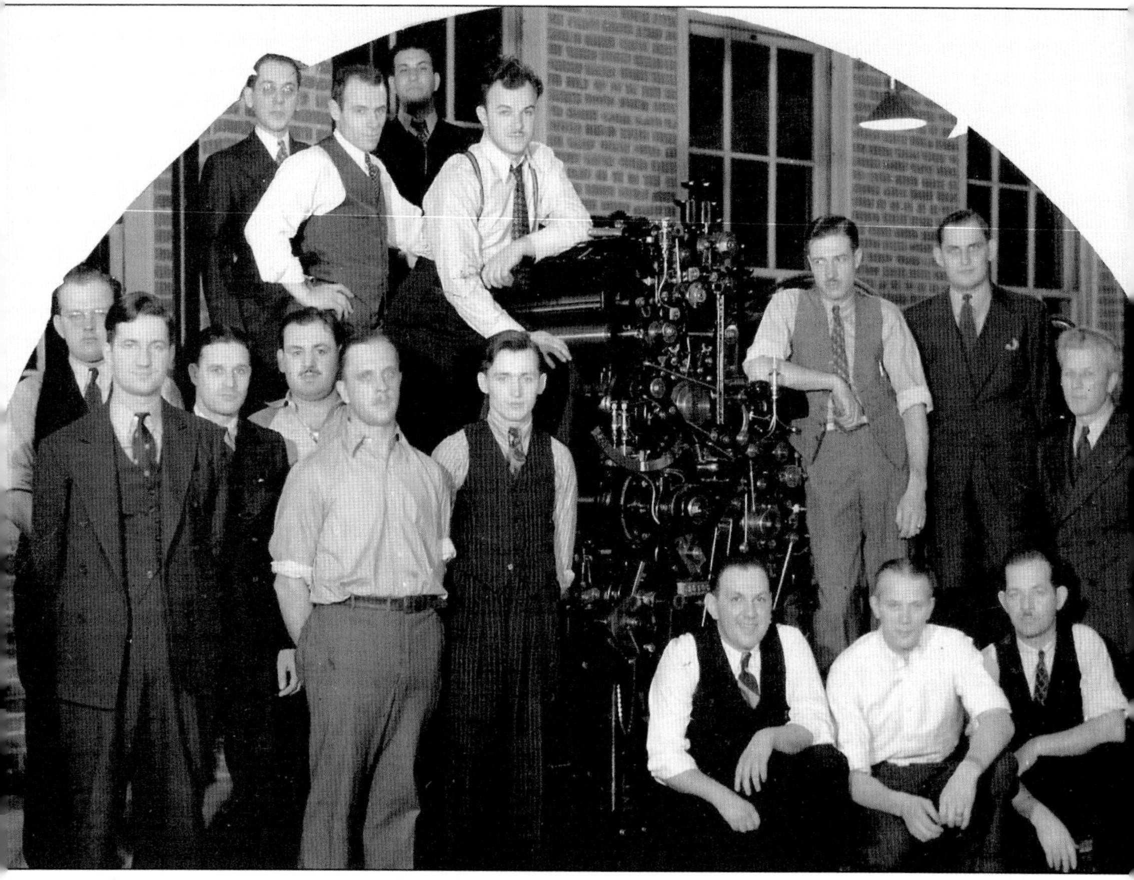

This *c.* 1890 picture was found in the archives, and is no doubt from the Voorhees Institute of Technology era. Notice that the men were in formal dress for class, a far cry from the relaxed styles that characterize higher education today. They seem to be standing in front of a printing press. The lithographic arts taught in this period have been largely replaced by computer-based layout and typesetting.

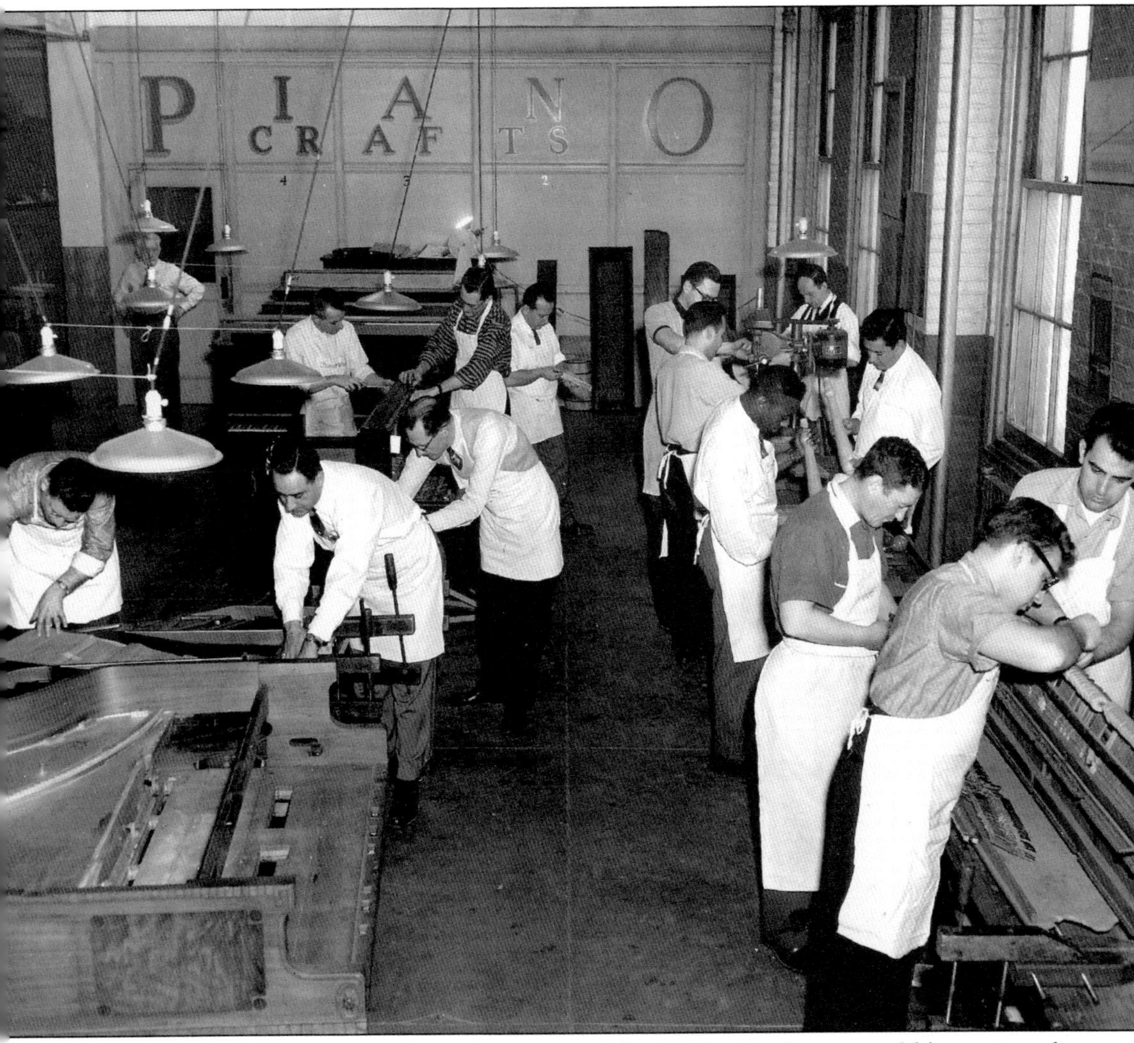

Displayed here is a piano crafting class around the 1890s. Students would be assigned the task of working together to construct a piano. It is possible that one class would complete a piano, but several classes could be assigned the task of completing one or several pianos. It is reasonable to assume that each student was taught a number of different tasks in order to learn the trade of piano crafting.

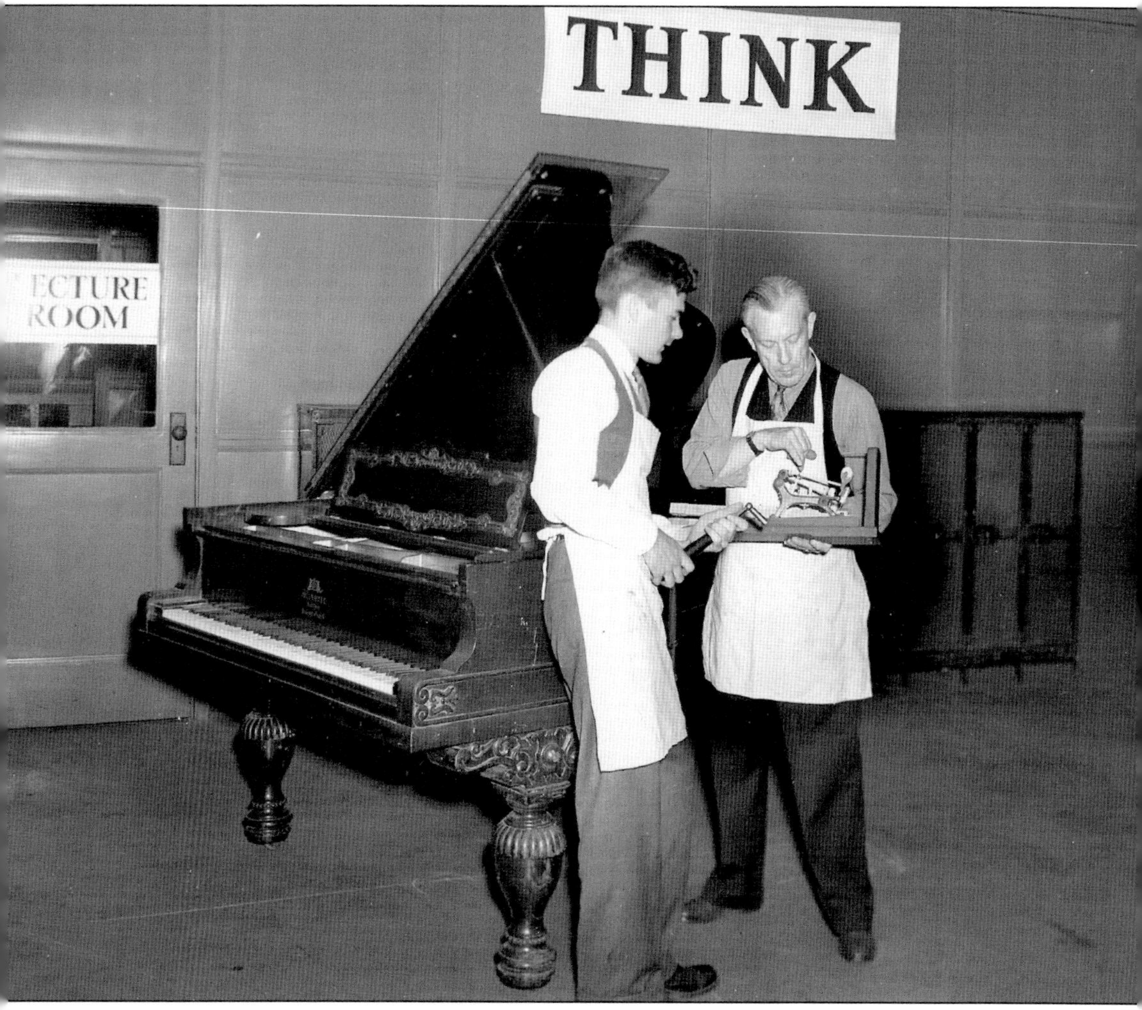

A completed product is shown here. Notice how ornate this piano is. The legs as well as parts of the body of the piano had the look of the arts and crafts period. This piano was probably built during the later part of the 19th century. Note that the piano is sitting outside of the lecture room.

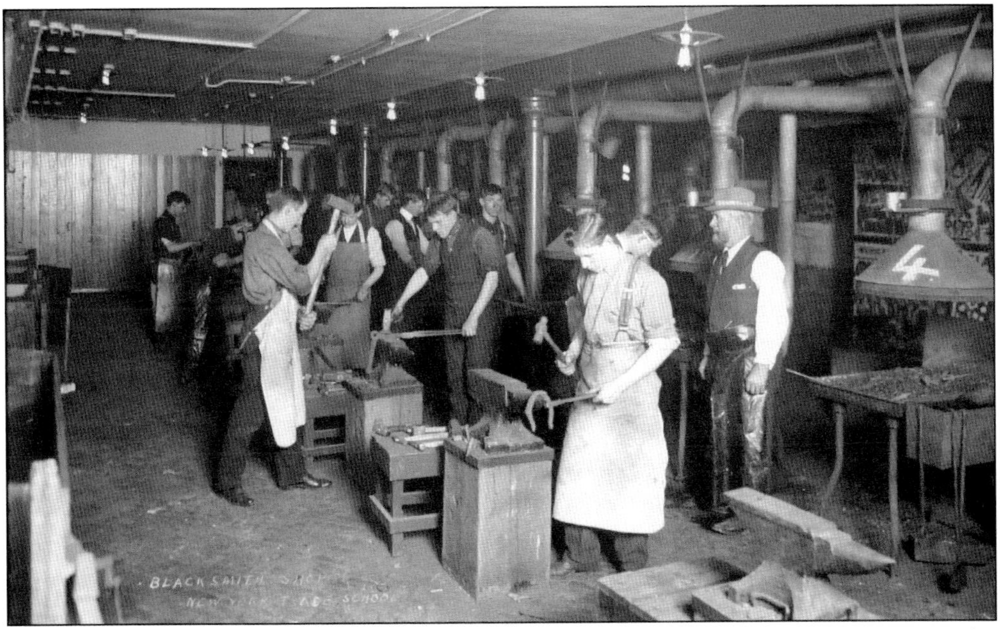

These students are learning the blacksmith trade. During the late 19th century, the automobile was not yet the dominant mode of transportation. The first gasoline automobile was sold in the United States in 1896, and before that, the primary mode of private transportation was the horse and buggy. Blacksmithing was a very lucrative trade, although there was considerable competition.

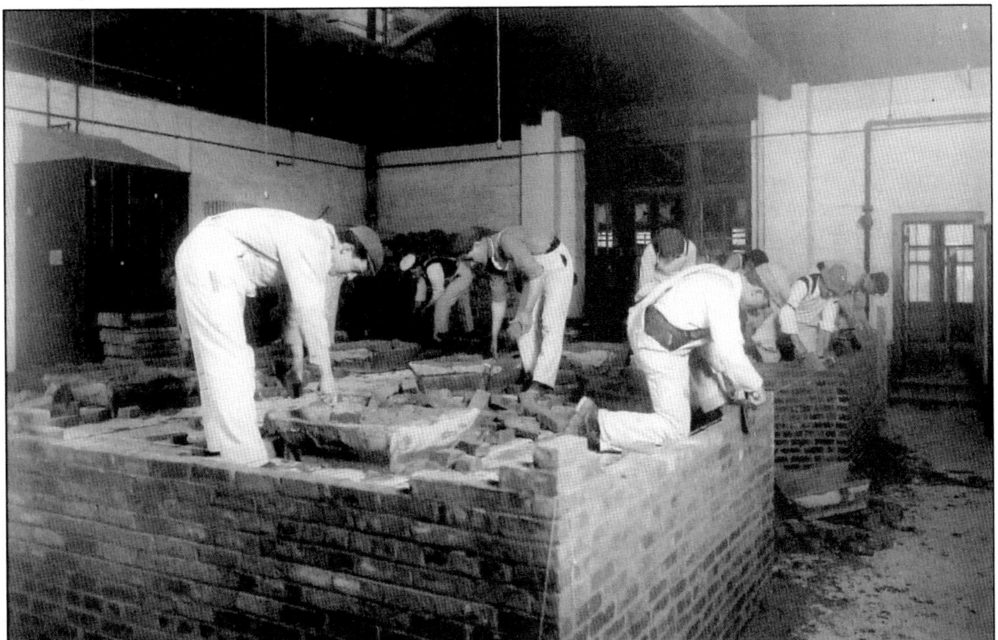

During the late 19th century, the building economy was booming in New York. Although this predates the era of skyscrapers, most commercial buildings were built of brick and mortar rather than wood. These students would have been quite marketable after completing their course of study.

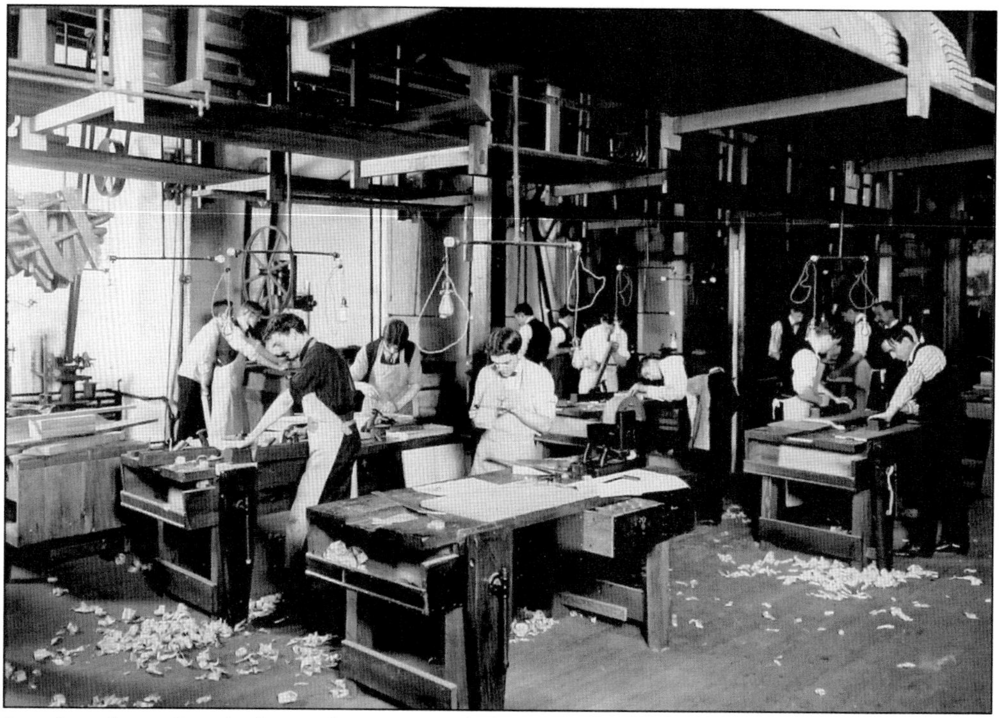

Another shop class is shown here around the 1890s, but it is not quite clear what these students are producing. Again notice that these men were dressed somewhat formally by today's standards. In this era, trades were open primarily to men and not to women, whose principal responsibilities focused on raising families.

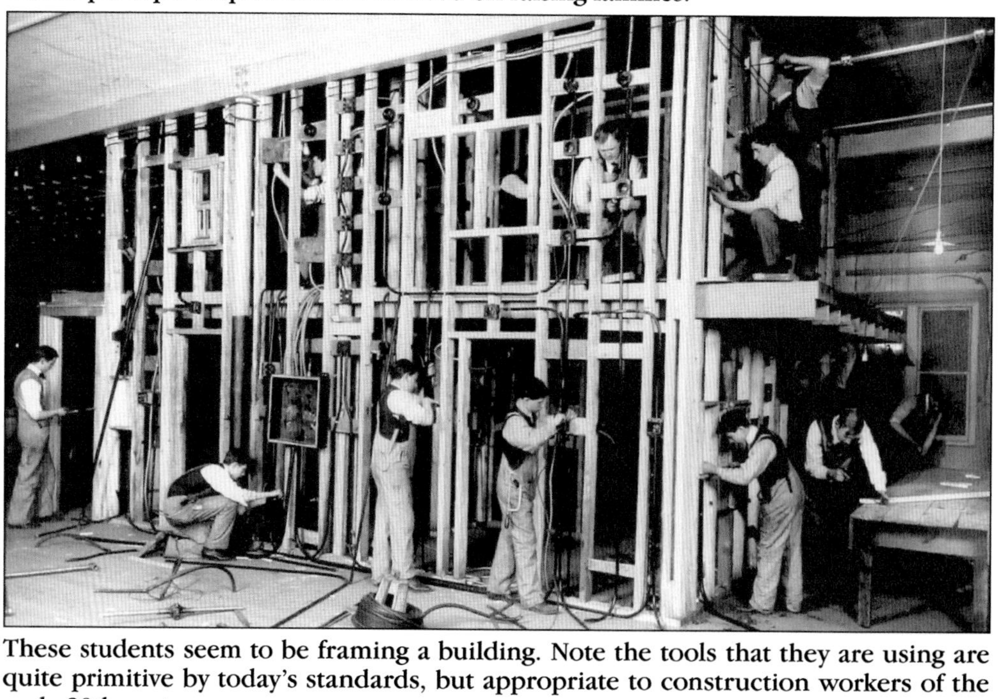

These students seem to be framing a building. Note the tools that they are using are quite primitive by today's standards, but appropriate to construction workers of the early 20th century.

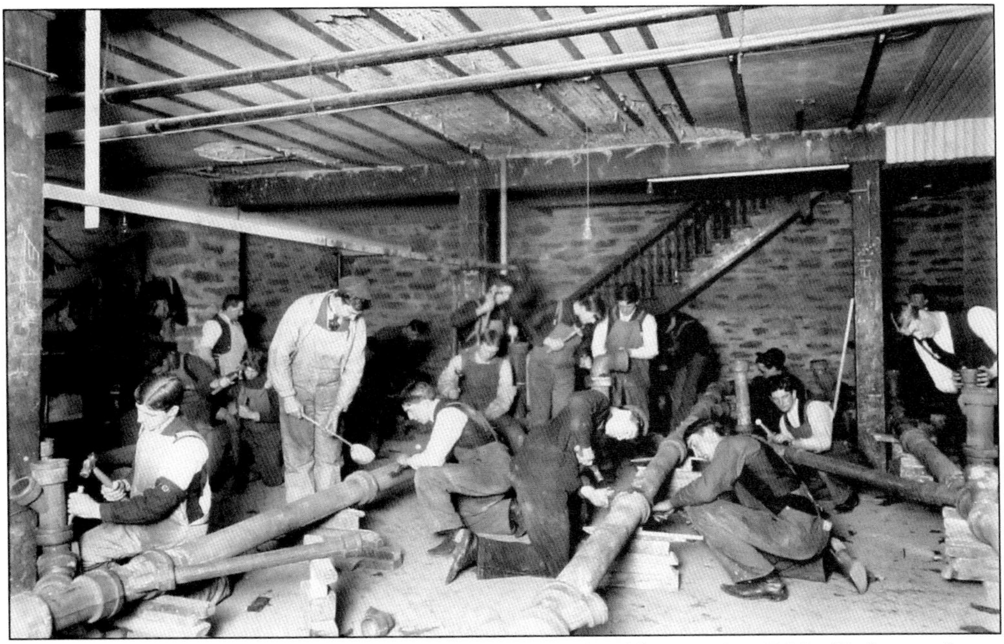

These students are learning to install plumbing in a building in the 1890s. Today students who would be involved in this kind of work would be required to wear hard hats and other safety guards.

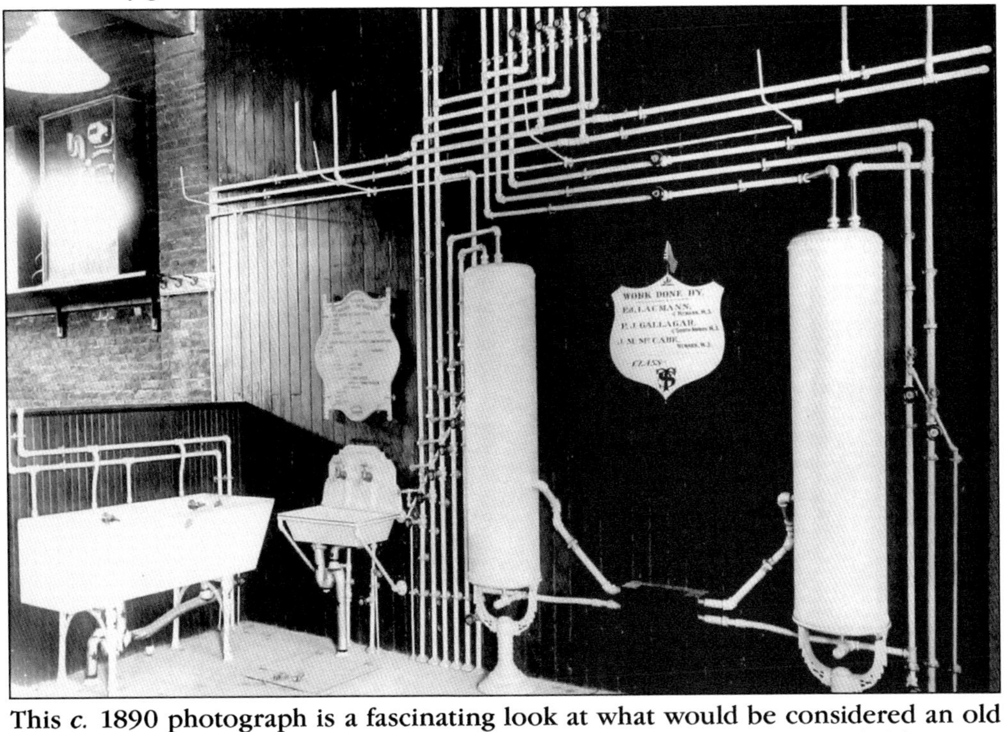

This *c.* 1890 photograph is a fascinating look at what would be considered an old fashioned wash tub and sink. In the center could possibly be some type of older water heater. Although the fixtures are quaint by contemporary standards, men capable of installing them were very much in demand in the late 19th century.

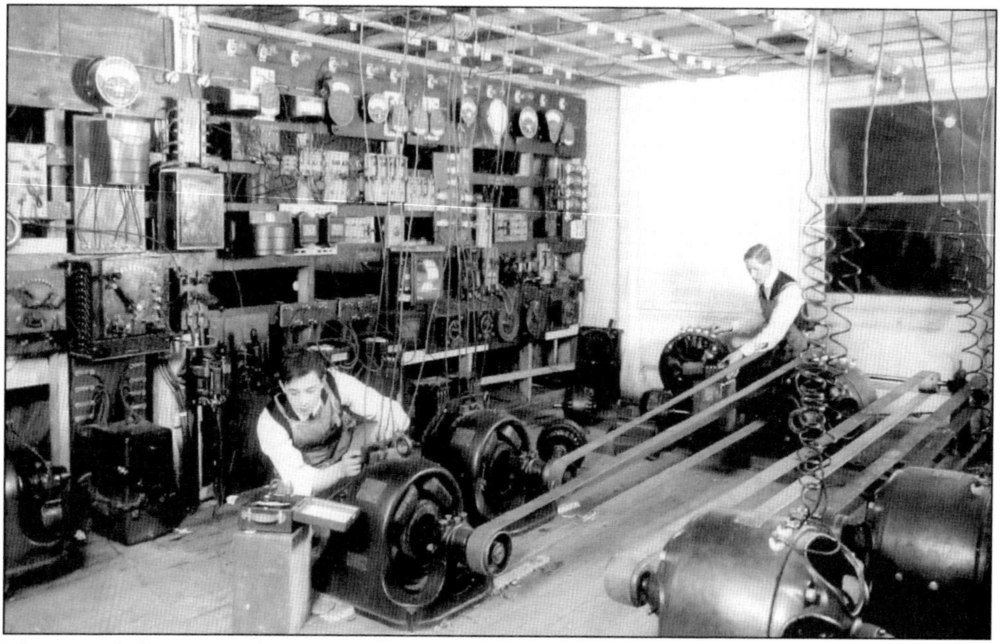

The era of electricity demanded new skills and a skilled workforce capable of serving the needs of the city. Students at the trade school acquired these skills as shown in this early photograph. It is difficult to discern what kind of class this is. Are these students in actuality using these machines to construct something or are they repairing these machines that look similar to a generator?

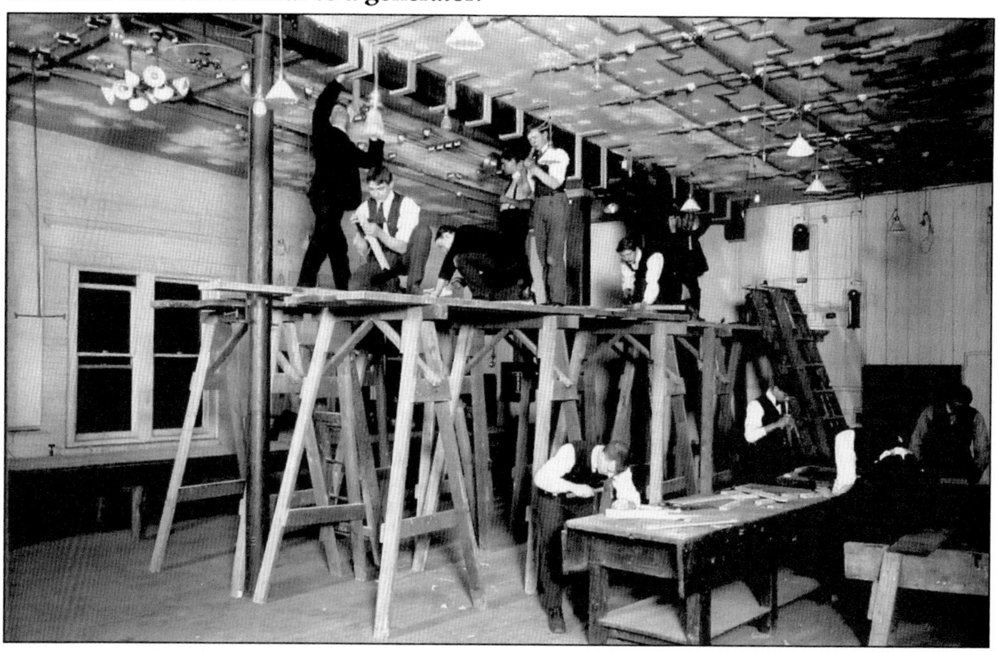

In this pre–World War I class, the students are creating lighting fixtures. By the late 1800s, electricity was being used in the workplace as well as in many homes. Electricity was often supplied by a new company called General Electric, later to become one of the dominant companies in the United States economy.

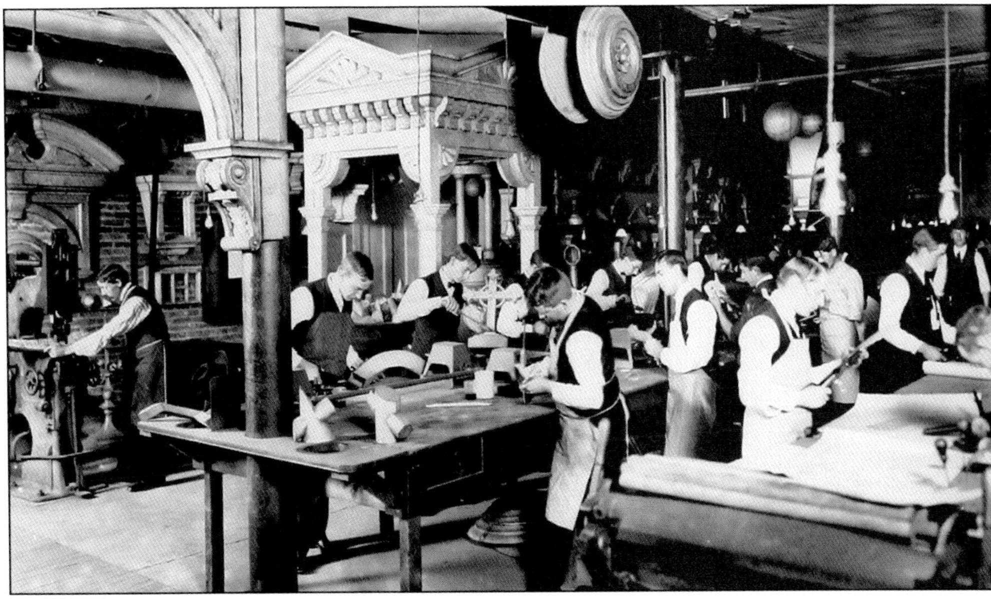

In this class around the 1890s, the students seem to be making ornate fixtures or props, perhaps for the theater. Today stagecraft involves laser optics and sophisticated engineering taught in few places, but done well in the Entertainment Technology Department.

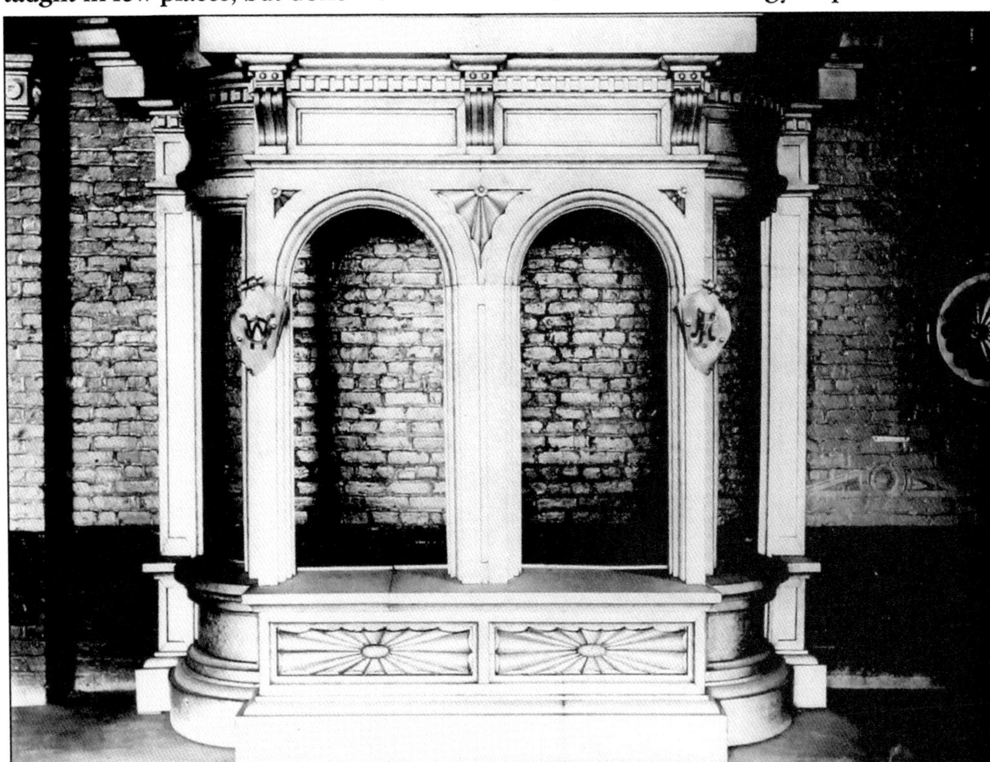

This ornate structure in all likelihood was intended to decorate a house. The ornateness of this piece dates it back to the late 19th century. Students are, in all likelihood, in a construction trades program.

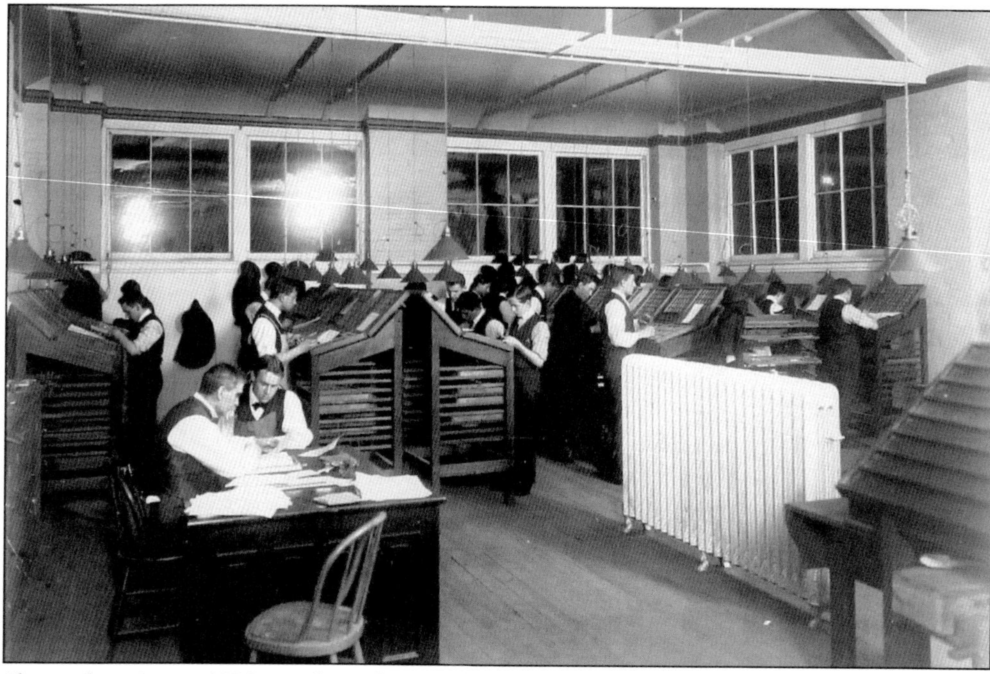

Shown here is a *c.* 1890 graphics class with what looks like an old cast iron radiator sitting in the center of this picture. It is highly doubtful that this was a room heater. Today the New York City College of Technology students study vastly more sophisticated systems of heating, ventilation, and air conditioning.

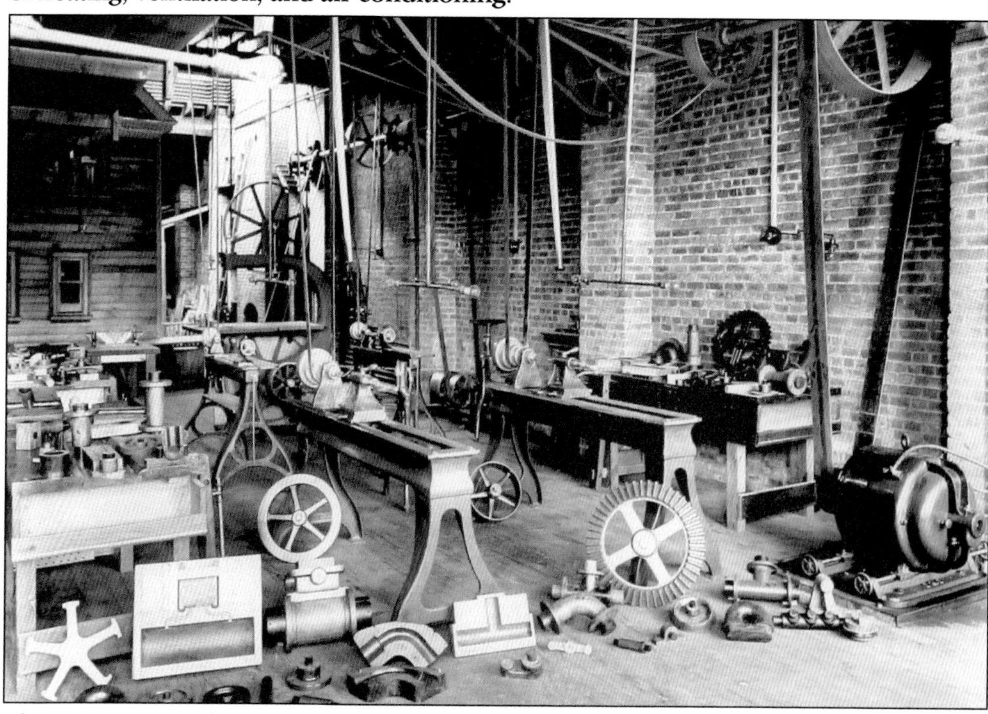

This is a picture of a shop class without the students present. However the machinery looks quite primitive, suggesting that it dates to the late 19 century.

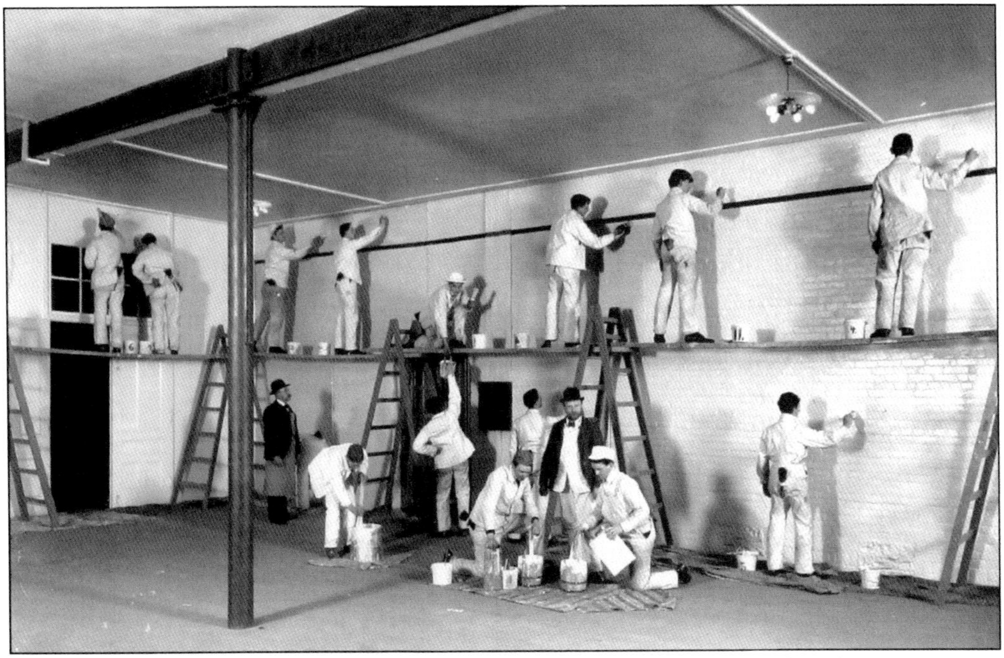

These students seem to be involved in painting, which was considered an important trade in the late 19th century. Notice that the instructors were wearing the traditional hat styles of this time period.

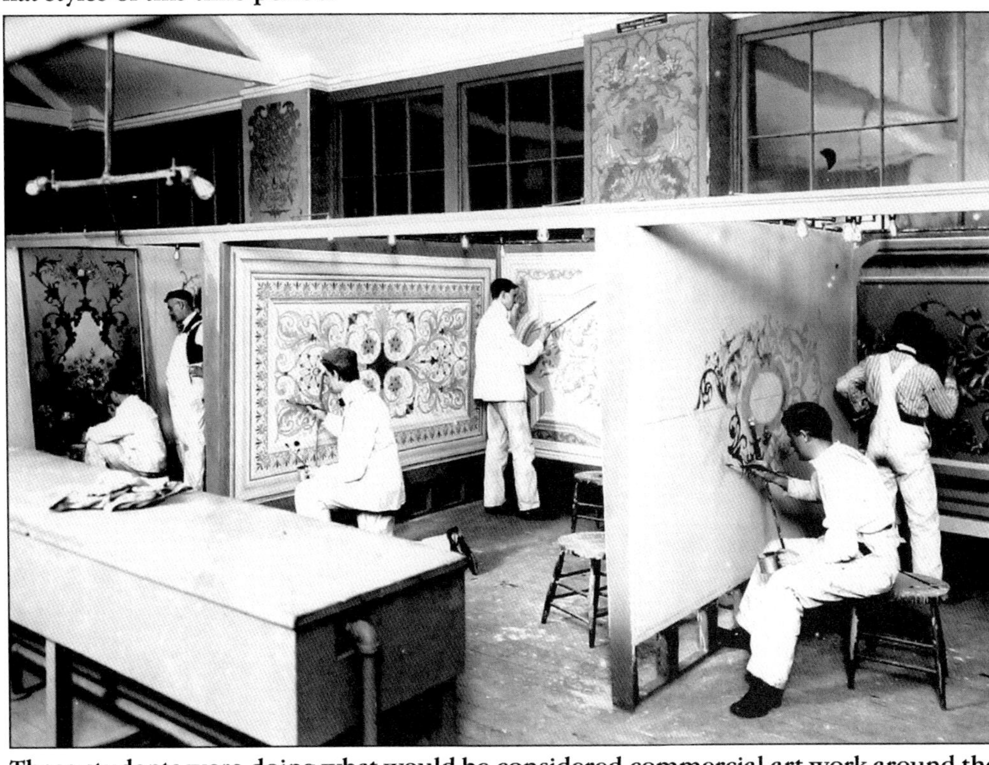

These students were doing what would be considered commercial art work around the 1890s. This was in all likelihood intended for a place of business.

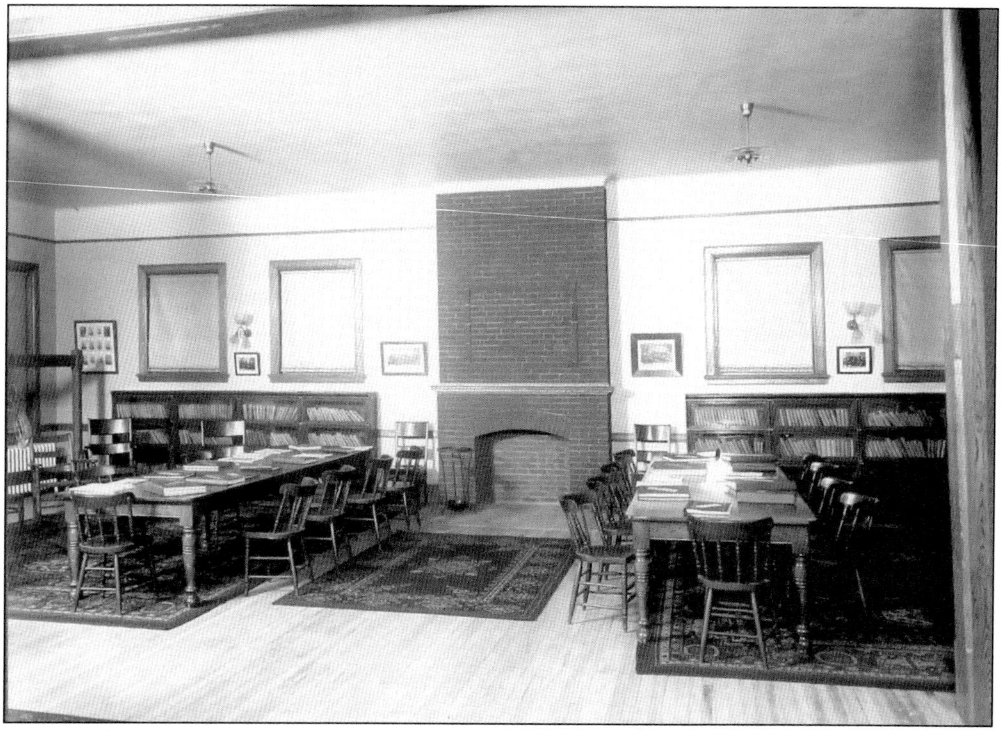

Pictured here is a lecture room from around 1890. Notice how tastefully the room was set up for the students, quite different from the utilitarian styles that characterize the era of mass education.

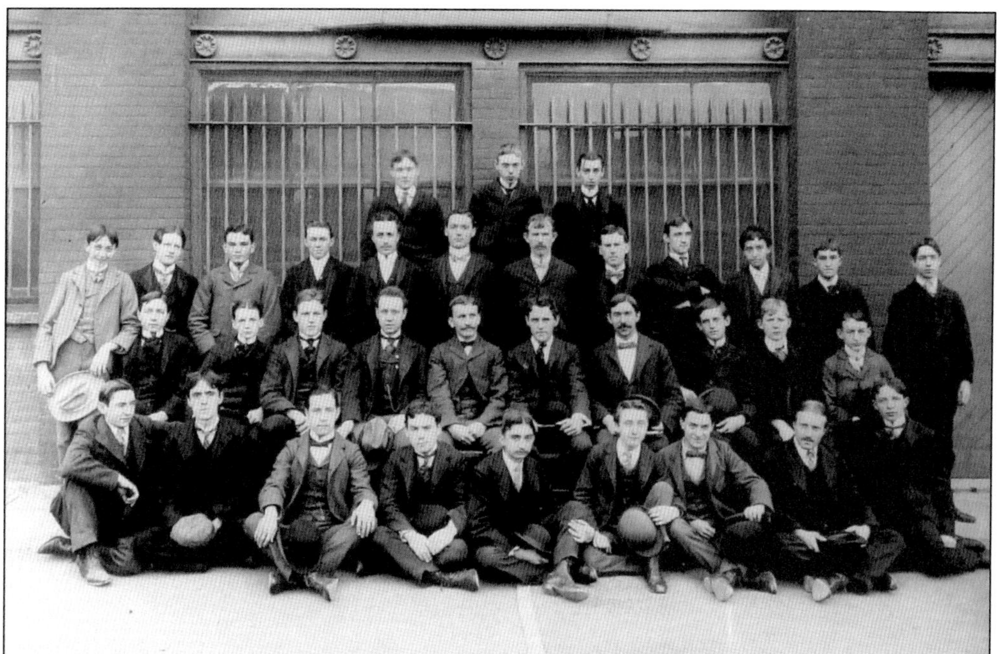

It is presumed that this is a graduating class dates back to the late 19th century. Notice the formal dress of these late–19th century students.

Two

Founding of the College and the Early Years 1946–1960

As World War II ground to an end, as the Allies celebrated their victory, thoughts turned to how to integrate hundreds of thousands of returning GIs into the post-war economy. The GI Bill benefits allowed the returning veterans to acquire an education to give them a foothold in this emerging economy. For those interested in the arts and sciences, elite schools turned these veterans into the intellectual luminaries of the 1950s and 1960s. But for those who were not bound for Princeton, Yale, or, in New York, for City College (known in those days as "the poor man's Harvard"), a different future beckoned. They needed to learn a craft, a profession.

In 1946, Gov. Thomas E. Dewey proposed legislation to assist these returning GIs. With his strong support, the New York State Legislature provided funding for five experimental institutes designed to meet that need. New York State Regents, the governing board for public education, had asked for 22 institutes; the governor and the legislature were more sanguine. The purpose was clearly stated, to provide "technical and sub-professional education in those areas in which business, industry, commerce and the professions need trained technical personnel, through curricula not to exceed two years in length." One of these five institutes was to be in New York City, and Brooklyn was designated as the location.

A small budget was allocated, about $165,000 for the first year. A board of trustees was appointed, including educators, businessmen, and representatives of the labor movement. Maj. Benjamin Namm, chairman of the board of the Namm-Loeser Department Store was elected chairman of the board of trustees of the new institute. Shortly thereafter, the board selected Dr. Otto Klitgord, a former administrator of the War Training Program and earlier a high school teacher, as the first director. Instruction began on February 5, 1947, in an aging high school building in downtown Brooklyn, for the initial 234 students. The New York State Institute of Applied Arts and Sciences, today known as New York City College of Technology (City Tech), took its first, tentative steps.

Instruction was initially in only a handful of departments: Mechanical Technology, Chemical Technology, Electrical Technology, and Structural Technology. Other departments were added as the young institution grew. In rapid succession, programs were developed in Commercial Art and Industrial Design, Marketing, and Dental Laboratory Technology. Dental Hygiene and Hotel Technology were added shortly thereafter. There were no frills, none of the amenities students expect today. Janet Lefler, one of the early instructors and later chair of hotel technology, spoke of the difficulties of that period: "When we opened the institute, we had no chairs for the students, so the mostly GI students sat on the floor or on top of the small grade-school desks." But the students stayed, and the students succeeded. Under difficult conditions and on a bare-bones budget, a strong and durable institution emerged.

The photographs in this chapter concentrate heavily on these early departments. As will be seen, many of the students were returning or active duty GIs. Decorum was the rule. Students wore ties and often industrial uniforms. Much was different from today. A newspaper cost 3¢, a subway ride a nickel. The Brooklyn-based revolution in which Jackie Robinson of the Dodgers broke the color line in Major League Baseball was still being planned. A consumer-oriented economy and modern tools of advertising and sales emerged. In these changing times, the young college adapted to allow its students to find a place in the new economy.

The New York City College of Technology is situated in what is today the exciting, resurgent center of downtown Brooklyn, rapidly acquiring a skyline that will rival Manhattan, London, or Tokyo. But this is today; yesterday was a different story altogether. To Manhattanites, Brooklyn was the frontier, a mixture of factories and tenement housing (and, to be sure, some very elegant townhouses), with even a few dairies, as distant from Manhattan as Omaha. Pete Hamill tells a story that is quintessential Brooklyn: "In Upper Flatbush, already two miles deep from the bridges, a young woman of Manhattan asked a druggist how she might get into certain territory well south of there. Without thought of irony, he began, 'Oh. You want to go to Brooklyn.'" Once one left Oz, it was all Brooklyn. In this chapter, one will find photographs intended to create a sense of this Brooklyn of the 1940s.

By the end of this period, enormous growth had occurred at the college. By 1963, the Community College of Applied Arts and Sciences had over 10,000 graduates. It had an enrollment of 6,500 students (4,000 of them evening students) and it was the largest community college in New York State. In 1964, the college became part of The City University of New York. Many changes were still to come, but the experiment of 1947 had succeeded; the college was meeting and extending its mission as it adapted to meet emerging needs in the post-war economy.

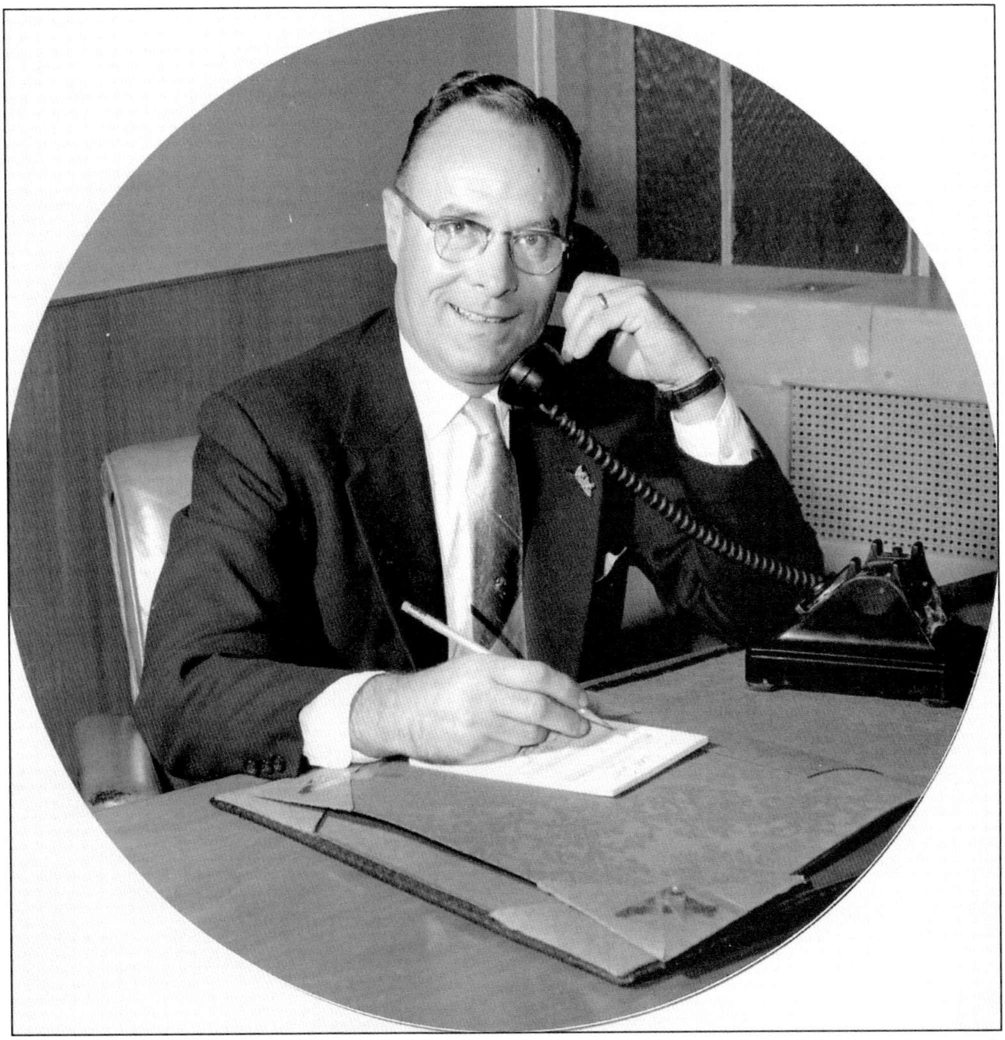

Pictured here is Dr. Otto Klitgord talking on the telephone. On September 30, 1946, Dr. Klitgord was appointed was the first director of the New York State Institute of Applied Arts and Science. Dr. Klitgord led the institute from 1946 until his death on April 19, 1960. By 1960, under Dr. Klitgord's leadership, the New York State Institute of Applied Arts and Science was considered one of the finest institutions of its kind in the United States, with over 7,000 students in attendance in both the day and evening classes. It is important to remember that the school was tuition-free until the early 1970s.

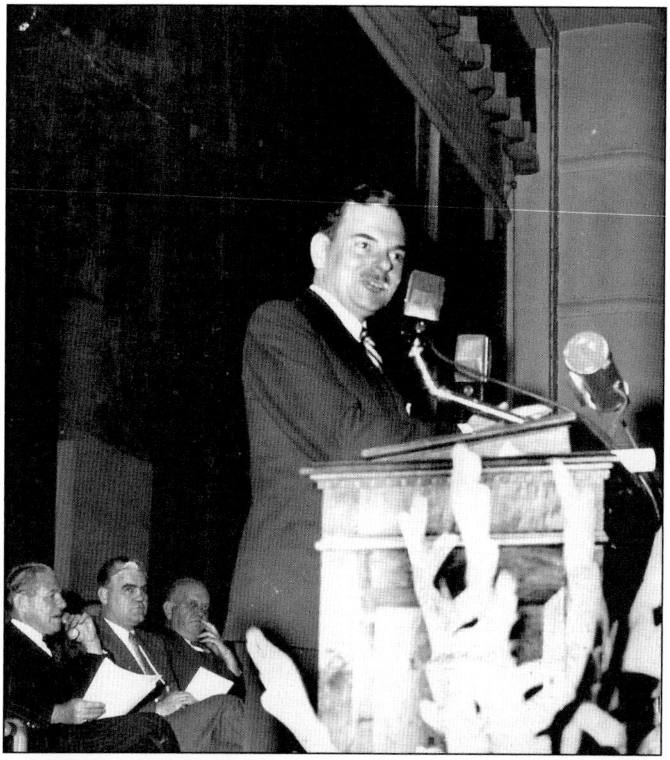

This was in all probability a luncheon commemorating the 10th anniversary of the founding of the college, held at the Waldorf-Astoria Hotel in New York City in October of 1956. Pictured at the podium is Gov. Thomas Dewey, a supporter of the community college movement and the proponent of the legislation that created the New York State Institute of Applied Arts and Sciences.

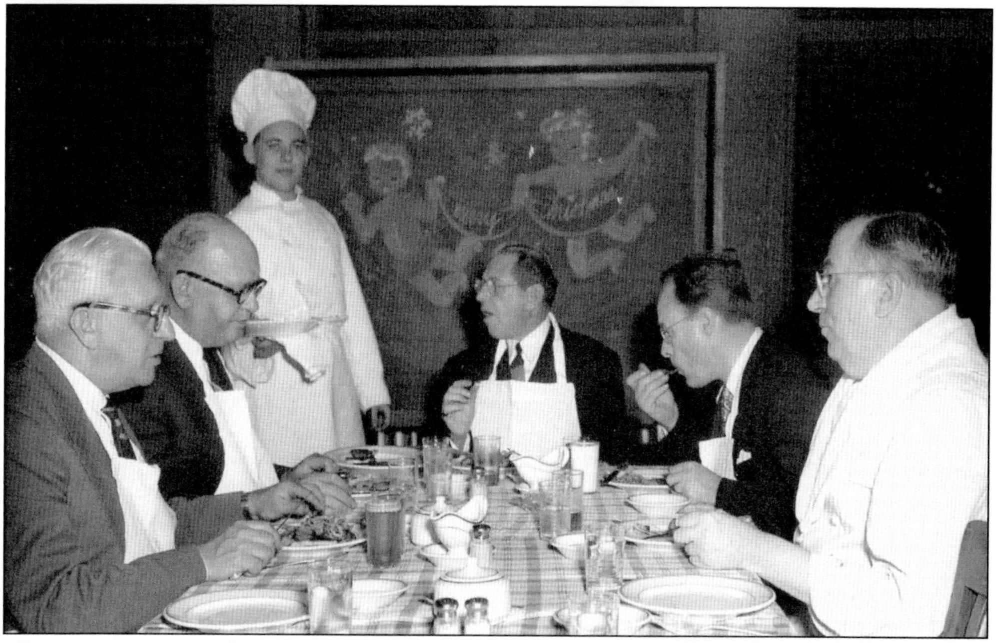

This picture was taken shortly before the Christmas season in the mid-1950s. This photograph was probably taken in the dining room in Franklin Hall, used for instruction in the early years of the Hotel Technology Department (today Hospitality Management). Pictured in the center is Benjamin Namm, first chairman of the board of trustees of the college. Seated second from the right is Dr. Otto Klitgord, first director.

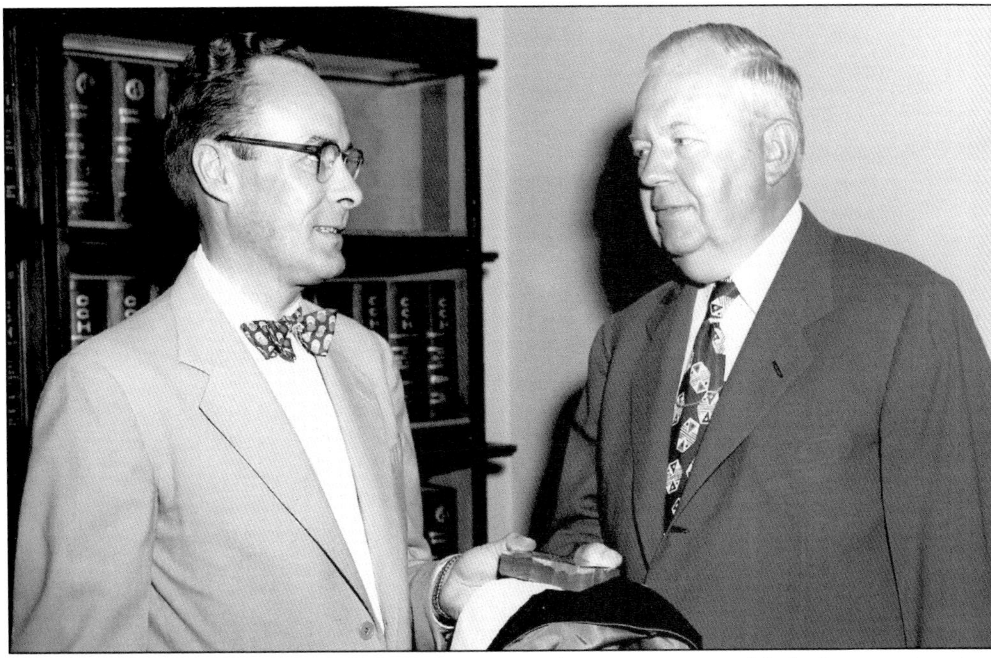

This is Dr. Klitgord to the left, holding a cap and gown, presumably before graduation. Dr. Klitgord was wearing his signature polka dot tie, which is found in many other early pictures of him. The man to the right is unidentified.

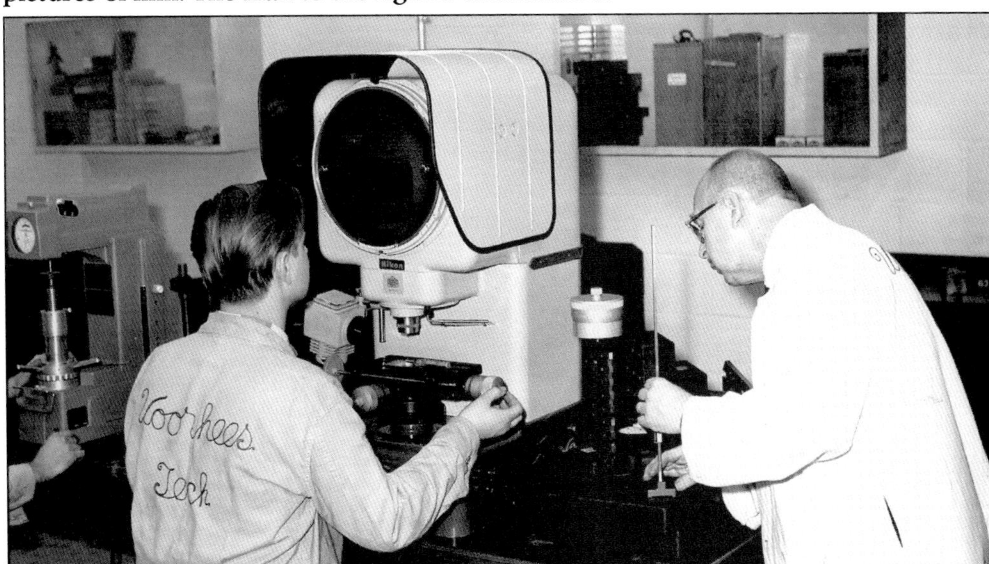

This is a student who is working on an early machine that probably dates to the early 1960s. The back of the uniform reveals that this is a student of the Voorhees Technical Institute. In 1961, the New York Trade School changed its name to the Voorhees Technical Institute, named after a famous industrialist, Enders M. Voorhees. Under Pres. Milton Bassin's leadership, the Voorhees Technical Institute was merged into the college in 1970. The identity of the college, then known as New York City Community College, remained intact, but it inherited a tradition that extended back to the late 1800s.

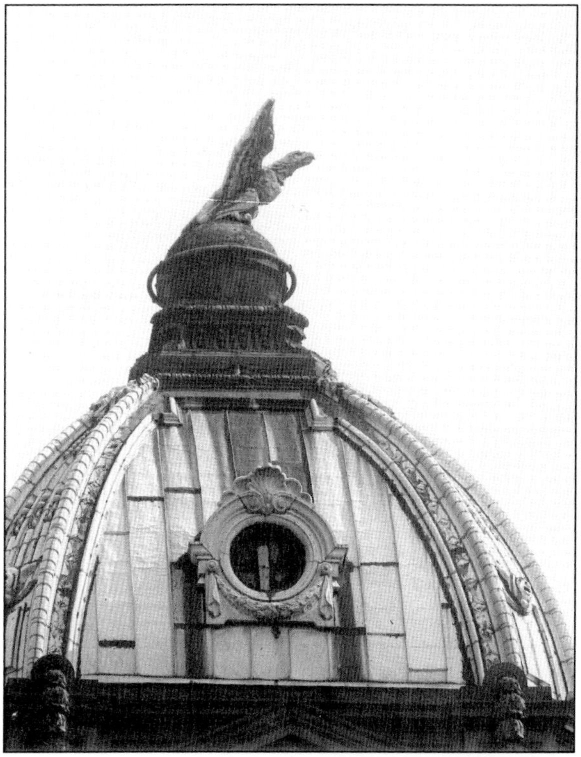

This is the proud eagle as it sat atop the Brooklyn Eagle Building at Washington and Johnson Streets in downtown Brooklyn. This was one of at least four eagles that adorned the structure since September 23, 1892. It was given to the college as a gift from the then defunct newspaper, the *Brooklyn Eagle*. Rumor has it that the eagle is stored in one of the many sub-basements of the college, but it may well be simply urban legend. It is interesting to note that with the renaissance of downtown Brooklyn, the *Brooklyn Eagle* resumed publication in 2003, after a 40-year hiatus.

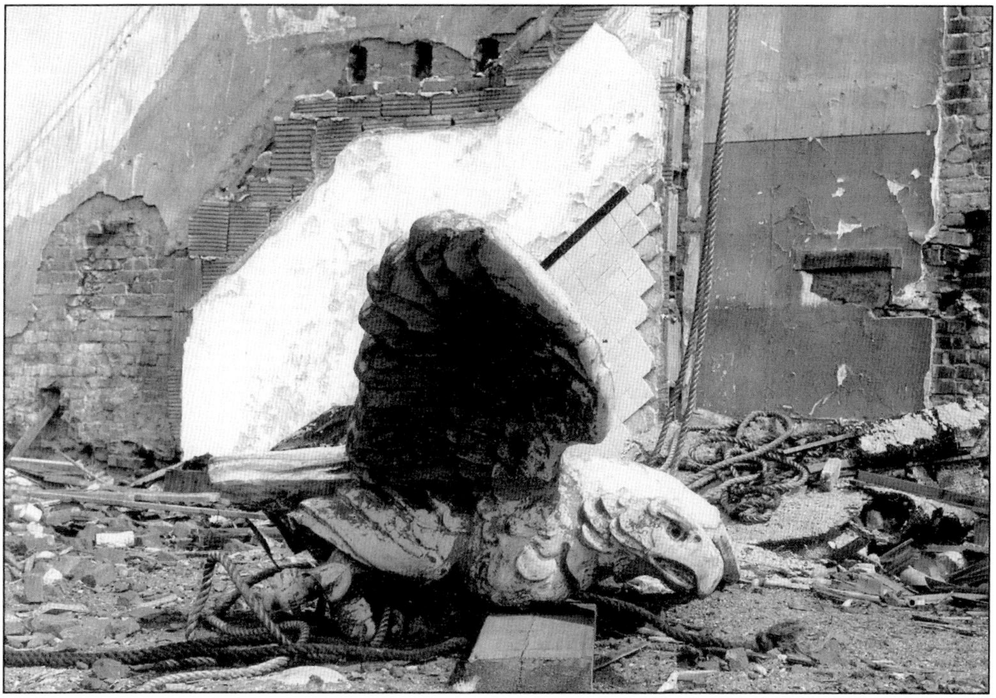

This eagle was no lightweight. It was a 200-pound monster that had to be lowered on a truck and then transported to the college. Although the *Brooklyn Eagle* ceased publication in 1955, the bird was not given to the college until 1956.

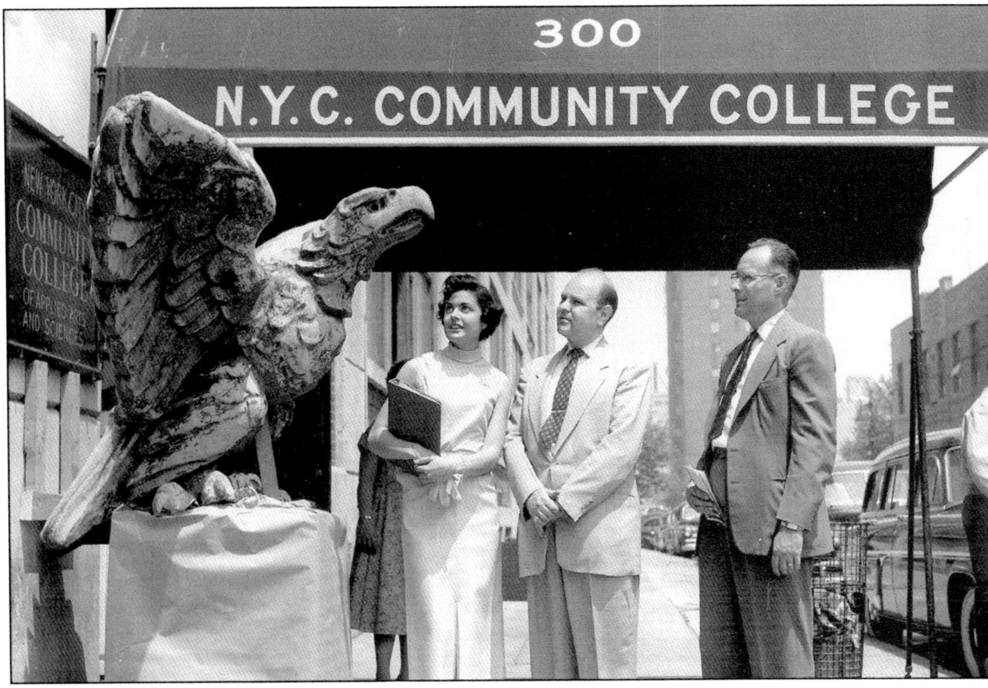

Dr. Otto Klitgord stands proud in front of the newly donated bird. Legend has it that the eagle stood in front of Dr. Klitgord's office for a number of years until it was removed. The student to the right is Elaine Peepe. The gentleman at the center is not identified, but Dr. Klitgord is on the right. This is not 300 Jay Street, the site of today's largest academic complex, as one might assume, but 300 Pearl Street, an earlier college site.

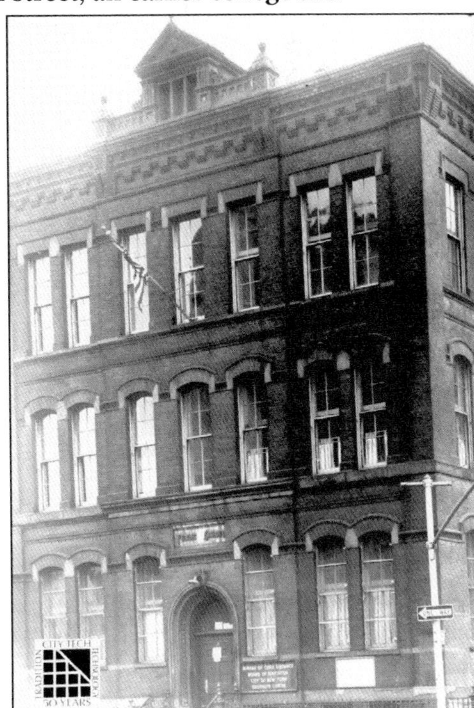

This is Public School 15, located at Schermerhorn Street and Third Avenue, the initial teaching space available to the college as it opened its doors. The first day of class was February 5, 1947. A total of 234 students attended that day in classes in the four initial departments, Chemical, Electrical, Mechanical, and Structural Technology. Other programs were added very rapidly, in Hotel Technology, Nursing, Dental Laboratory, and Dental Hygiene. The building dates back to the 1850s and is almost an archetype of the 19th century urban schoolhouse. From 1947 until 1953, the college was called the New York State Institute of Applied Arts and Sciences, reflective of its initial mission.

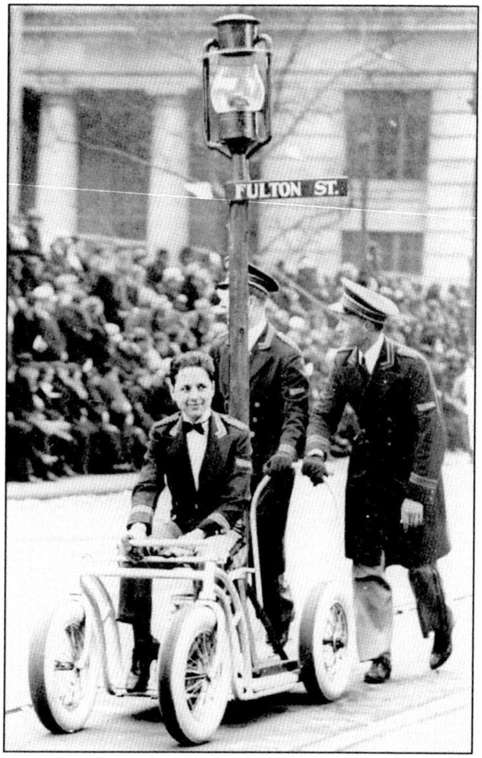

Pictured here is a street celebration on Fulton Street in downtown Brooklyn, two or three blocks from the college. The event is difficult to guess, but the celebration occurred in February 1947, the same month that the college offered its first classes.

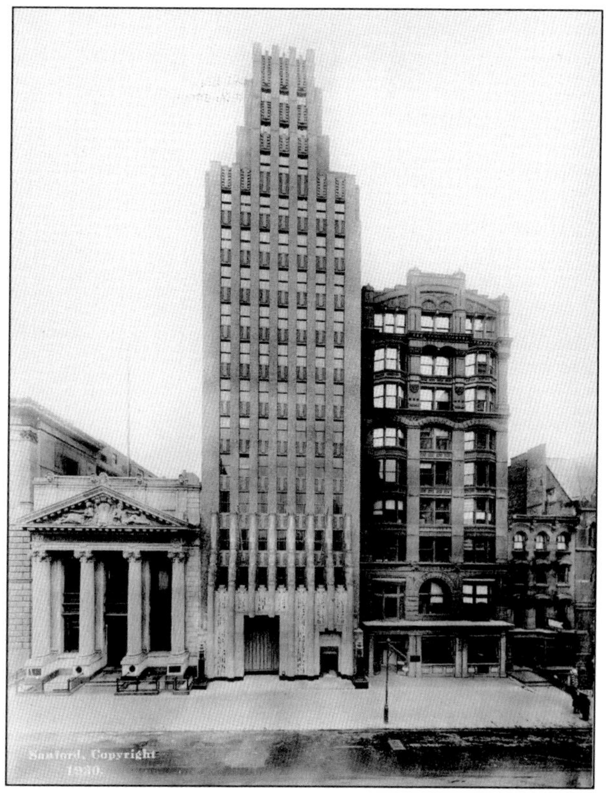

Montague Street in downtown Brooklyn is shown in 1947. Today this site is the meeting point of Brooklyn Heights, one of the more exclusive residential areas in New York City, and the MetroTech Center, a business and commerce hub that has been described by the *New York Times* as the site of "the renaissance of downtown Brooklyn."

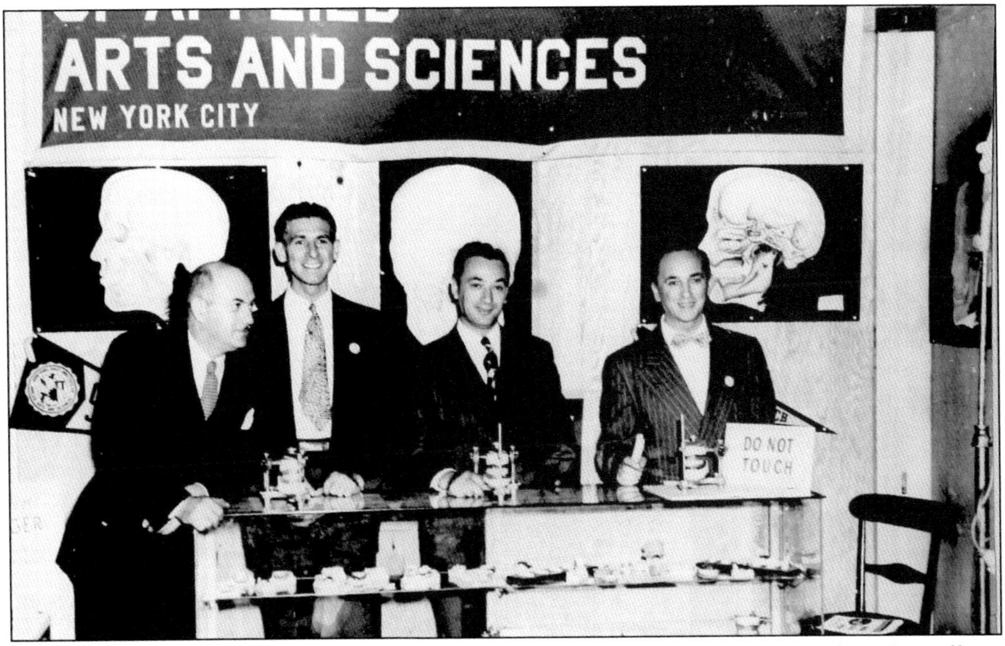

This banner suggests that the picture was taken between 1947 and 1953, when the college was officially known as the New York State Institute of Applied Arts and Sciences at New York City. This looks like a presentation in what was then referred to as the Dental Laboratory Department. In 1950, there were 141 male students and only 3 women. At that time, there would have been a large number of students who were veterans of the Korean conflict enrolled at the college. Dental laboratory was originally closely linked with the U.S. Air Force, which supplied the initial instructors and many of the initial students.

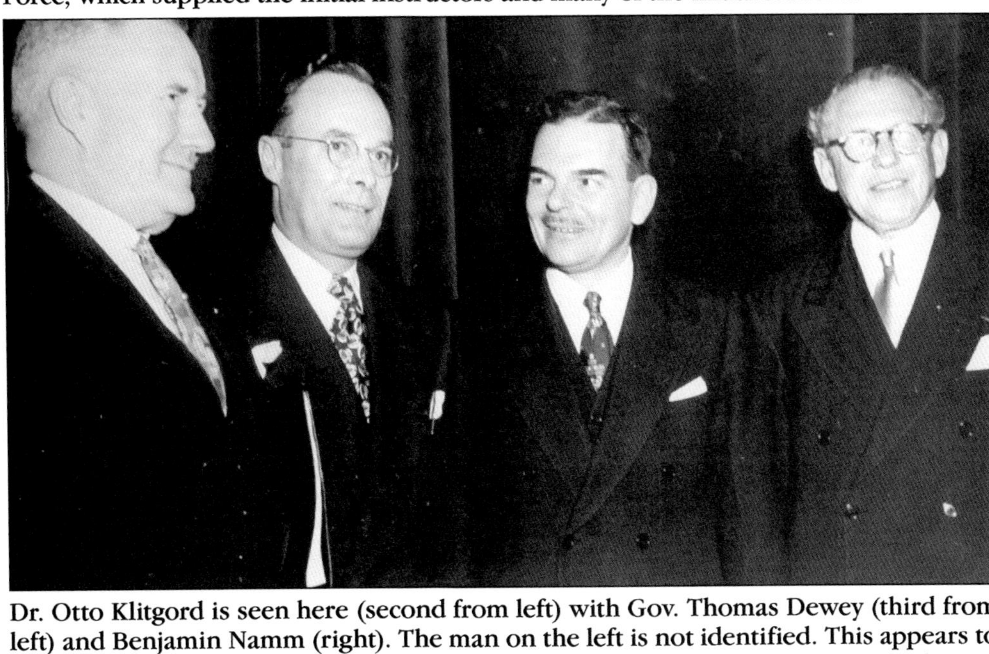

Dr. Otto Klitgord is seen here (second from left) with Gov. Thomas Dewey (third from left) and Benjamin Namm (right). The man on the left is not identified. This appears to be a picture of the dedication ceremony of the first day of classes at the New York State Institute of Applied Arts and Sciences, February 5, 1947.

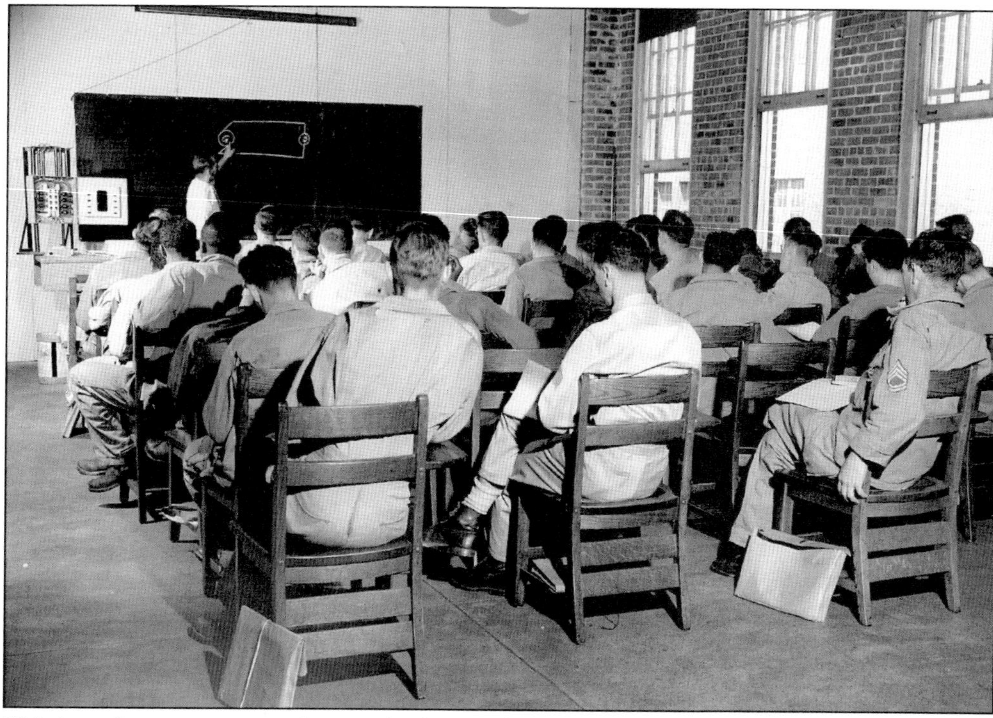

This is a classroom scene during the late 1940s or early 1950s. These men appear to be wearing some sort of uniform. During the early years, strict dress codes for a number of the departments were strictly enforced. Some prescribed dress and uniforms exist today, especially for students in the health care fields and for those in hospitality management.

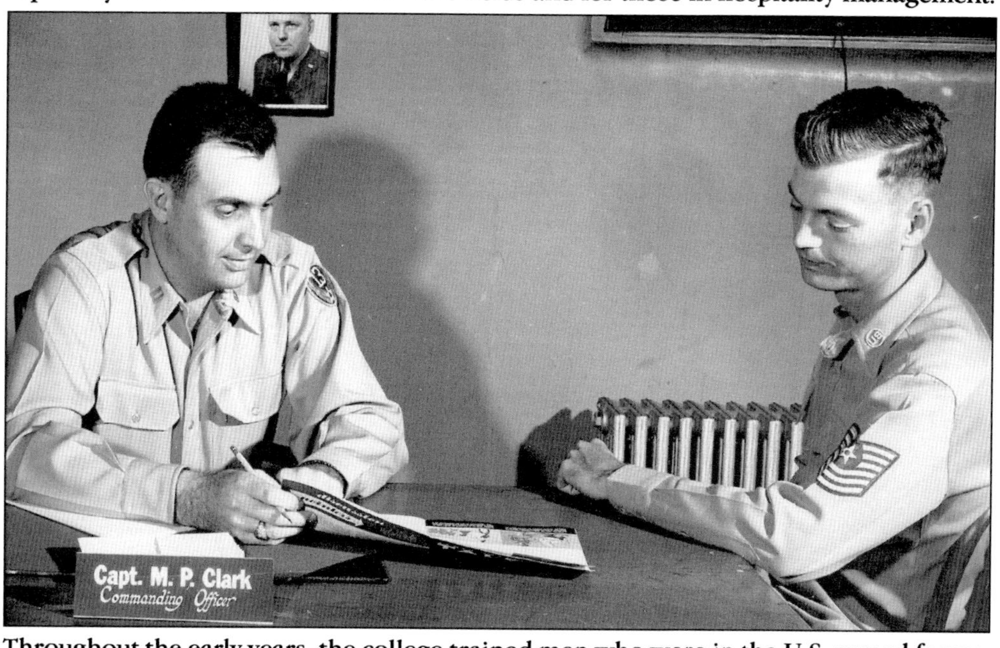

Throughout the early years, the college trained men who were in the U.S. armed forces. Here we see a member of the U.S. Air Force speaking to Capt. M. P. Clark, identified as a community service officer around the 1950s.

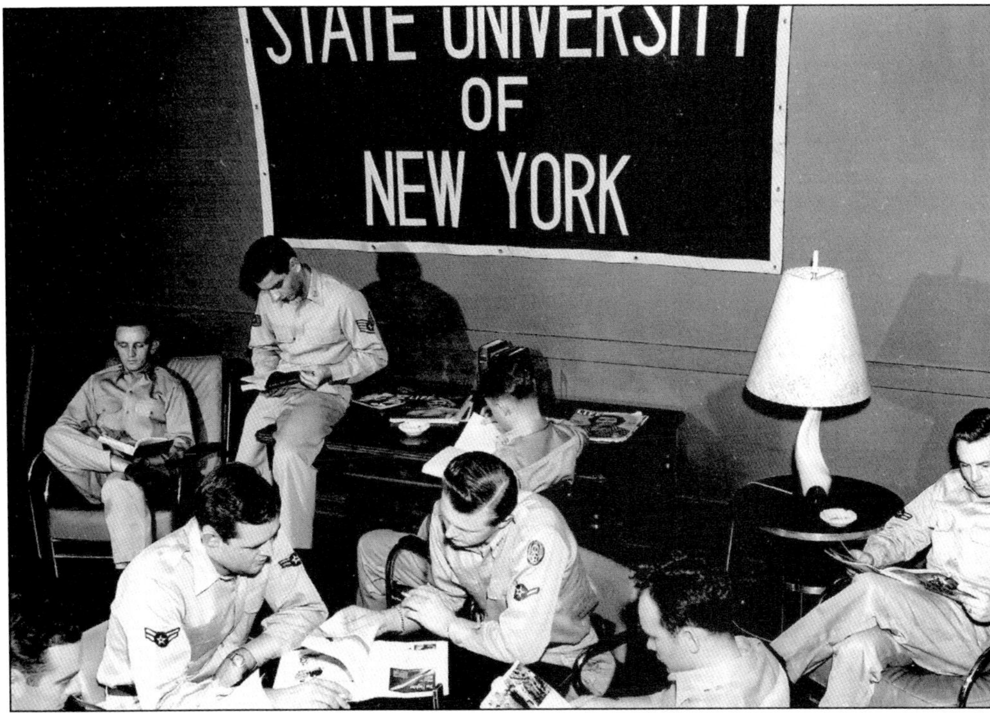

This *c.* 1950 picture shows more members of the U.S. Air Force enjoying a lounge created specifically for them. During the semester, these military personnel would be housed at the old St. George Hotel in Brooklyn Heights. This picture was probably taken inside the hotel. The St. George, a once elegant hotel, declined into a sorry state of disrepair before it was restored as a privately owned residence for college students in the 1990s.

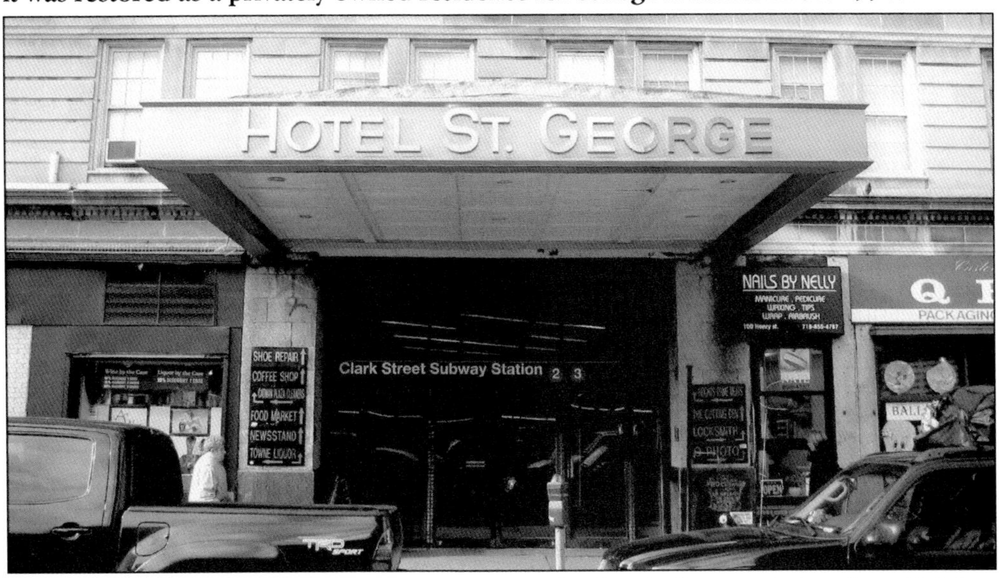

The St. George Hotel, located on Henry Street in the decidedly upscale Brooklyn Heights, shares a history with the college. During the 1950s, students in the military were housed in the St. George Hotel and classes were held there. If one were to visit the hotel today, there are no traces of the City Tech.

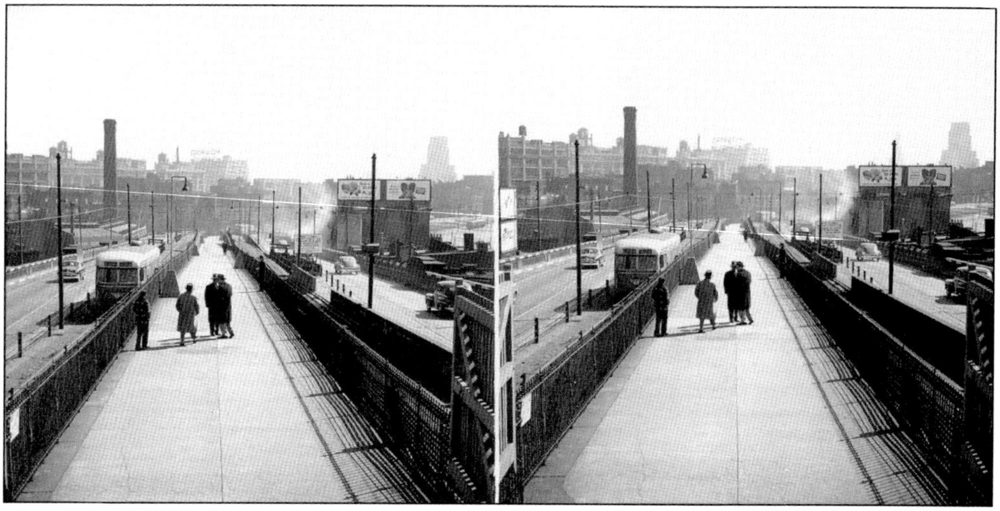

This view of the grimy, industrial Brooklyn of the 1940s was taken from the Brooklyn Bridge. The main academic buildings of the college today are literally steps from the end of the walkway of the Brooklyn Bridge. These twin pictures were designed to be seen through a stereoscopic viewer to create a three-dimensional view. They were still very common at the time.

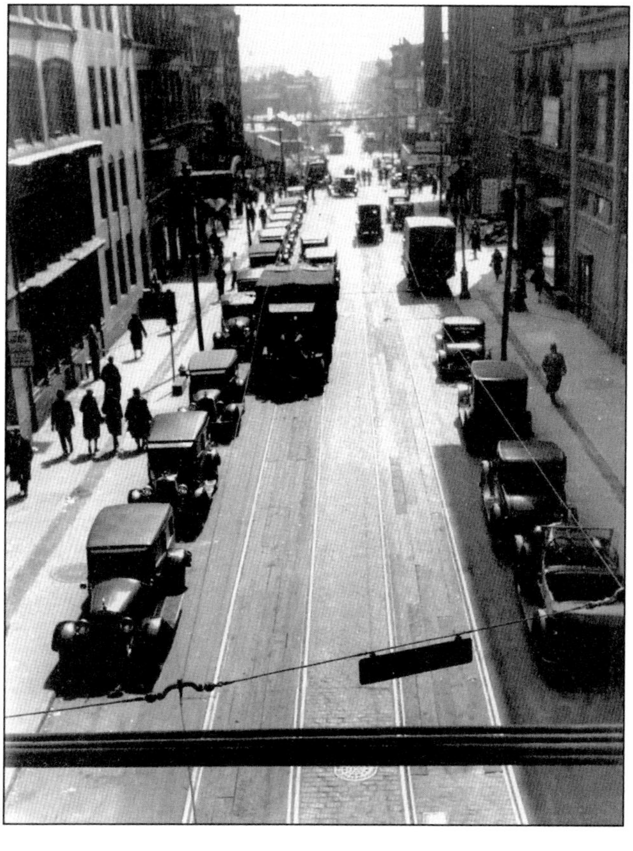

This 1940s street scene was taken from Jay Street in front of where today's Namm Hall stands. Note the trolley tracks. The Brooklyn trolleys produced one of America's best-loved sports teams, the trolley-dodgers, giving a name to the Brooklyn Dodgers.

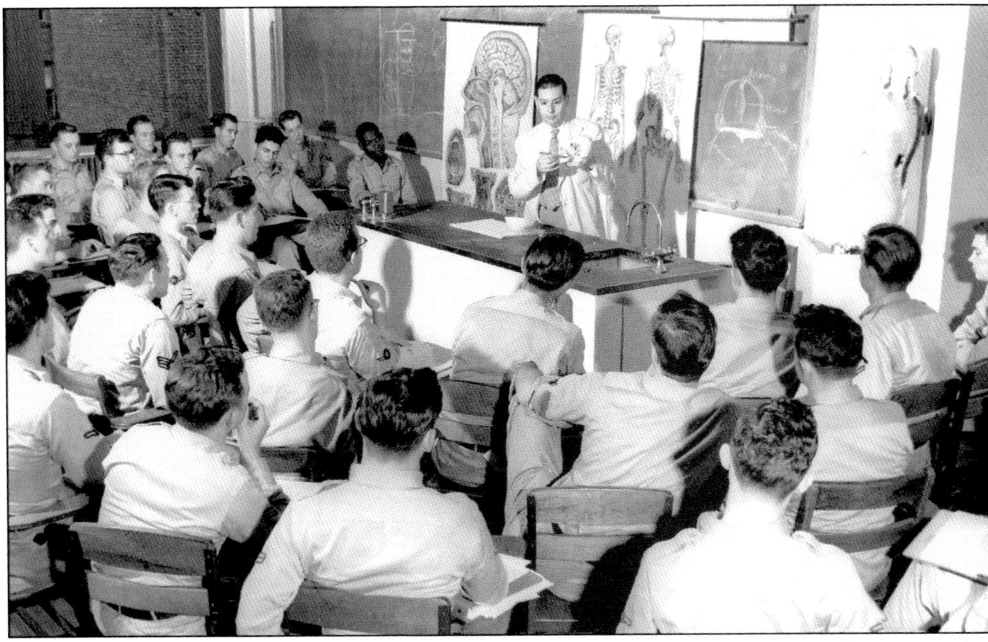

These are air force military personnel sitting through a science class. A significant number of students in the military were trained in what was then called dental laboratory. Students who were trained in this profession would graduate and get decent paying jobs in a dental laboratory. Today the program resides in the Restorative Dentistry Department. Students still learn traditional skills, but also learn to create computer-generated models of teeth, which can then be produced in highly robotized production facilities.

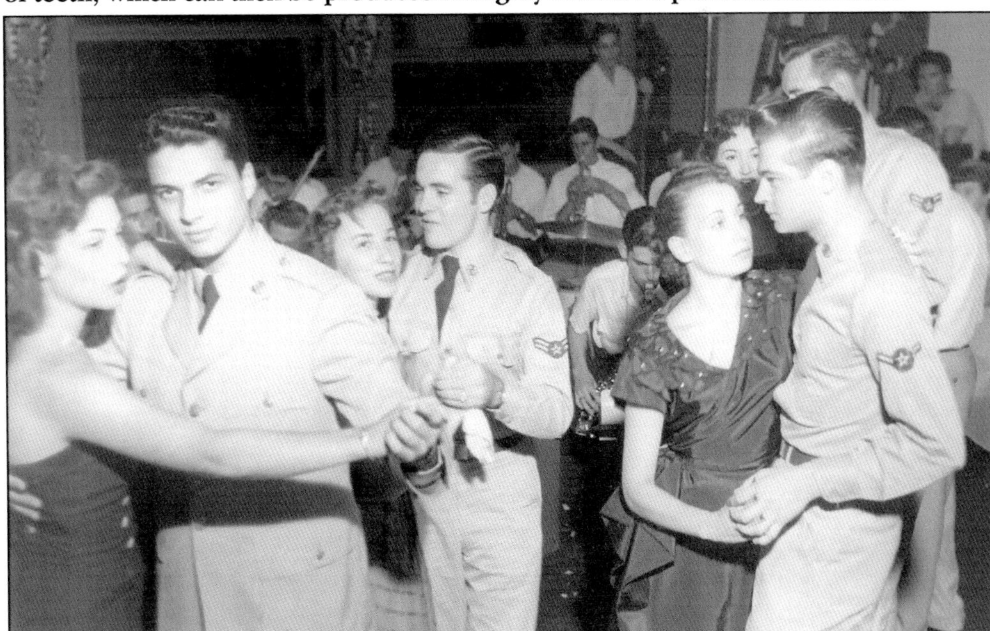

The college provided numerous social and recreational activities for the military students who attended. This is a formal dance that took place during the 1950s, an era of formality that would seem altogether alien to current generations of college students.

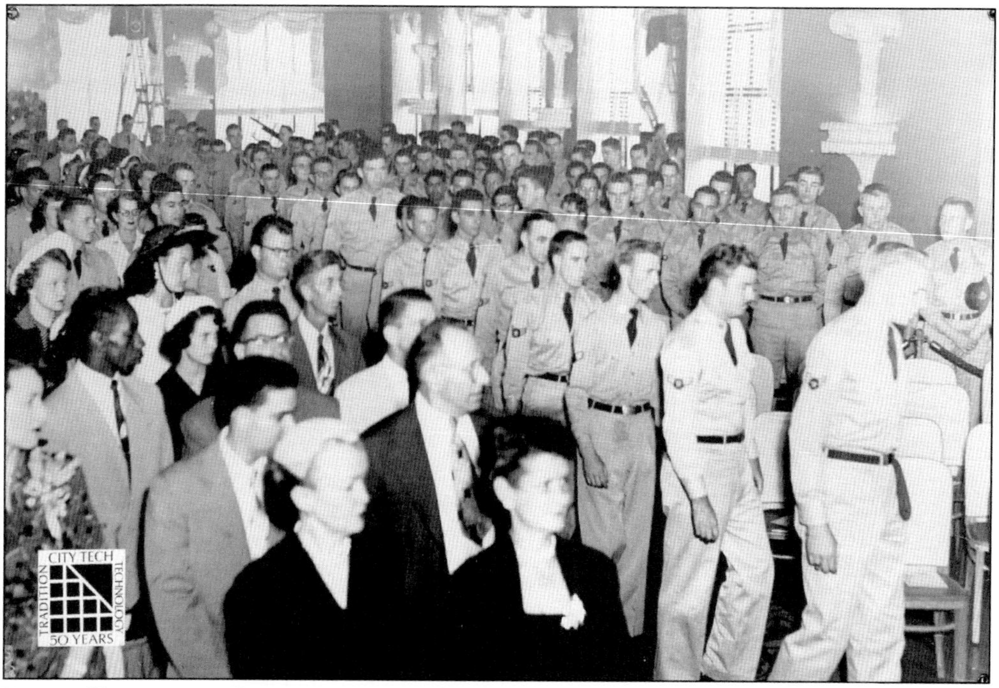

Pictured here is a graduation ceremony for the air force military personnel who graduated from the college during the 1950s.

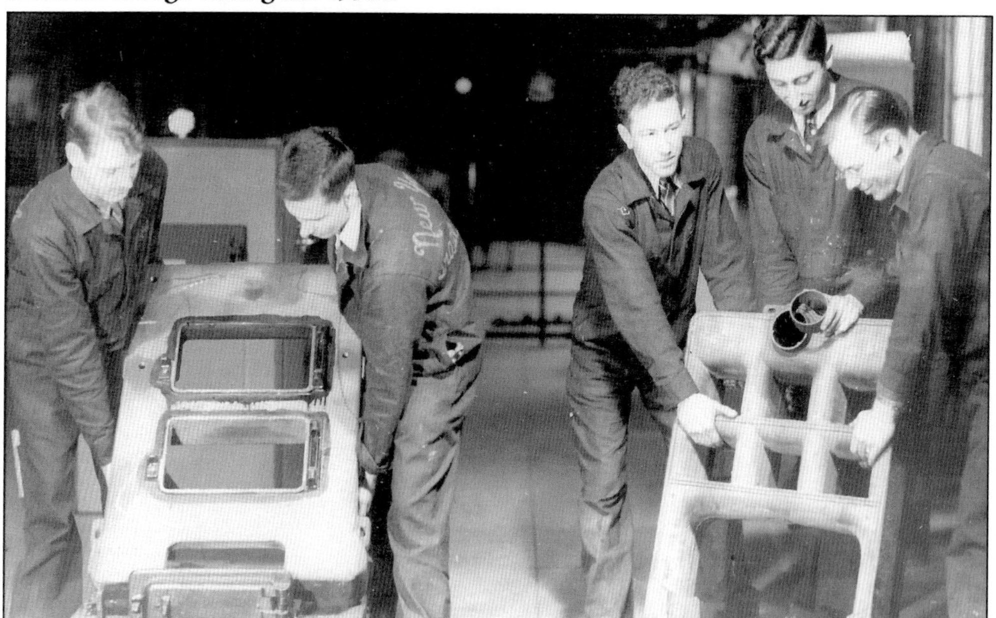

Students shown here are in the college program originally called structural technology. The Structural Technology Department would actually put up buildings. In this photograph, the students seem to be involved with some type of heating unit. Clearly written on the back of their work clothes is New York State Institute. Today radically more advanced programs prepare students in Construction Management and Civil Engineering Technology, Environmental Control, Facilities Management, and Architectural Technology.

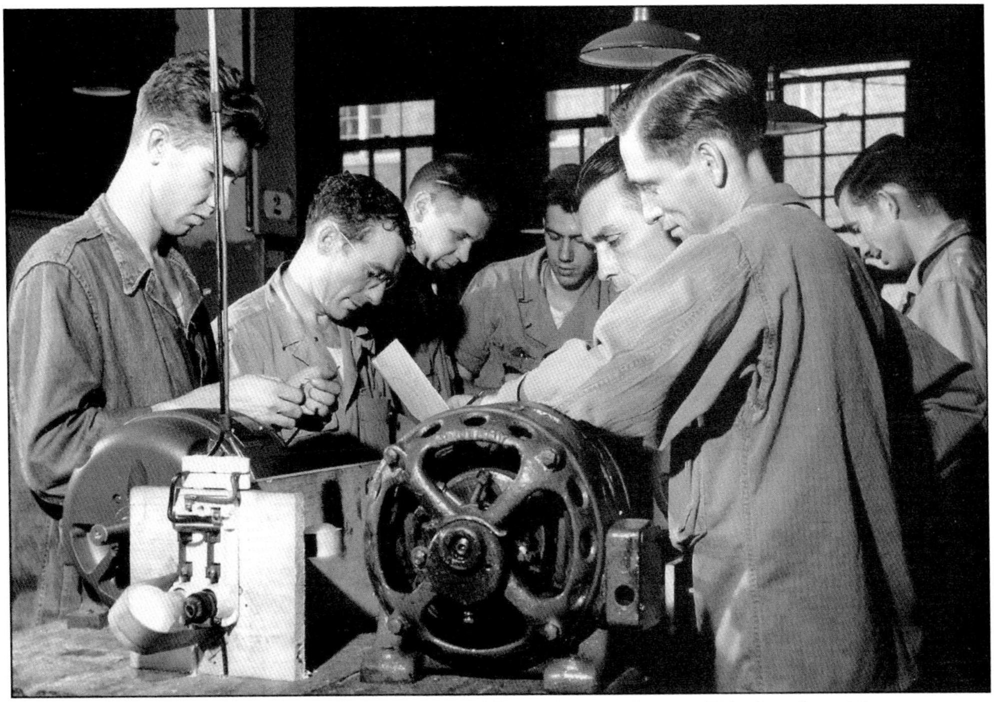

The students who are shown here are possibly in the Mechanical Technology Department. The department today offers degrees in mechanical engineering technology and industrial design. As in other degree programs at the institute, basic industrial skill sets have been supplemented with, but not entirely replaced by, the cutting-edge skills of the era of computer-based technologies.

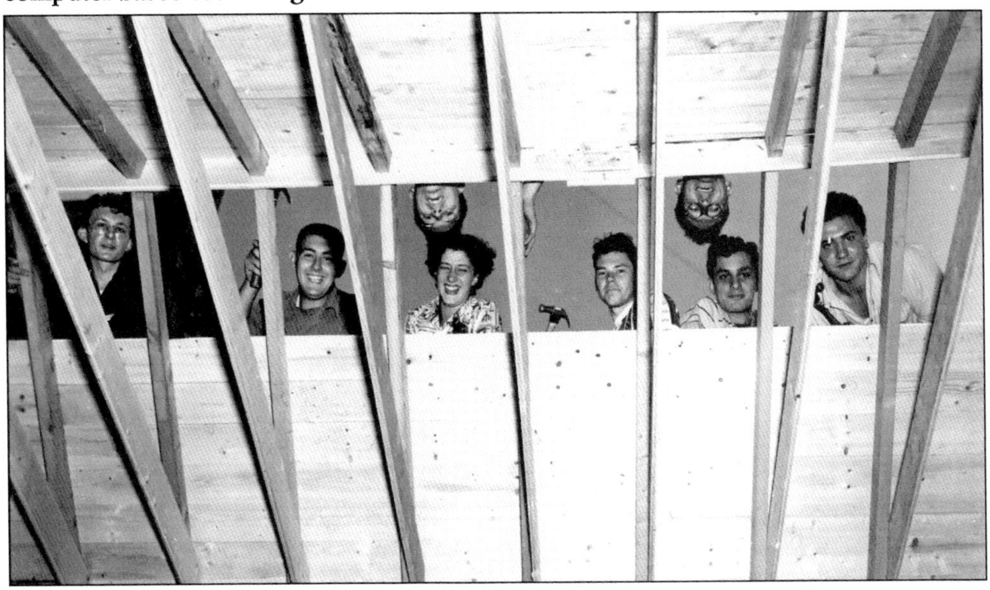

These students in the Structural Technology Department are actually constructing buildings in the school yard. The students would design the building and would frame it to almost a completed structure. Here we see students peering in from the roof of the building that they built.

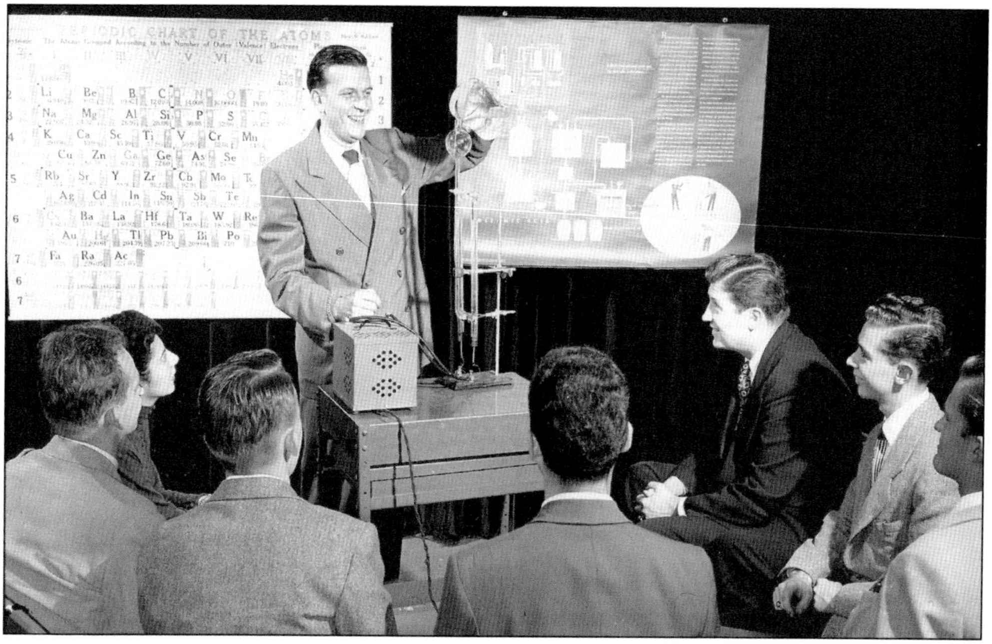

Students in this picture from the early 1950s appear to be learning chemistry. Again note the extreme difference in dress from current college students. Chemical Technology was one of the original areas of study at the institute.

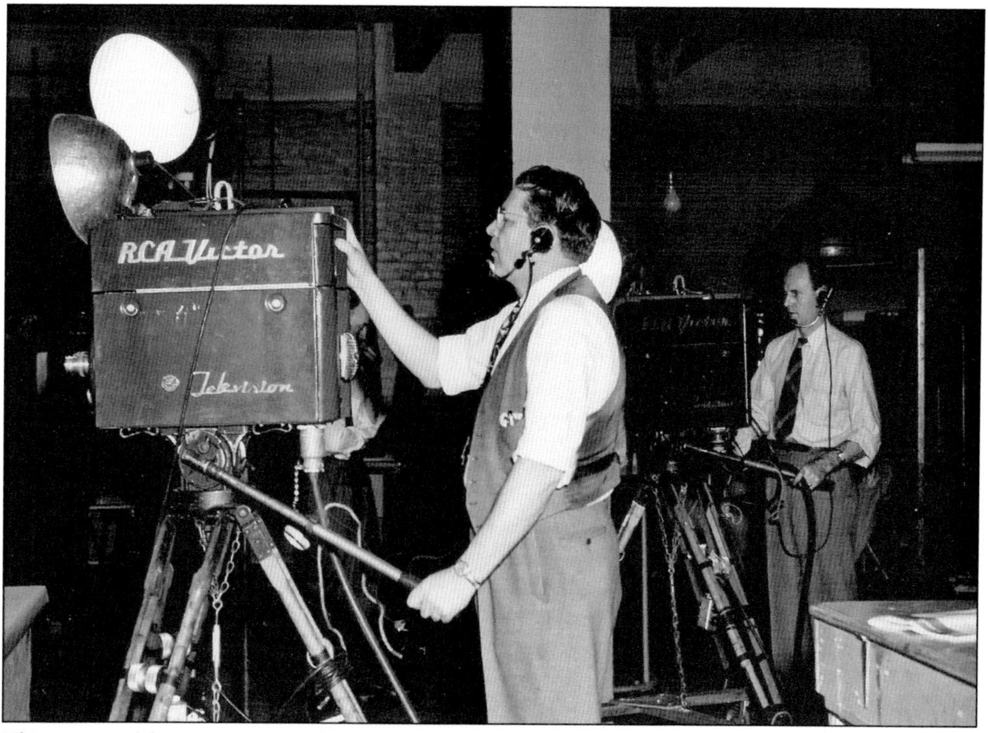

This is an old RCA Victor television camera. The picture appears to depict part of the Commercial Art and Advertising Production Department, from which the current Advertising Design and Graphic Arts Department evolved.

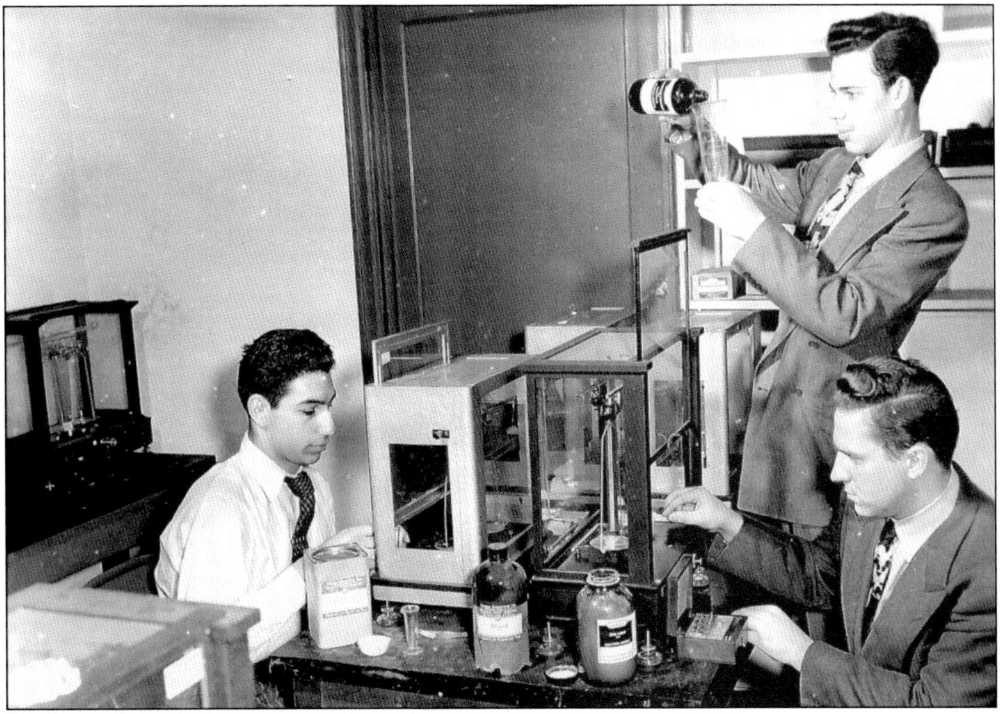

This chemistry class is pictured during the 1950s. Notice that two of these students are wearing suits and one student is wearing a lab coat. Chemistry and biology are central to many of the technologies today, just as they were a half century ago.

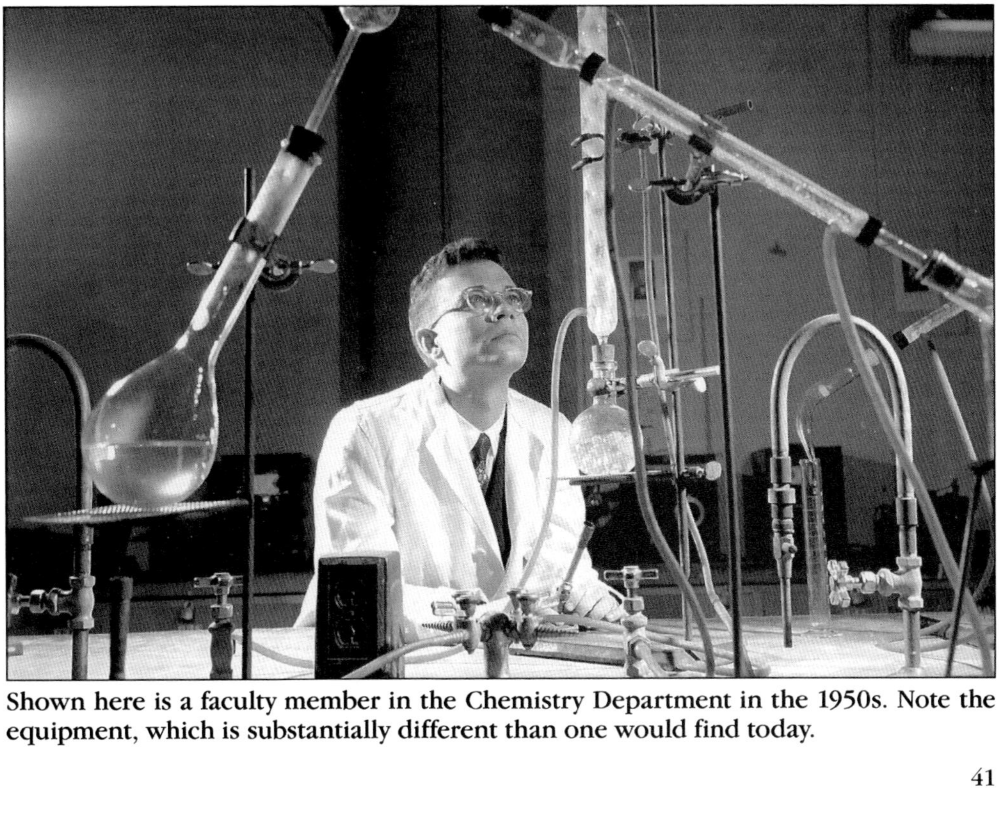

Shown here is a faculty member in the Chemistry Department in the 1950s. Note the equipment, which is substantially different than one would find today.

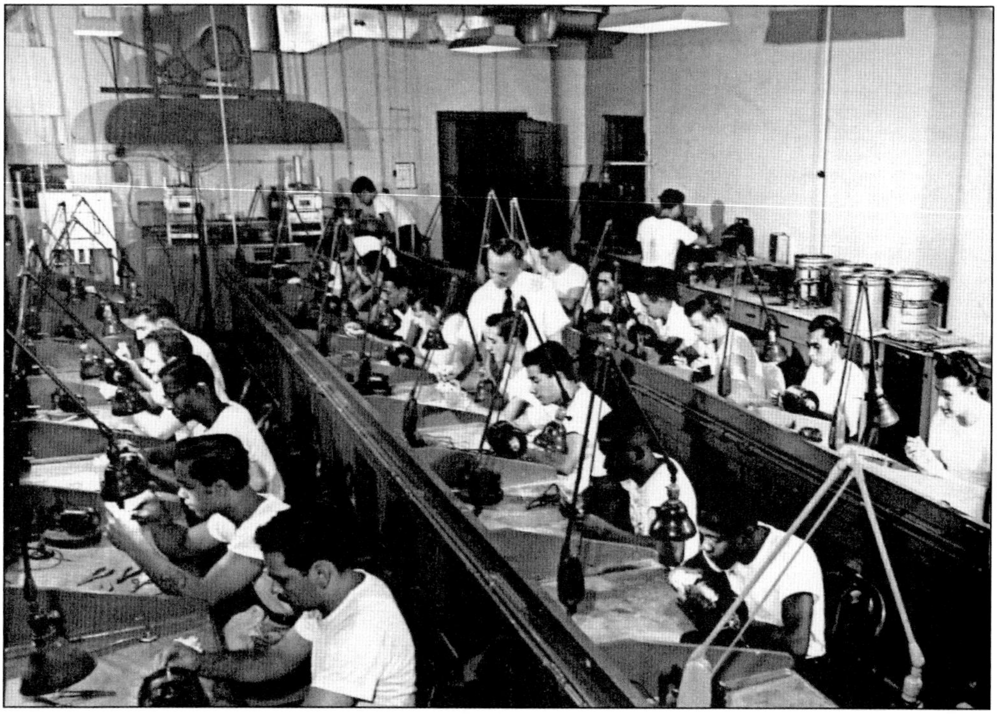

Students are shown in the dental laboratory during the early 1950s. This is a far cry from the classroom activity one would find today.

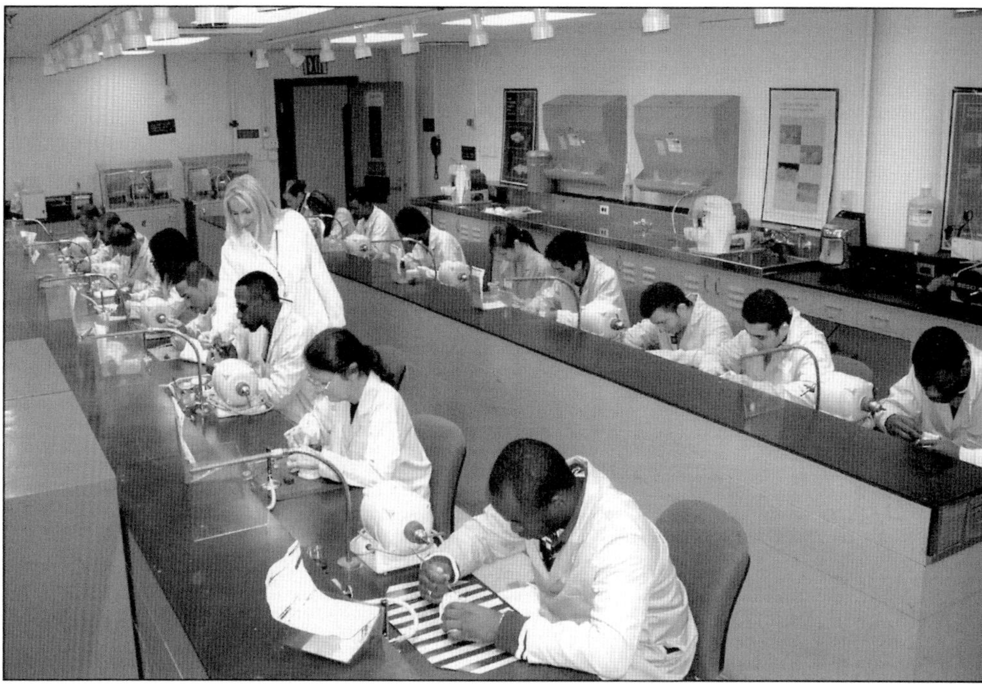

Shown here is precisely the same classroom as in the previous picture. Note the modern equipment and the far greater student diversity than found in the institute. What is the same? Notice the attention that the instructor gives to the work of each student.

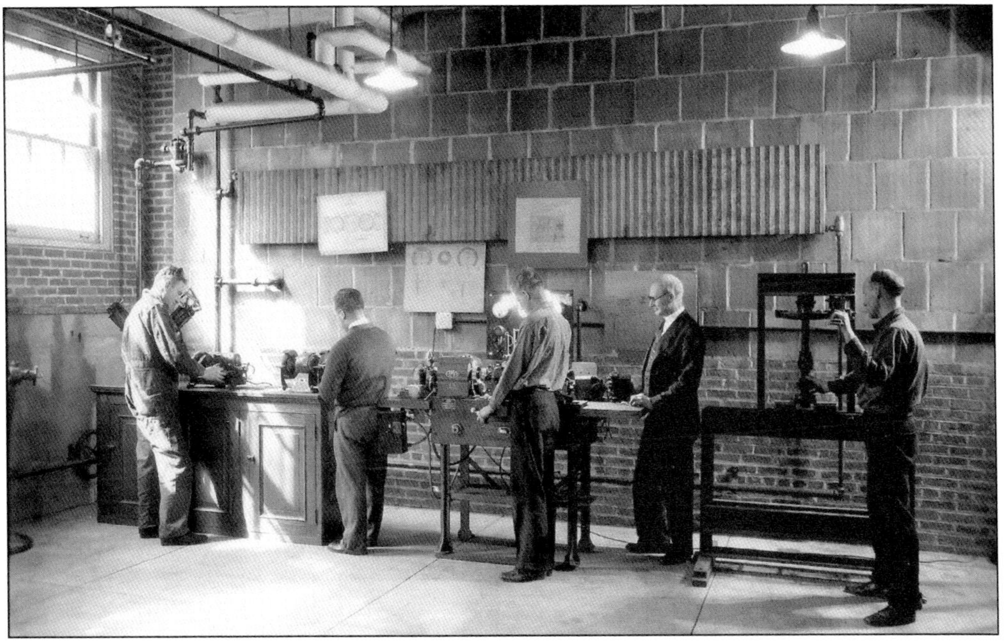

This picture depicts students in the Electrical Technology Department during the late 1940s or early 1950s. Notice that the students were wearing work clothing in order to take part in class.

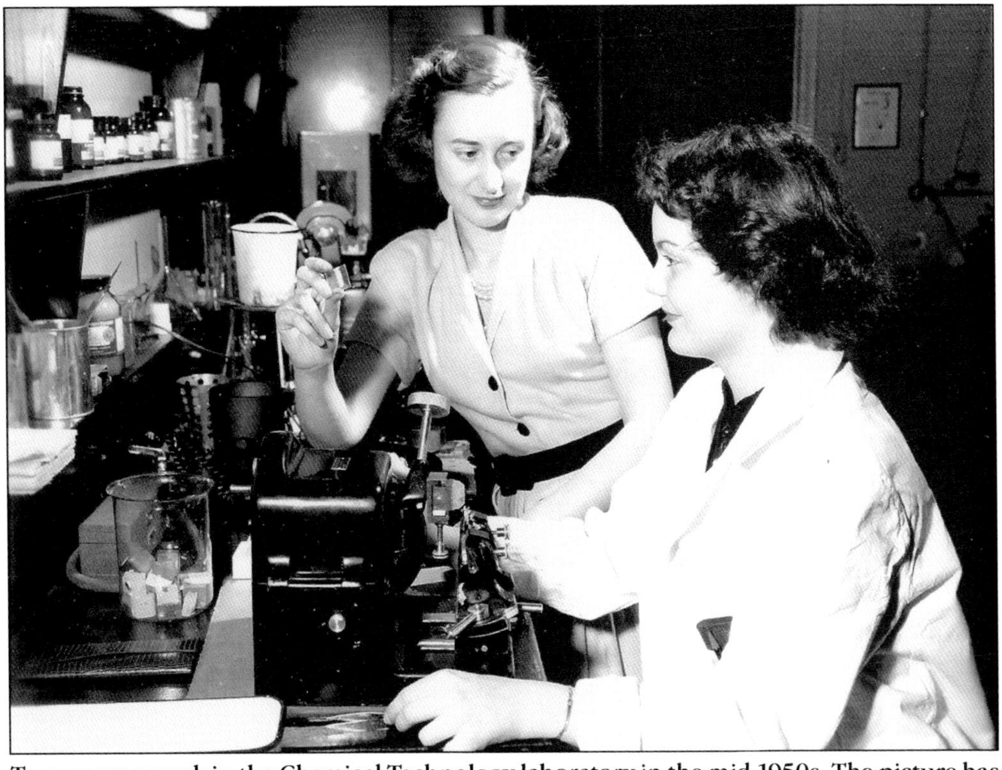

Two women work in the Chemical Technology laboratory in the mid-1950s. The picture has something of a staged feeling to it and may have been taken for publicity purposes.

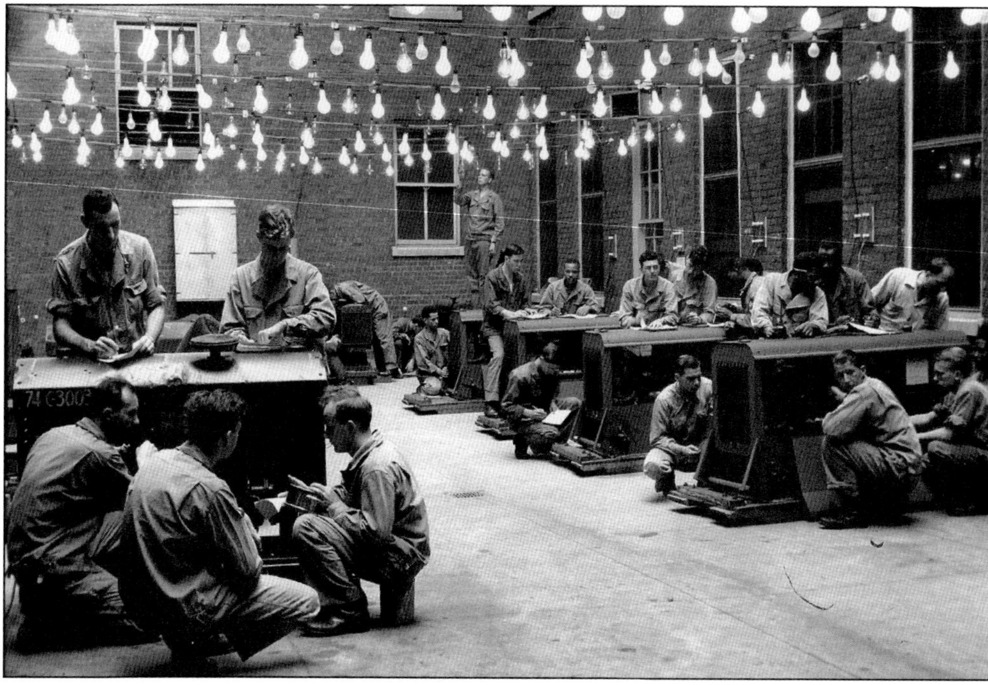

Students in military uniform work in a Mechanical Technology laboratory in the early 1950s.

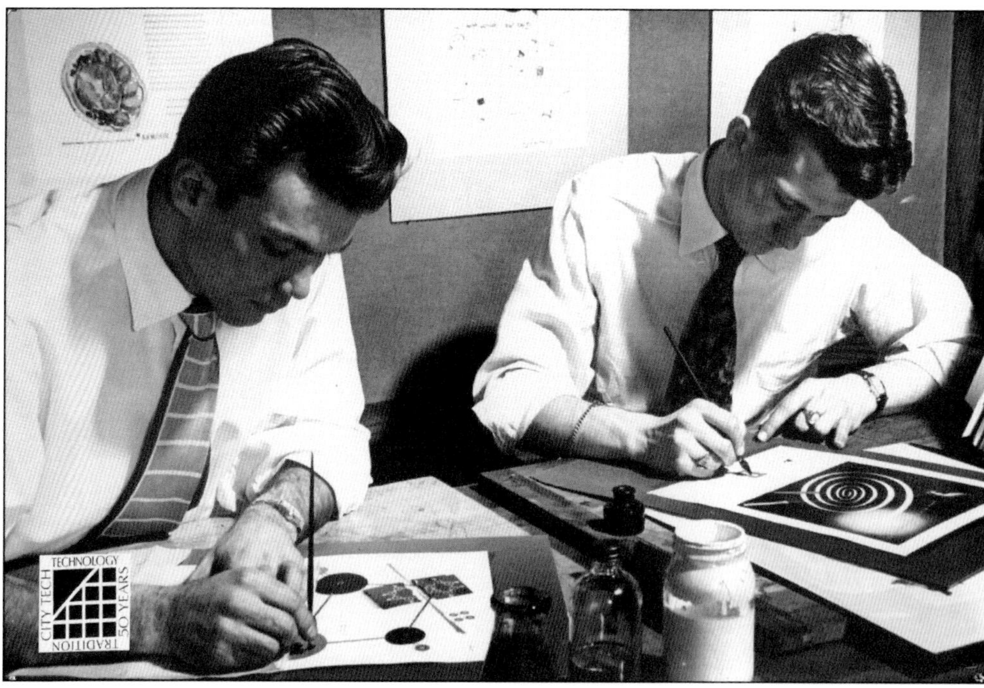

These two students are in the Commercial Art Department. This was the only department that trained students to become commercial artists as well as the advertising field. It is today the largest department at the college and, according to a recent article in *Advertising Age*, is unique in its diversity.

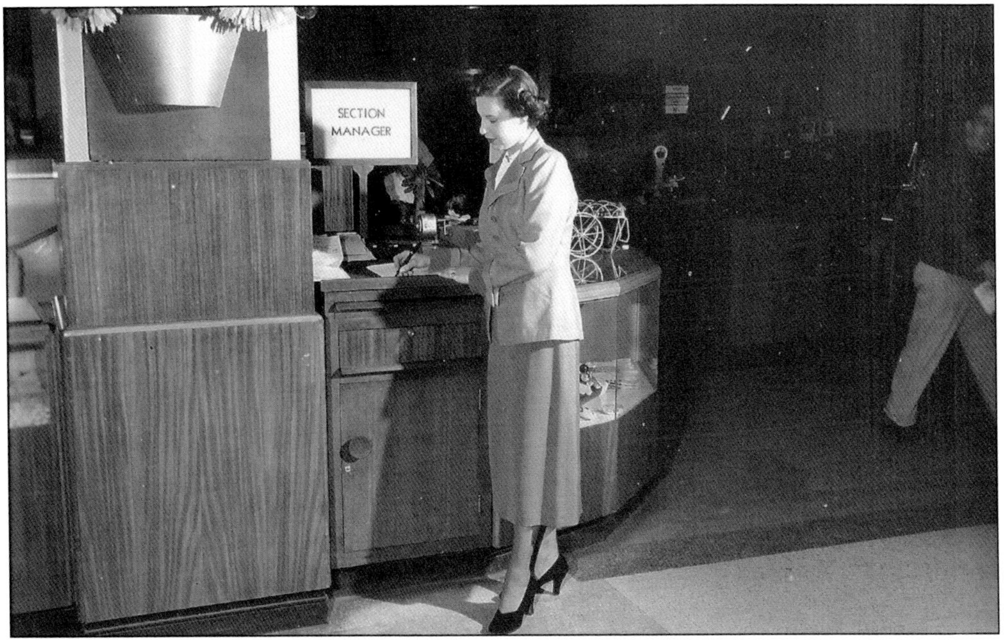

This picture was taken during the early 1950s. The sign says, "section manager." The student is from the early Retail Distribution and Commerce Department, started in 1948. The department, today labeled simply the Business Department, currently enrolls over 1,000 students and houses three separate majors: accounting, marketing management and sales, and fashion marketing.

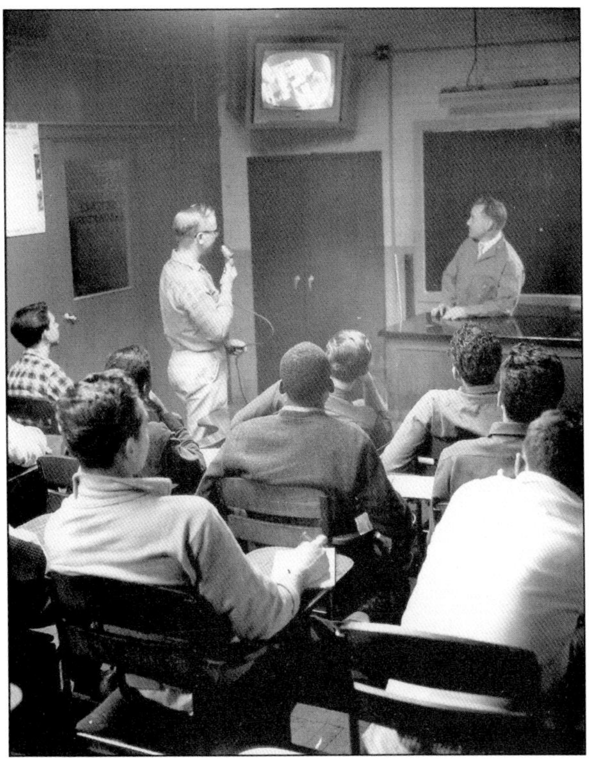

This shows a class in Communication Arts and Skills Department in the late 1950s. Today's degree requirements include substantial training in the liberal arts, including both english and speech.

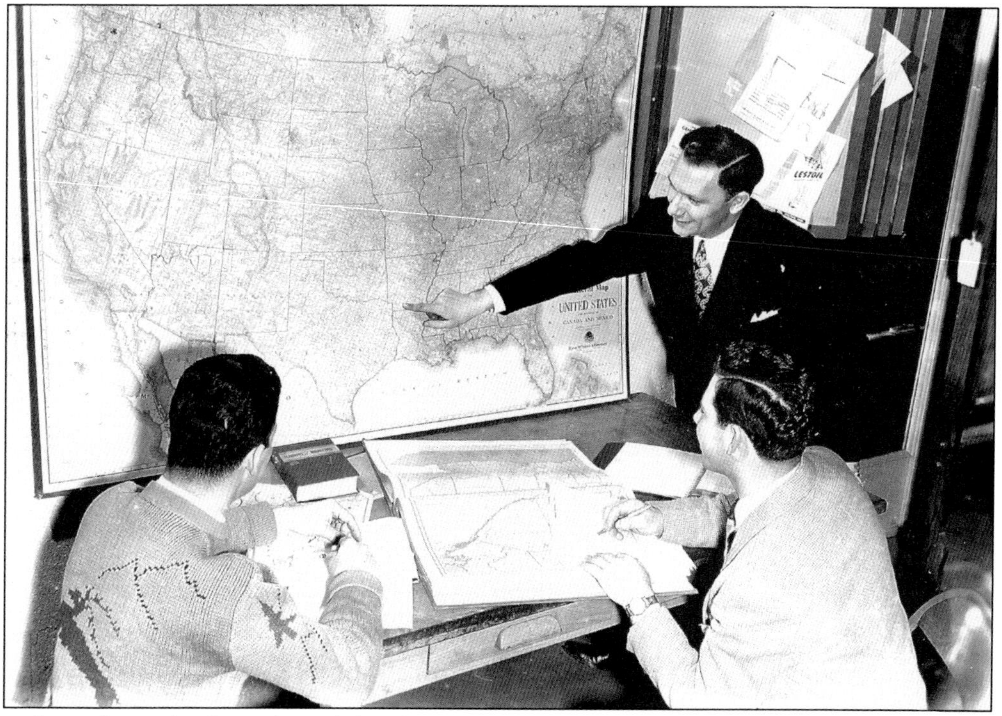

Judging from the formality of the dress, this picture was taken in the early 1950s. The map would suggest that this could have been a course in geography, American history, or American government.

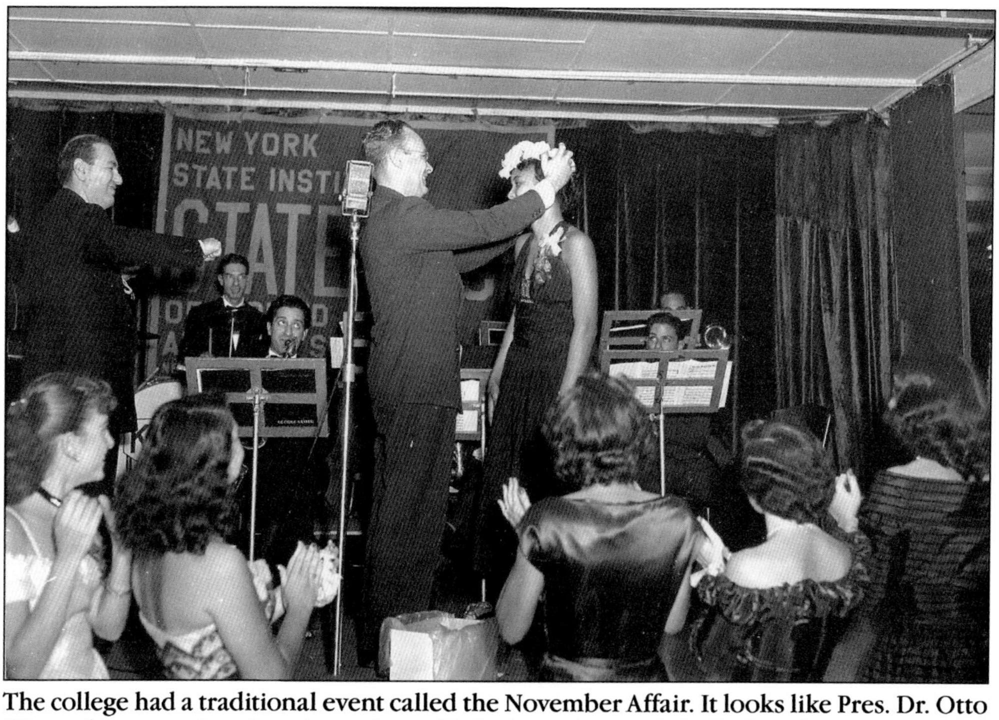

The college had a traditional event called the November Affair. It looks like Pres. Dr. Otto Klitgord is crowning the winner here. Today's students might find such events quaint.

Three

A College in Search of an Identity 1960–1980

In the middle years of this history, the college grew rapidly, and its structure and affiliation changed just as rapidly. The college began 1968 as part of the State University of New York system, and carried the nickname SUNY Tech. The college had grown to 4,000 day students and 7,500 evening students. There was no tuition and apparently only spotty record keeping, especially for the evening students. The large numbers for the evening session included much of what is today seen as Continuing Education, training for students with no degree aspirations, who either sought entry into a profession or were attempting to improve their job skills.

By the end of 1969, the administration of the college had passed from state control to New York City control, as part of the recently merged City University of New York (CUNY). By 1971, the college—under the banner of New York City Community College—had grown to an estimated 15,000 students. It was the first public community college in the city of New York, and one of the largest of the 1,150 community colleges in the United States.

The 1970s were a tumultuous era for the college, and a decade during which it experienced a serious challenge to its survival, one of two such crises. As the college passed from the SUNY system to the CUNY system, its funding passed from the state to the city. In theory, this should have posed no problem. However, no one at the college anticipated the fiscal crisis of the City of New York. For years, New York City had existed beyond its means, building up substantial debt. But by the mid-1970s, bills came due and the pyramid of debt posed a threat to all public institutions. For a variety of political reasons, the federal government initially refused to participate in the bailout necessary to the survival of the nation's largest city. Severe austerity measures were instituted and much of the decision-making for the city government rested in the hands of the Municipal Assistance Corporation, led by financier Felix Rohatyn, and the Emergency Financial Control Board of New York state. The necessary budget reductions were to include a $32 million rescission of the budget of the City University of New York.

Plans included a furlough for all faculty at the college, elimination of all liberal arts courses, and other draconian reductions. The college entered a period of retrenchment, where decisions had to be made on staff reduction, program closings, and other austerity measures.

At the same time, the student population had grown rapidly, propelled by the open admission policy instituted for the university in 1972. By 1975, enrollment had grown to over 18,000, counting both daytime and evening sessions. The college was operating in rented space spread throughout downtown Brooklyn. Before this crisis ended, tuition was imposed, enrollments became less swollen, and the college seemed once again on track.

But there was another crisis yet to come. The extended budget crisis of the city eventually reduced the college to a point where its very existence was in doubt. This college, which had gone from state control to local control, appeared to be heading for a sad ending, as New York City reduced its funding of community colleges. However the college was well served in this crisis by its new president, Ursula C. Schwerin. The first president to be a graduate of the college, Schwerin was also the first woman president of a technical college in the United States. After a period of frantic negotiations, demonstrations, and near despair, control of the college shifted once again to the State of New York.

In retrospect, this crisis laid the groundwork for the college as it is known today. The name of the college changed again in 1980, from New York City Community College to New York City Technical College. The charter of the college was amended by the New York State legislature to designate it as an "urban technical institute" and the college shortly thereafter became a bi-level institution, authorized to grant both associate and baccalaureate degrees. Budgetary responsibility was assumed by New York State, as it is for all senior colleges of the CUNY system.

The crisis was averted, but for some years the new charter ill defined the institution. Although the college was authorized to award bachelor of technology degrees, it remained an overwhelmingly associate-level institution. In 1992, of slightly over 10,000 students at the college, fewer than 400 were enrolled in bachelor's degree programs. A senior college in name, the transition of the New York City College of Technology to full senior college status was still on the horizon.

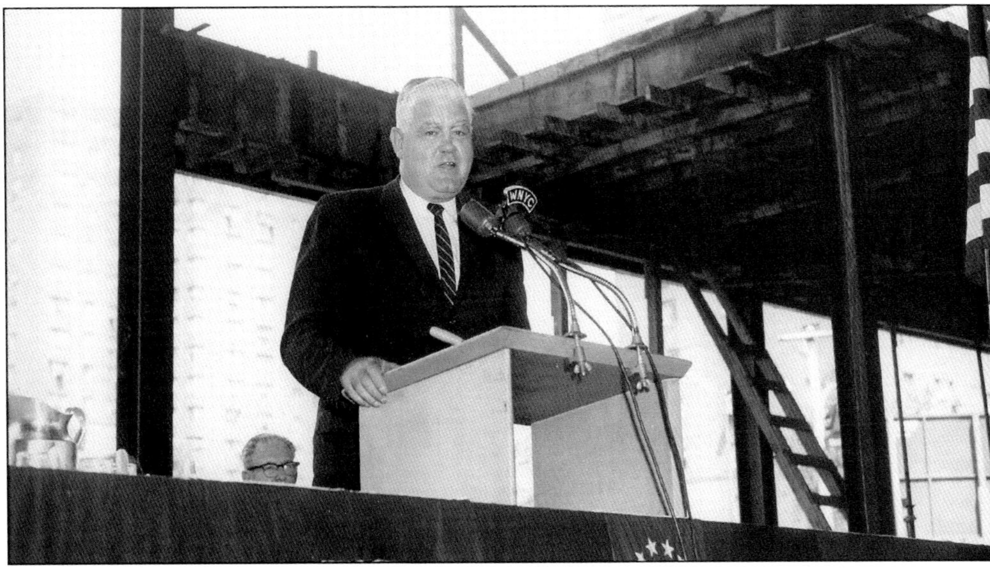

This is a picture of the New York City College of Technology's second president, Lawrence Jarvie. Dr. Otto Klitgord's untimely death in April 1960, while touring Puerto Rico for research that he was conducting, shocked the college. In August 1960, Jarvie assumed the helm of the college. President Jarvie's tenure was short lived, only serving the college for 16 months before he resigned. At the time of Jarvie's resignation, New York City Community College, as it was then called, was the largest community college in the State of New York. Here President Jarvie is dedicating Klitgord auditorium, completed in 1962 and named for the founding director of the college.

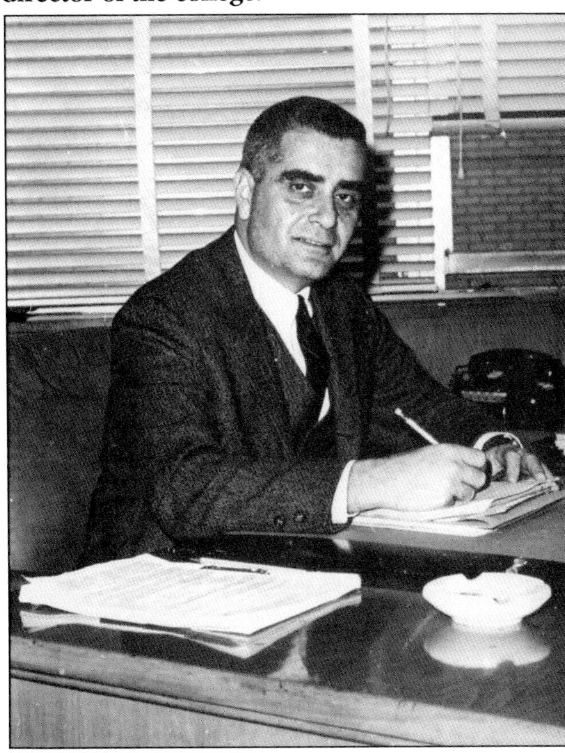

Milton Bassin was the third president of the college. Among his several accomplishments was the successful incorporation of the Voorhees Technical Institute into the college. Enrollments grew enormously during his years. The Bassin years were marked by the social upheavals found at almost every college of the period.

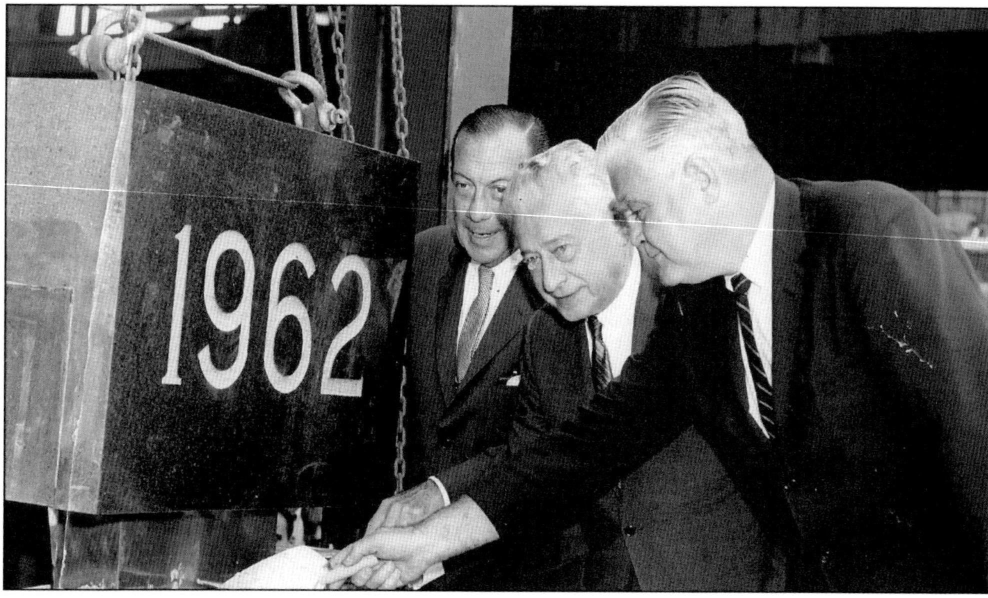

Laying the cornerstone for the Klitgord auditorium and gymnasium are Mayor Robert Wagner to the left, Brooklyn Borough president Abe Stark in the middle, and New York Community College president Lawrence Jarvie to the right.

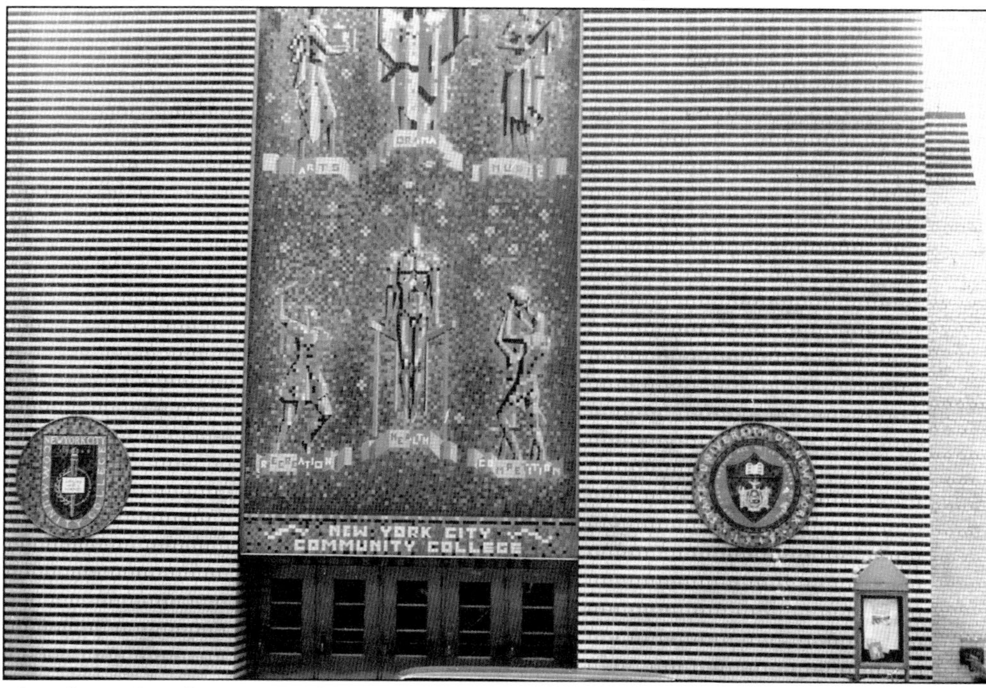

The Klitgord auditorium is shown as it looked shortly after its 1962 completion. It looks almost identical today, over 40 years later. This building is set to be torn down in the future to make room for expansion. On its site will rise the first academic facility constructed by the City University of New York as a public-private partnership. The sign above the entrance doors says, "New York City Community College," one of the half-dozen names of the college during its 60-year history.

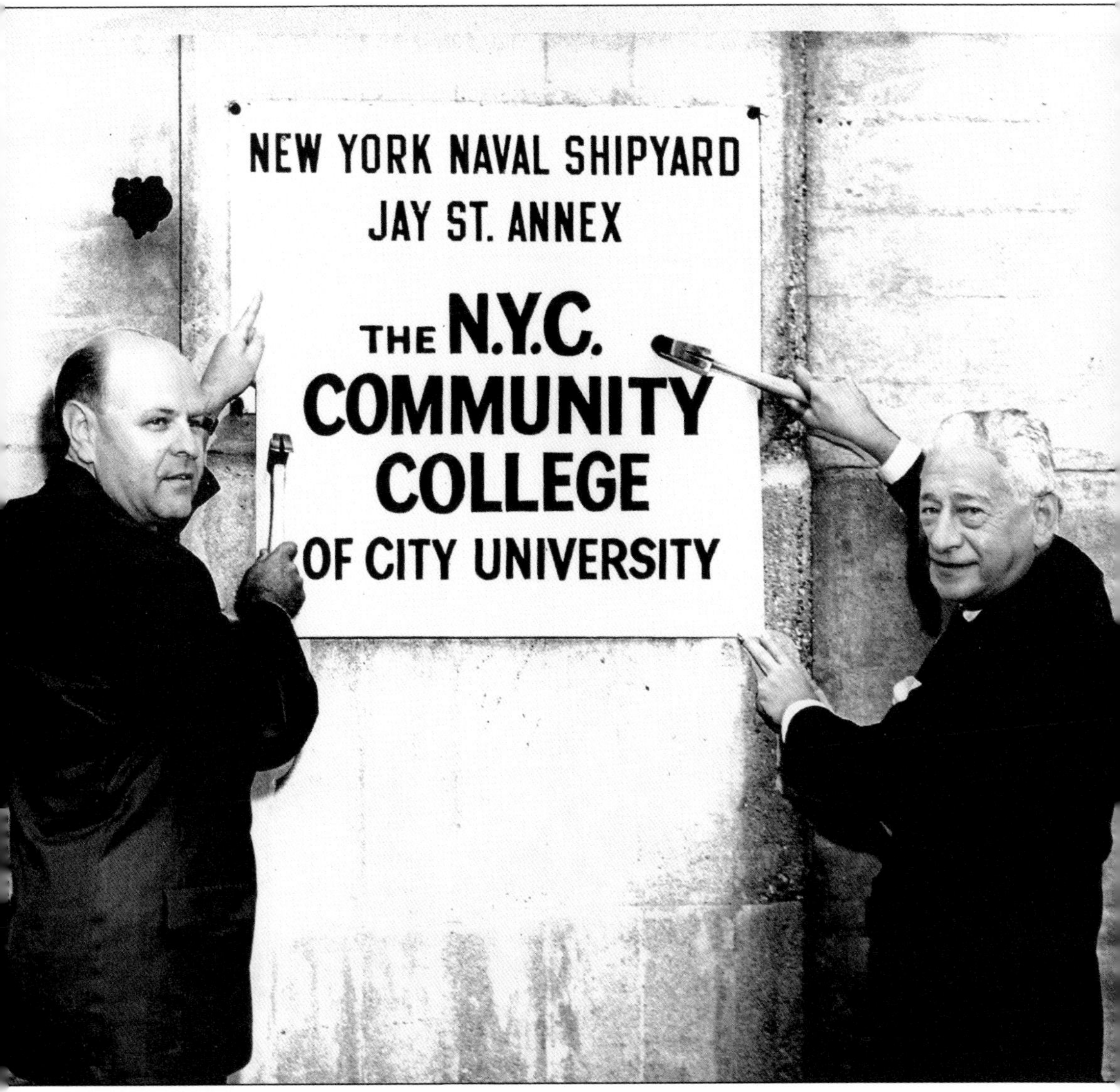

Dr. Murray Block, the acting president of the college, and Brooklyn Borough president Abe Stark proudly affix the sign of the new owners on the New York Naval Shipyard Jay Street Annex. Later this building would stand next to Namm Hall, which would not be occupied until 1969. The college was given the building by New York City for the expansion of its facilities. As this picture was taken, the Namm Building was under construction. Dr. Block, although never becoming the president of the college, served as acting president twice in his career. Acting Pres. Dr. Block assumed the role initially after Dr. Otto Klitgord's death in 1960 and subsequently after President Jarvie resigned in 1960. Dr. Block was considered an excellent leader. On April 15, 1964, during Dr. Block's second tenure as acting president, the college officially became a member of The City University of New York system. This university system is the largest and the most distinguished urban university system in the country. In 1965, Dr. Block was part of the ground-breaking ceremony of Namm Building, an 11-story academic complex that houses a large percentage of the instruction of the college today.

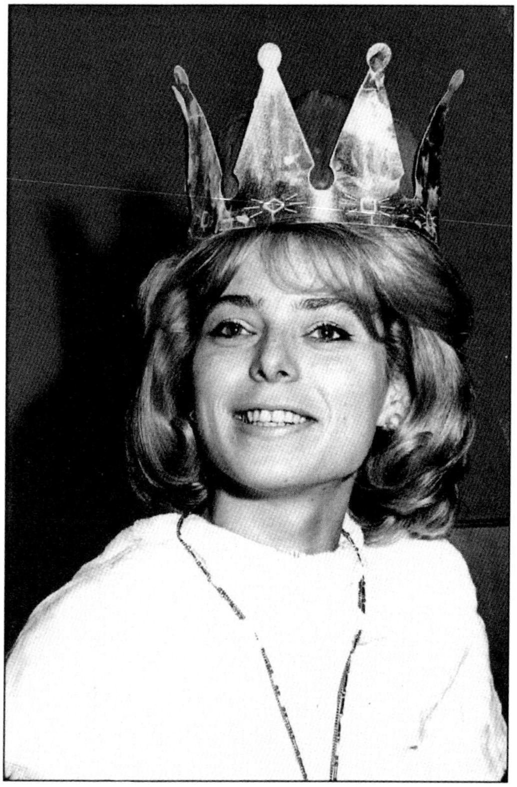

In the early 1960s, the big social event at the college was the November Affair. Miss Community College of 1963, chosen by ballot, was a 20-year-old dental hygiene student, shown here.

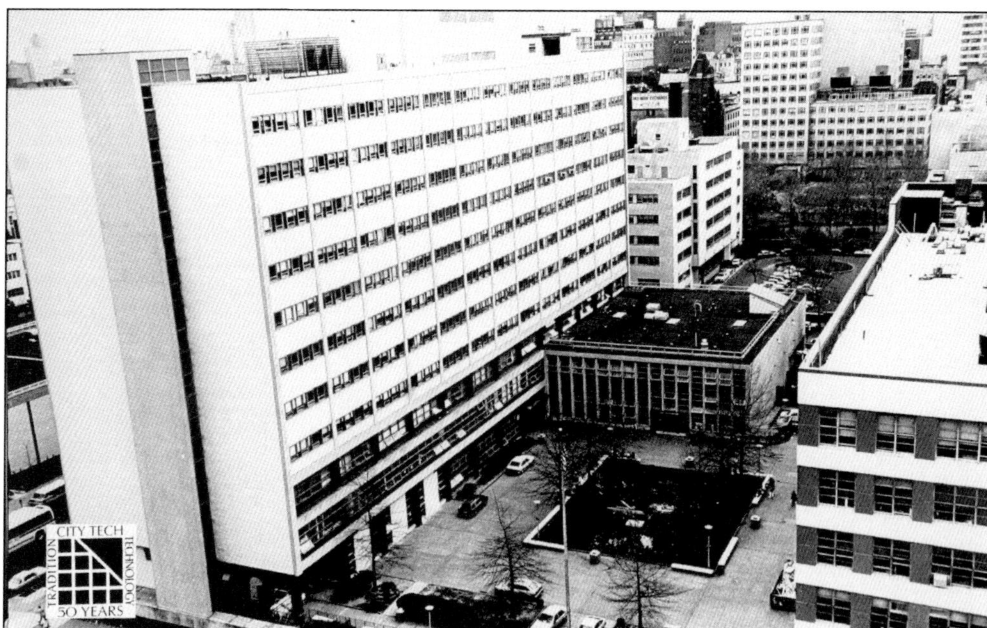

The Namm Building is shown at its completion in 1969. Notice that the Atrium was not built at this time. In the 1980s, the Atrium, a six-story, airy glass building was constructed linking Namm Building with the so-called Pearl and General Buildings, creating nearly a square block of linked academic facilities.

This sign announces construction of the Atrium during the Koch administration and while Mario Cuomo was governor. Edward Koch was mayor from 1978 until 1989.

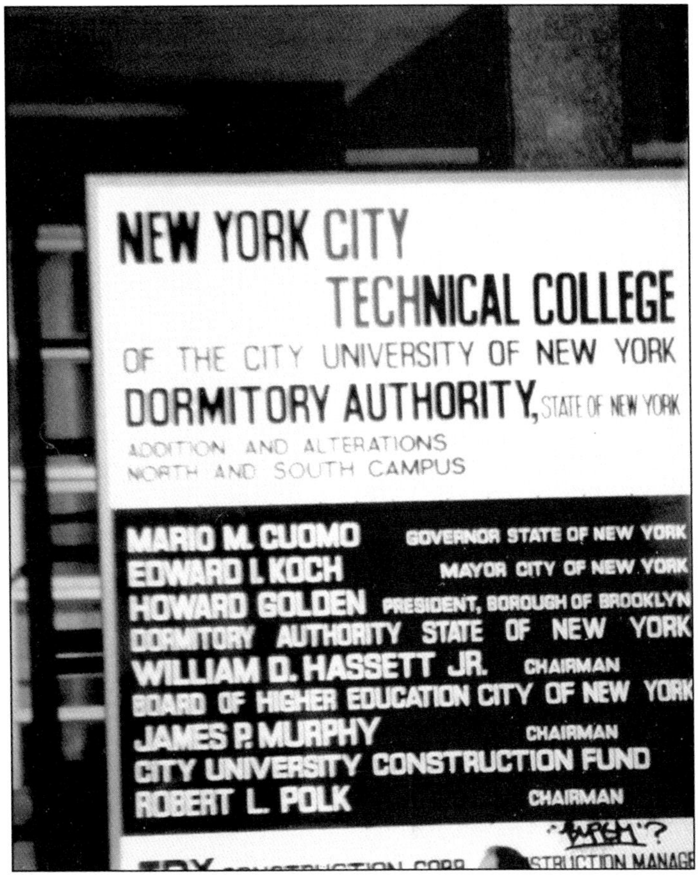

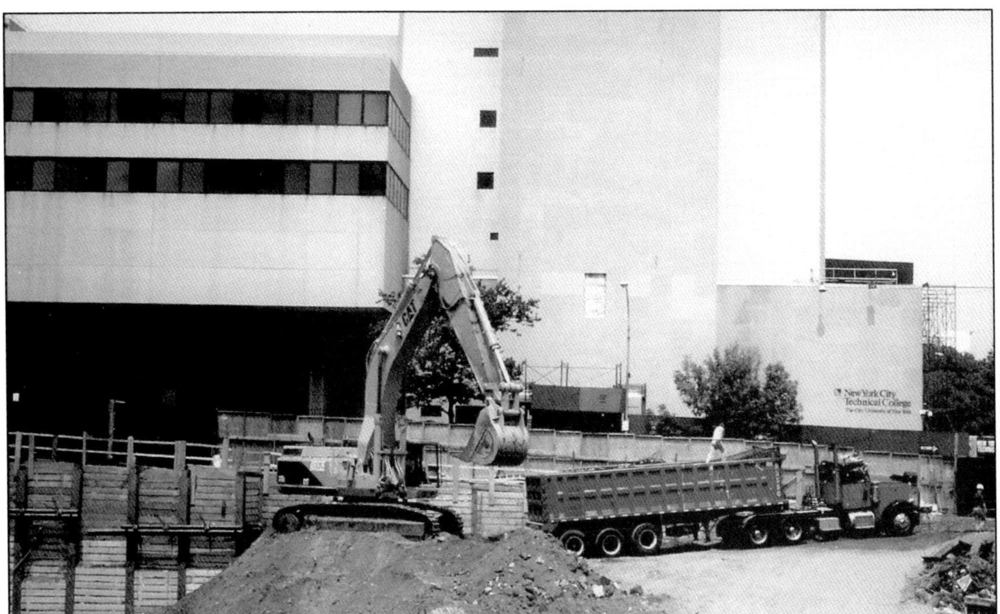

This picture was taken during the construction of the Atrium building, probably 1985.

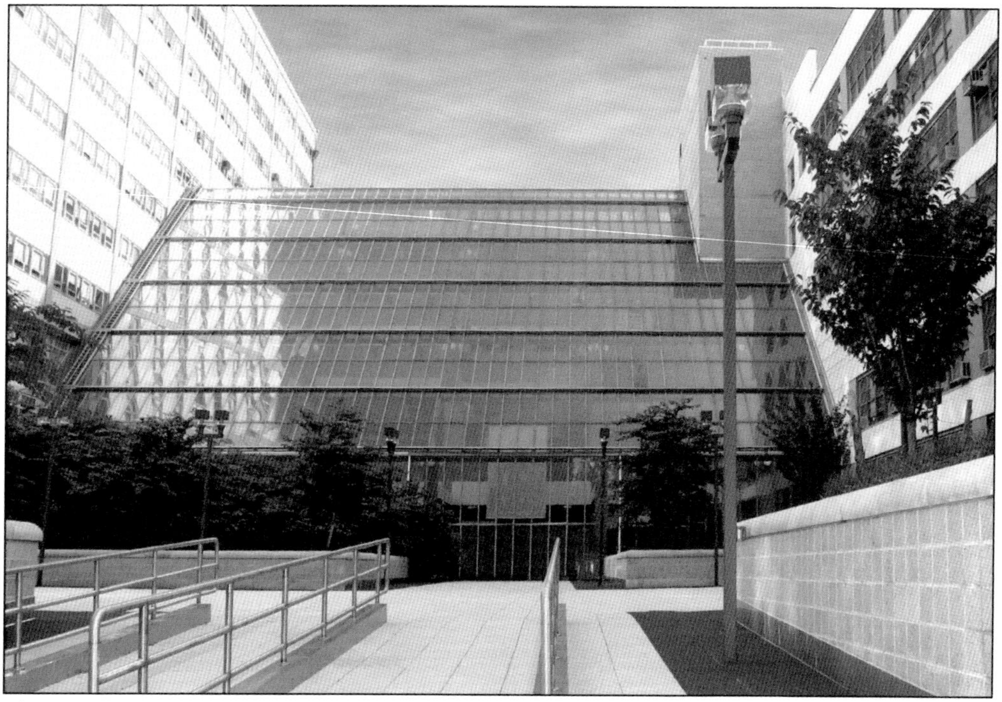

The Atrium was not constructed until the mid-1980s. The Atrium walkway makes it possible for students to get to the Pearl and General Buildings with greater ease. Here the Atrium, often used as a symbol of the college, is seen in all its glory, in a photograph enhanced by a graphic artist.

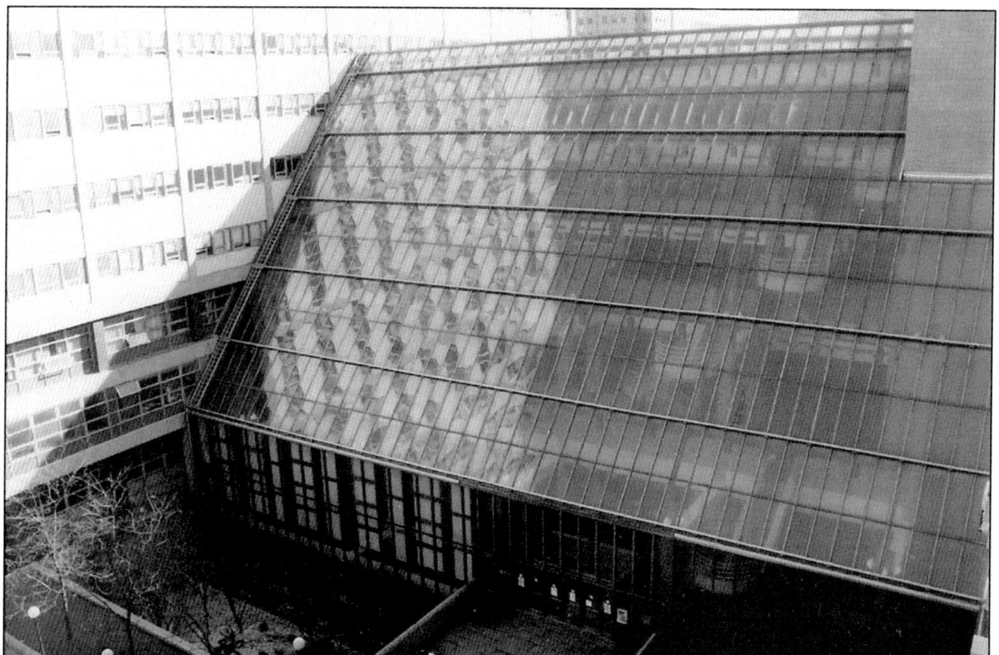

This is a close up of the Atrium. Notice that the facade of this building was constructed out of thick glass, which gives the building its airy appearance throughout the year.

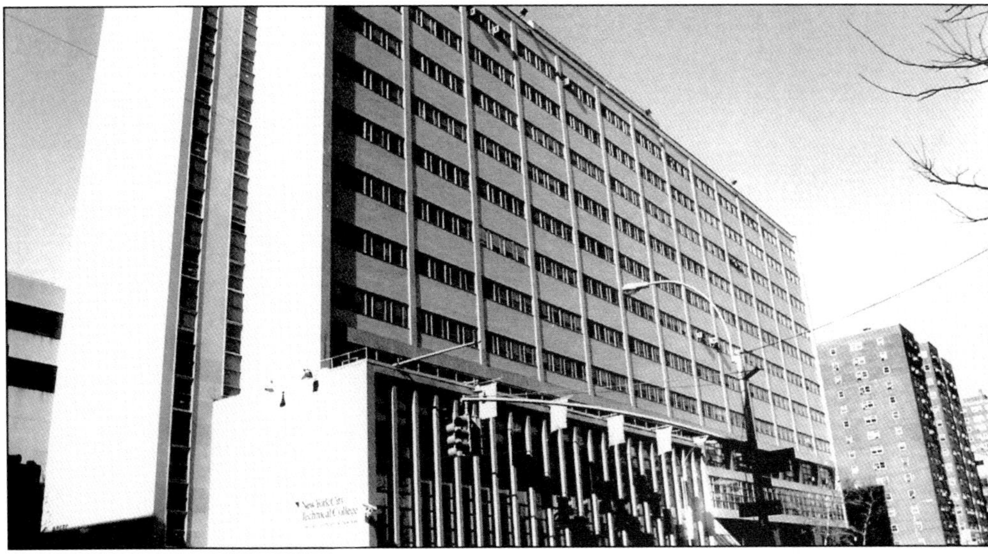

The Namm Building is shown wrapped in scaffolding. Before the end of 2007, the building is set to receive a new facade and windows, and will have significant improvements to its HVAC. Its original slate facade lasted over 40 years. The college is now going through major renovations that will also include a new facade and other enhancements to the Voorhees Building, which houses the engineering technologies, a new bookstore, and in the near future, construction of a major high-rise facility on the current site of the Klitgord gym and auditorium.

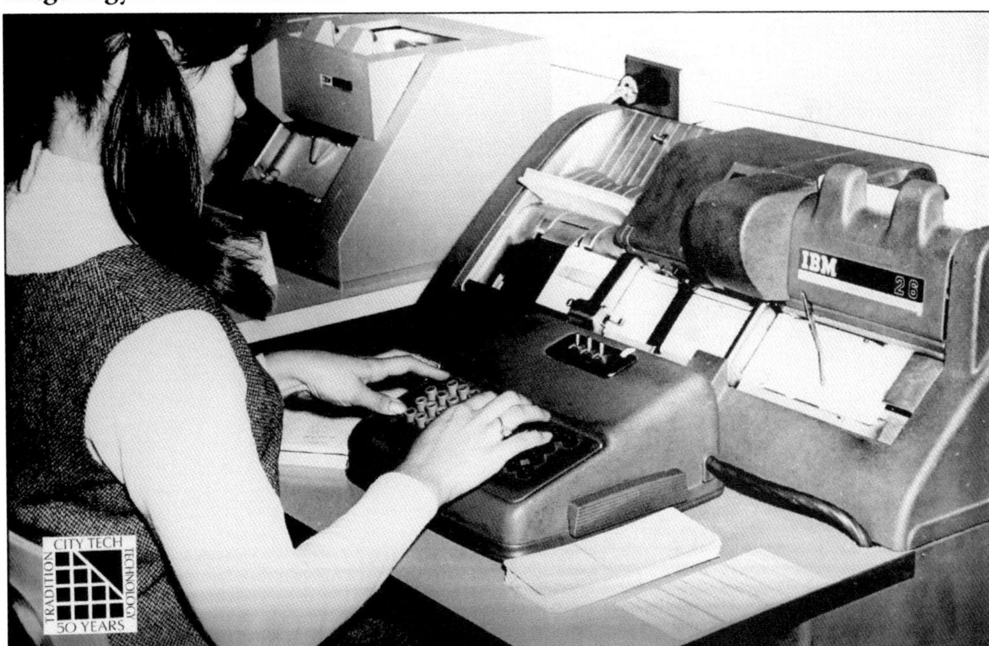

This young woman works on an old IBM punch card machine; this picture is from the late 1960s or early 1970s. Today's students cannot imagine that a few years ago, computers were run by these decks of cards and had only continuous paper print-outs rather than the graphical interfaces that current computer users take for granted.

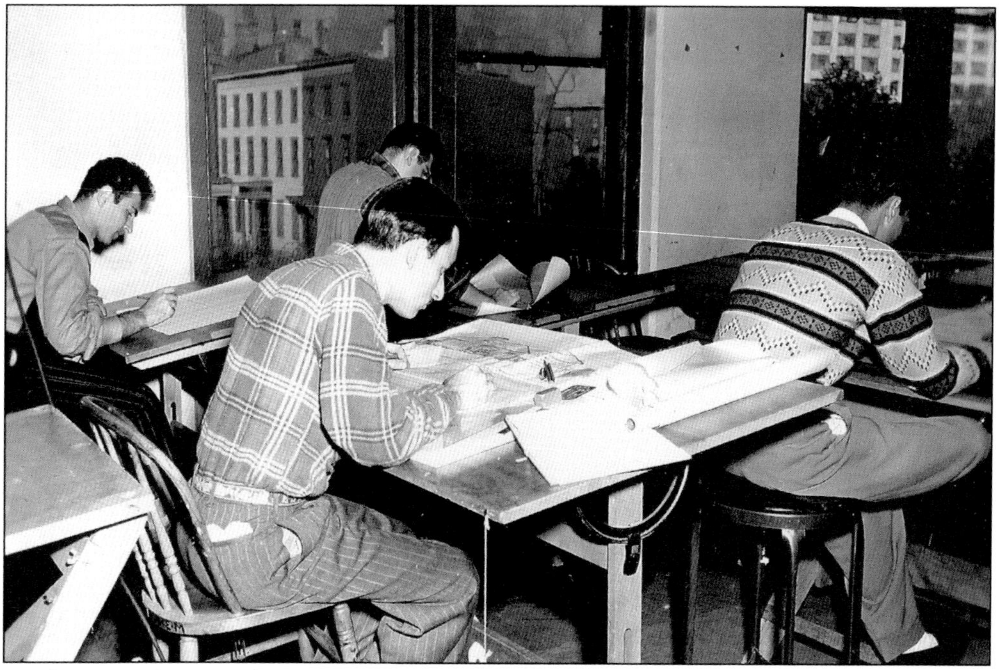

Students in the Graphic Arts Program are shown around the 1960s. In a relatively few years, students have seen this program change from leaded type set by hand to computer-based layouts normally routed to digital presses. Students from this program continue to staff the enormous printing industry around New York, and while studying can participate in a quality assurance lab sponsored by the New York Times.

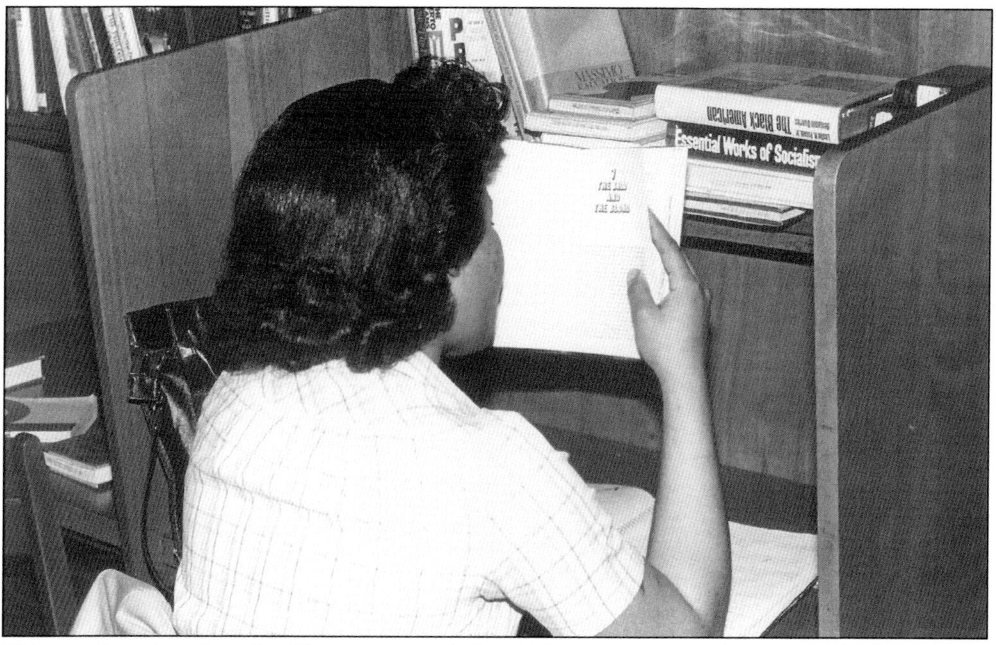

This student is using the library around the 1960s. As every other part of the college, the library today takes advantage of digital resources that would have been beyond the imagination of the student in this photograph.

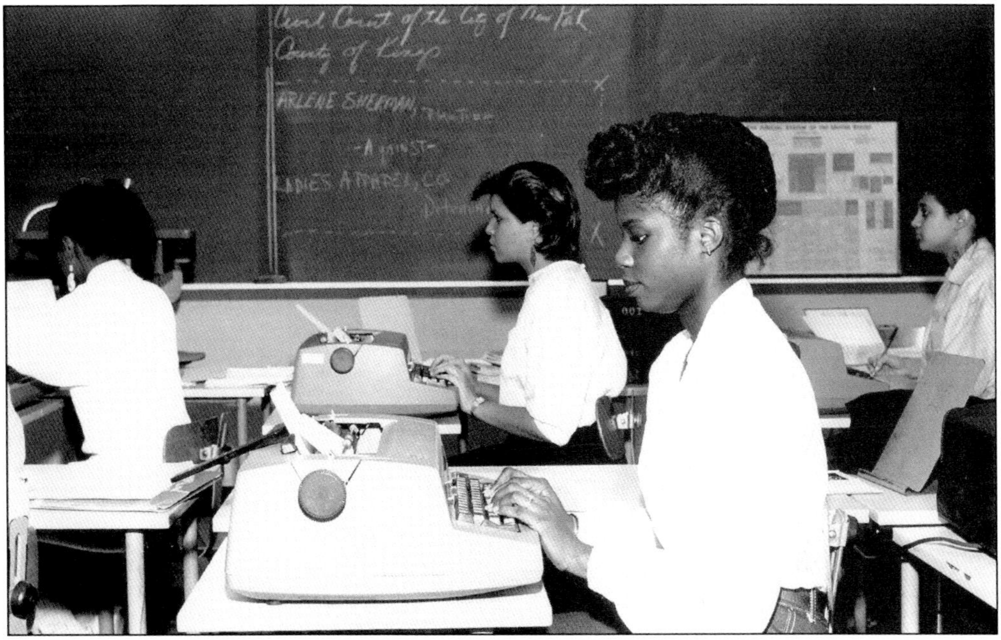

Pictured here are students in the Secretarial Science Department. This program ended in the mid-1990s. The electric typewriters seen here date this picture from the late 1960s to the early 1980s. While the skills learned by these students remain valuable today, the information age revolution has made them more easily accessible, eliminating the need for the program.

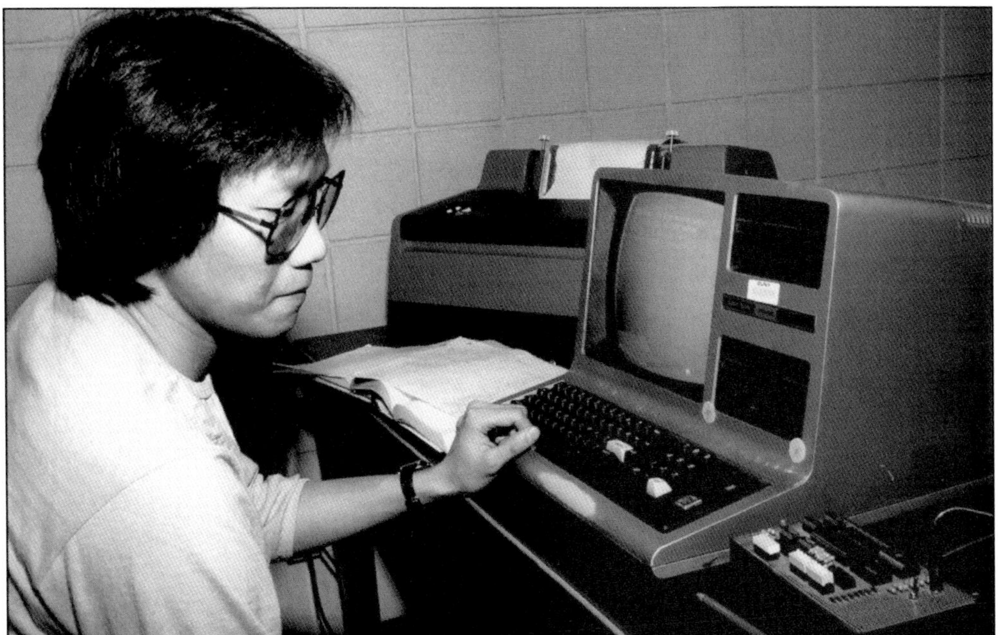

A student in this picture is working with an old computer, dating back possibly to the late 1970s. It appears to be a one-piece univac console and might today find a home in a computer museum.

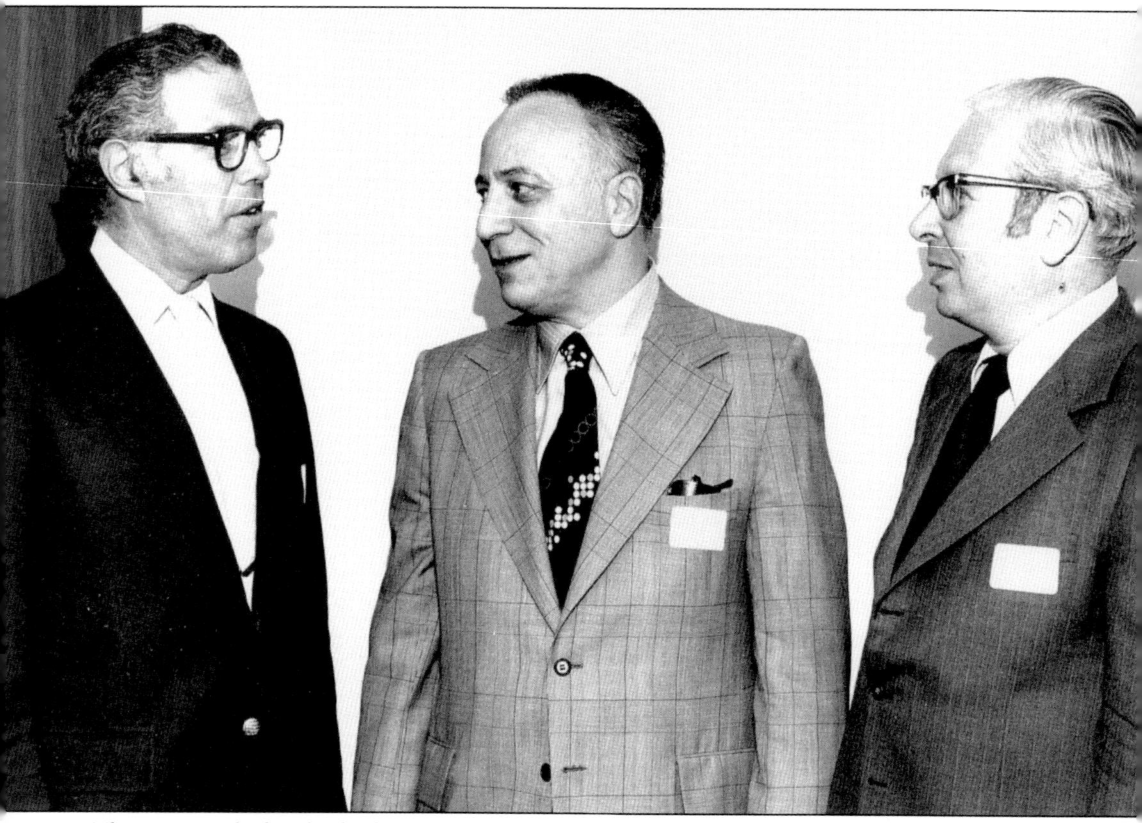

The man with the thick glasses on the left is the fourth president of the college, Herbert Sussman, who was at the helm from 1972 until 1977. President Sussman went on to assume an administrative position in the San Francisco Community College System. During his tenure, his most important accomplishment was keeping the college afloat during the New York City fiscal crises of the 1970s.

Four

A Mature College with a Clear Mission 1980–Present

If the New York City College of Technology entered the last decade of the 20th century as an institution in search of an identity, it left the decade with that identity firmly in place. Throughout its earlier history, the college had spent much of its energy explaining what it was not: not a trade school, not a community college, and not a place for students unable to meet the demands of a liberal arts college. In its most recent period, the college has been able to proudly proclaim what it is: the sole college of technology of the largest urban university system in the country.

In earlier periods, visitors and even college staff would marvel at the sophistication of the programs of the college and describe it in clichéd terms like, "the best-kept secret in Brooklyn," the sort of description frequently applied to schools that have not quite found their niche. But in the 1990s, as well-paid employment was no longer a given for the graduates of traditional liberal arts colleges, the New York City College of Technology was able to clarify its image: in the areas it served—the technologies, health care, business, entertainment and design, public service, and especially computer-related fields—the New York City College of Technology was uniquely positioned to provide its graduates with the passport to a satisfying and lucrative career. This would have been no surprise to residents of Japan or Germany, where training in technology had long been a prestigious career path, but it was new for the United States.

By the early 1990s, enrollment had shrunk to a little over 10,000. But as the realignment of the American economy, caused by the information age revolution, took hold, the college grew steadily. The new students were not at the college by default or because they had no alternative to an associate degree program, they were attracted to the New York City College of Technology by the strength and the uniqueness of its majors.

New programs were added, to meet emerging needs of the economy: data processing grew into two separate applied computer programs, Microcomputer Business Systems and Computer Information Systems; new baccalaureate programs were added, often but not always as continuations of existing associate degree programs; and curricula were modified to reflect the new trends in areas of technology.

Students responded to these changes. Between 1992 and 2006, as the overall student population at the college increased from 10,000 to almost 13,400, enrollment in bachelor's degree programs increased from less than 400 to nearly 4,000. Some older industrial programs were jettisoned, and programs reflecting emerging workforce needs were added. Programs in Computer Systems, Computer Engineering, and computer-enhanced Advertising Design became the largest at the college, eclipsing previous leaders. As the mid-1990s crisis in health care staffing deepened, many of the strongest students chose to enter these fields. Stronger students passed licensure exams immediately, found employment even before graduation, strengthened the reputation of the programs, and lead even better qualified students to the doors of the college.

New programs in Entertainment Technology, Health care Administration, and Applied Mathematics took the college in previously unexplored directions. Certificate programs were added in a dozen areas, to serve the small but important population who need job enhancement but not full degrees. Some of the traditional programs like Hotel Technology, refined considerably into associate and baccalaureate programs in Hospitality Management, added considerable luster to the image of the college. Students in the culinary arts portion of the curriculum now regularly win regional and national recognition and may be found in almost any high-end restaurant in New York.

Curricular reform and development were coupled with basic changes in approach to both pedagogy and process. Grant funding allowed the creation of learning communities to better integrate new students into college. A new student advisement center made sure that students received the attention they needed in selecting courses. Registration became a process done first on the telephone and later via the internet, taking students off needless lines and empowering them in the process. A revised master plan promised the college new facilities to meet surging enrollments.

Partially in response to these developments, the college approached one more name change. This time the change was not because the college was going to be bounced to another administrative structure and not because it was demanded to secure its funding. This was a name change sought by the college to gain greater recognition of its role in high-tech workforce development and to distinguish it from the many schools of lower ambition that call themselves technical colleges. On July 12, 2002, Gov. George Pataki signed legislation passed by the New York State legislature changing the formal name of the college to the New York City College of Technology.

In this chapter, one will find depictions of the work done by the New York City College of Technology students today. If one compares these pictures to those of the earlier periods, it is clear that much has changed. However much has also remained the same. The New York City College of Technology is still an engine of workforce development in the leading technologies. It still provides a home for a diverse and growing population—many are new immigrants, as in the trade school described at the start of the book. It is impossible to predict the changes that the New York City College of Technology will undergo in its second 60 years, but it can be said with some certainty that it will grow to meet emerging social and workforce needs.

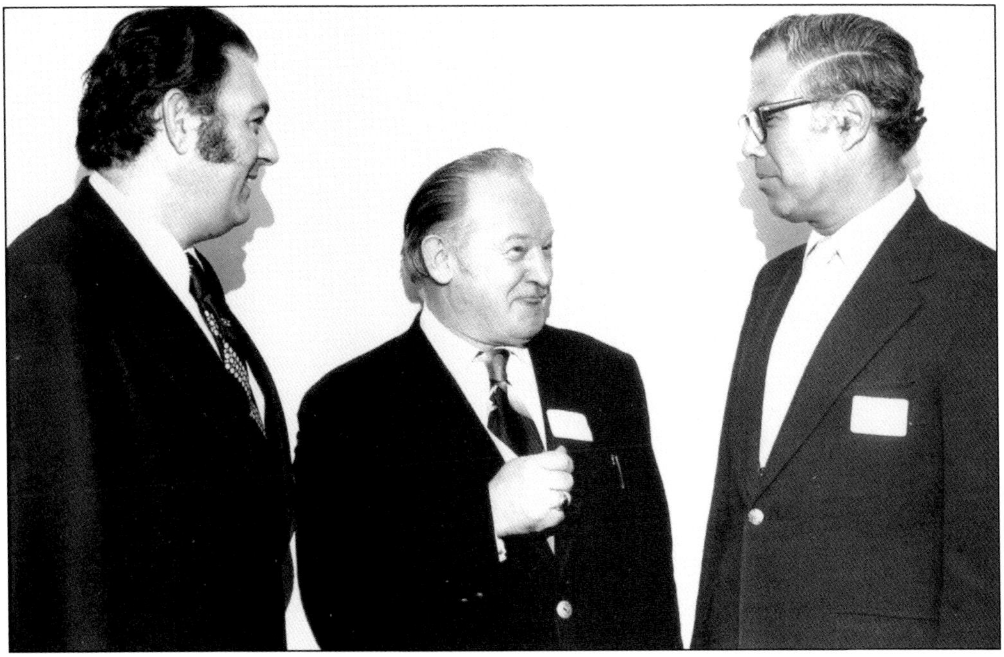

Pres. Herbert Sussman is seen here on the right. With President Sussman are Ozzie Ademic (left), who was on the president's advisory commission and, Prof. Seymour Foreman (center) of the Construction Technology Department.

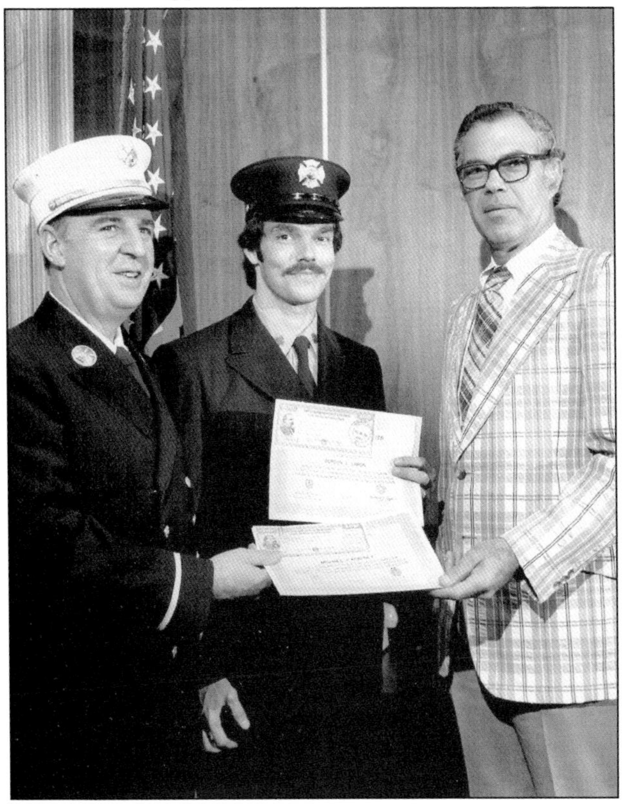

The caption on the back of this picture reads, "The feeling is definitely 'mutual' for these New York City firefighters who received top scholarship awards in the fire protection technology program at New York City Community College." At the 35th commencement, campus Pres. Herbert Sussman (right) presented the uniformed Fire Associations Scholar Award to Battalion Chief Michael Kearney (left) and another award to Fireman First Grade Gordon J. Symon (middle).

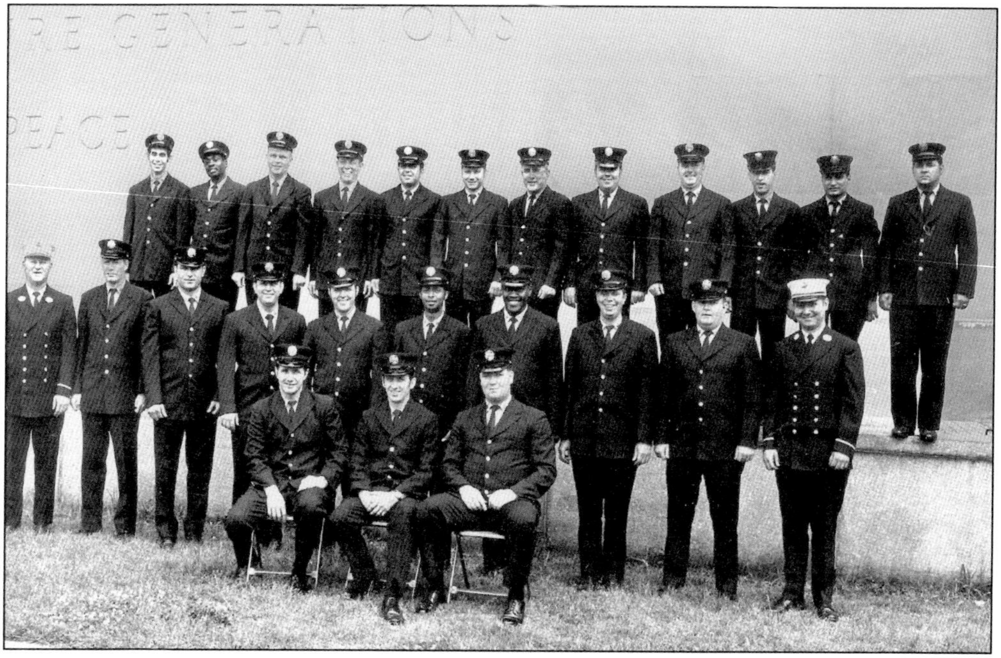

During the 1970s, the college ran a program in Fire Protection Technology for New York City firefighters. This is a graduation ceremony for individuals graduating from this degree program. Today many firefighters return to the college after leaving the Fire Department to prepare for a second career.

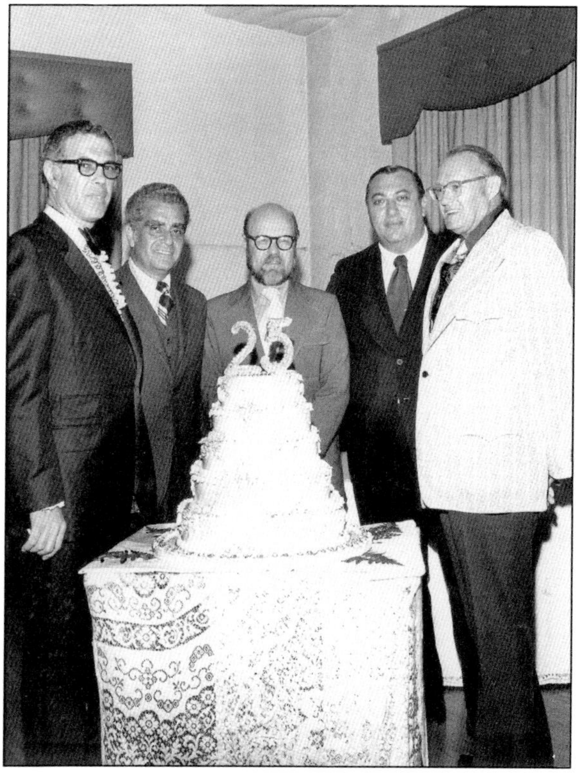

This cake celebrated the 25th anniversary of the college that occurred in February 1972. The man on the left was the new president of the college, Herbert Sussman.

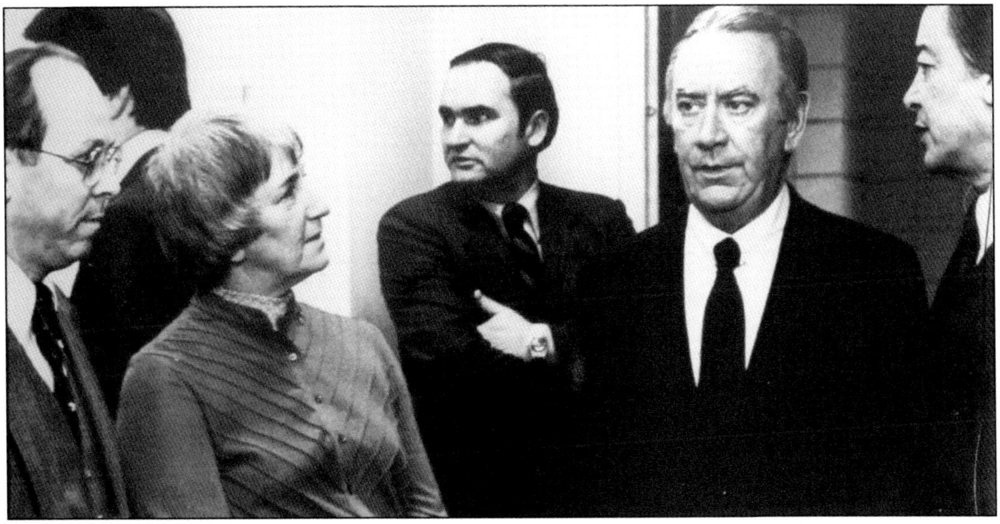

Pres. Ursula Schwerin became the fifth president of the college. She began as a student in the Dental Hygiene Department. Dr. Schwerin's picture can be found in the 1957 college yearbook, and she received her Associate Degree in 1958. President Schwerin went on to New York University, where she received her bachelor of science, masters of arts, and doctorate degrees. President Schwerin became the first woman president at the New York City College of Technology, only the second woman at that time to become president of a CUNY college and the first woman in the United States to become president of a technical college. In this picture, President Schwerin is with Gov. Hugh Carey (second from right), who signed legislation on July 2, 1980, granting the college senior college status.

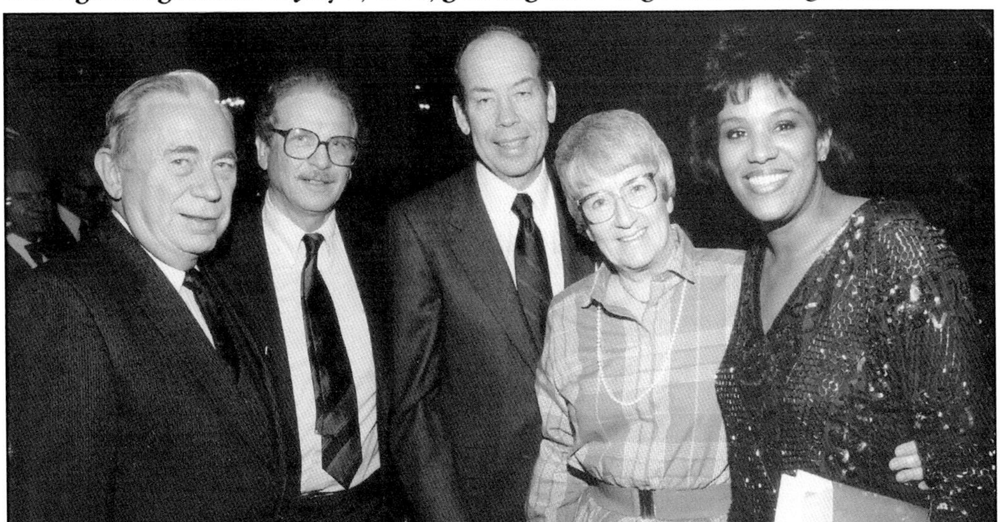

This picture was taken in 1985 at the first Best of New York Awards dinner, sponsored annually by the New York City College of Technology Foundation. Seen here, from left to right, are dinner honoree Eugene Lutney, at that time chairman and chief executive officer of Brooklyn Union Gas Company; Andrew Namm, who was then president of the foundation; William Ferguson, who was then president of the New York Telephone Company; President Schwerin; and Carol Martin of Channel 2 News, who was the master of ceremonies.

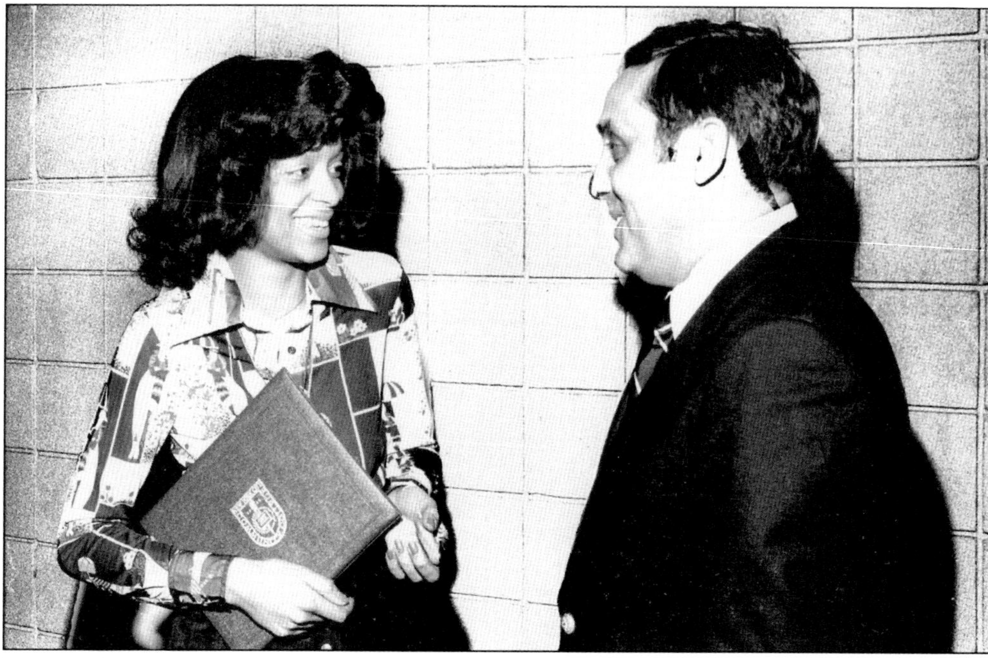

The caption on the back of this picture reads, "Ann L. Pyles, who managed a west side disco but felt she had much to learn about record keeping . . . picks up her graduation certificate at a ceremony for 31 upward-bound enterprisers who completed a free training program given by New York Community College." The picture is dated February 6, 1975.

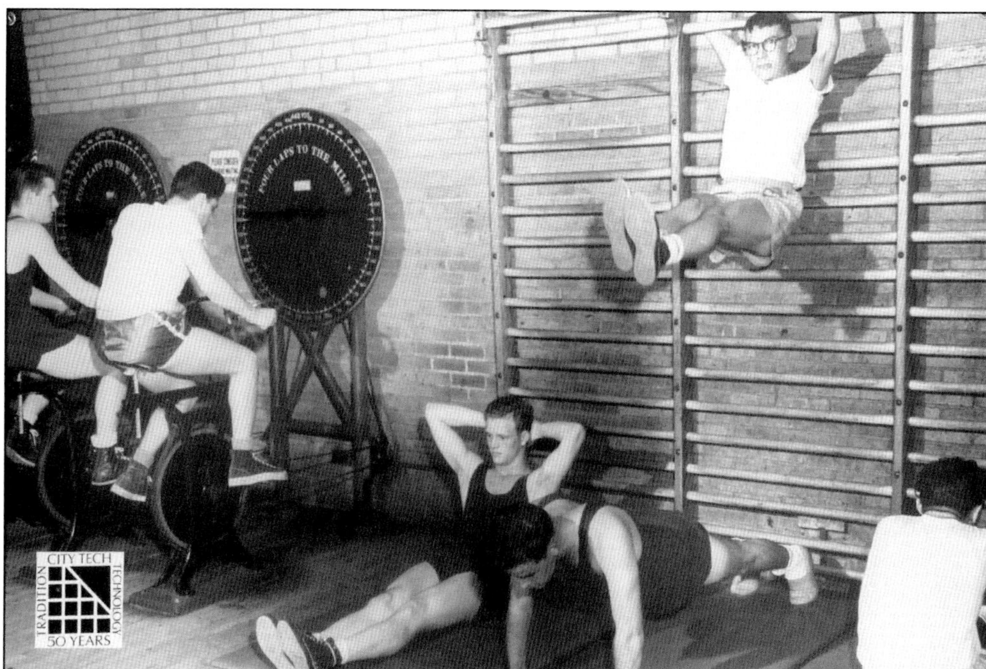

The students seen here are working out in the Klitgord gym. The equipment used in this picture dates it as far back as the late 1950s.

Today the college has a Division IV NCAA basketball team, which won the CUNY Athletic Conference Championship in 2005. Before entering NCAA competition, the college competed in the National Junior College Athletic Association and garnered many honors.

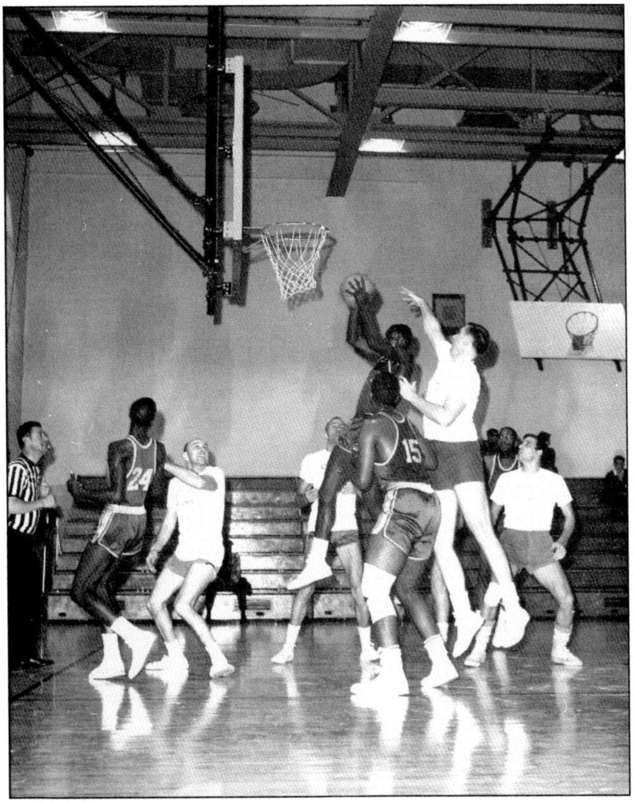

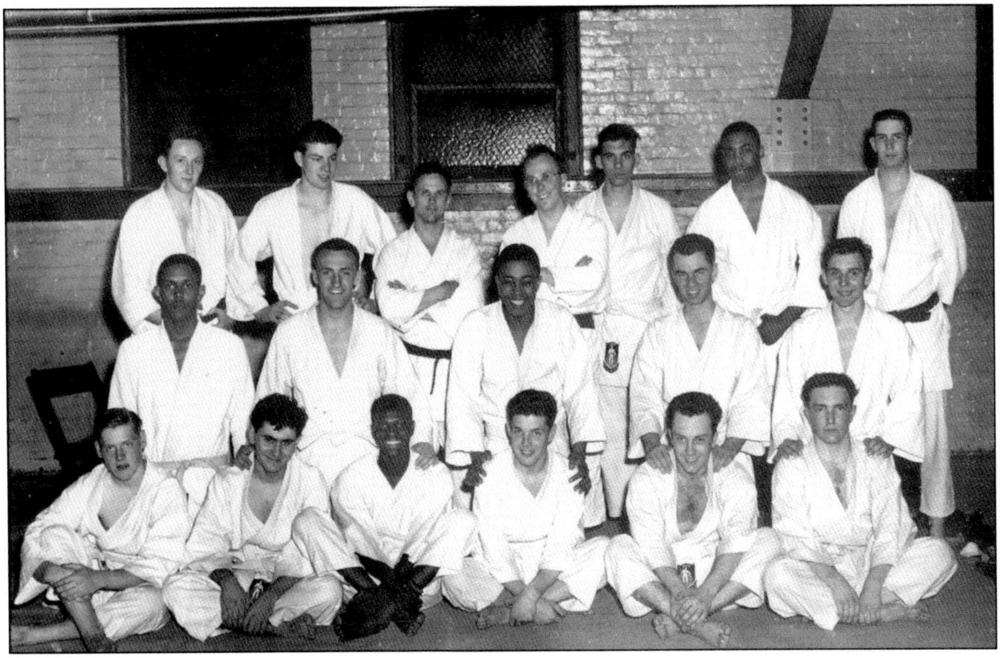

The college offered karate as one of its catalogue offerings. This picture dates the 1970s or 1980s. With the discontinuation of the Health and Recreation Department, such activities became purely recreational, without academic credit.

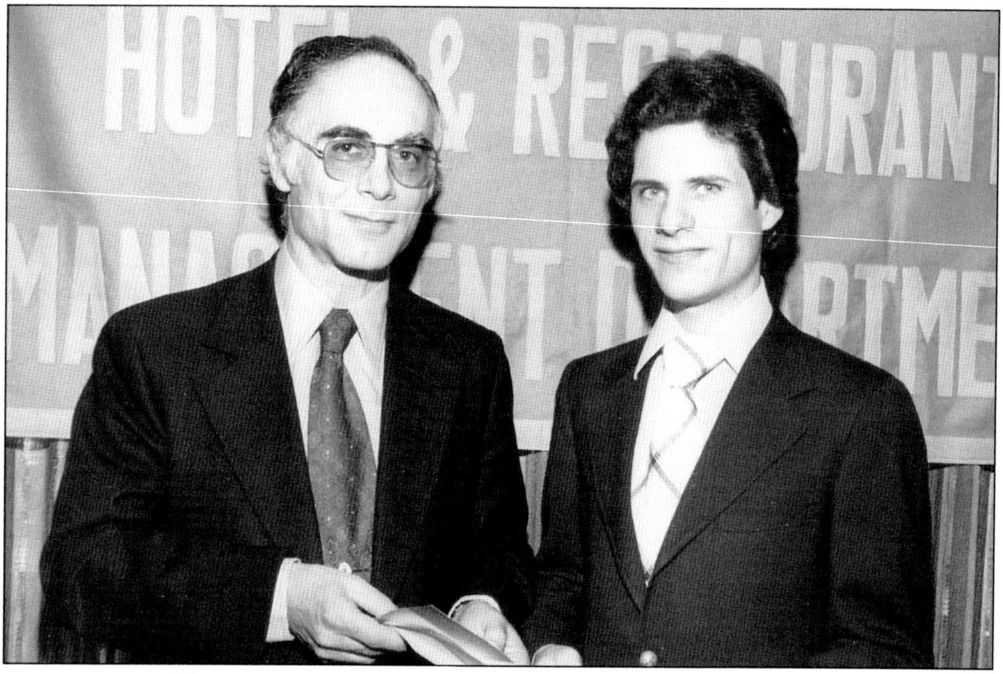

During a special luncheon for graduating students at New York City Community College's hotel and restaurant program, Michael Romano (right) receives the Chip Award, given by alumnus Rocky Aoki of the Benihana of Tokyo restaurant chain in memory of Prof. Felice Chiapperini, program chairman from 1969 to 1974. The award was presented by David Sabo, executive vice president of the Benihana organization. The award was given in 1976. Romano went on to become executive chef of New York's famed Union Square Café.

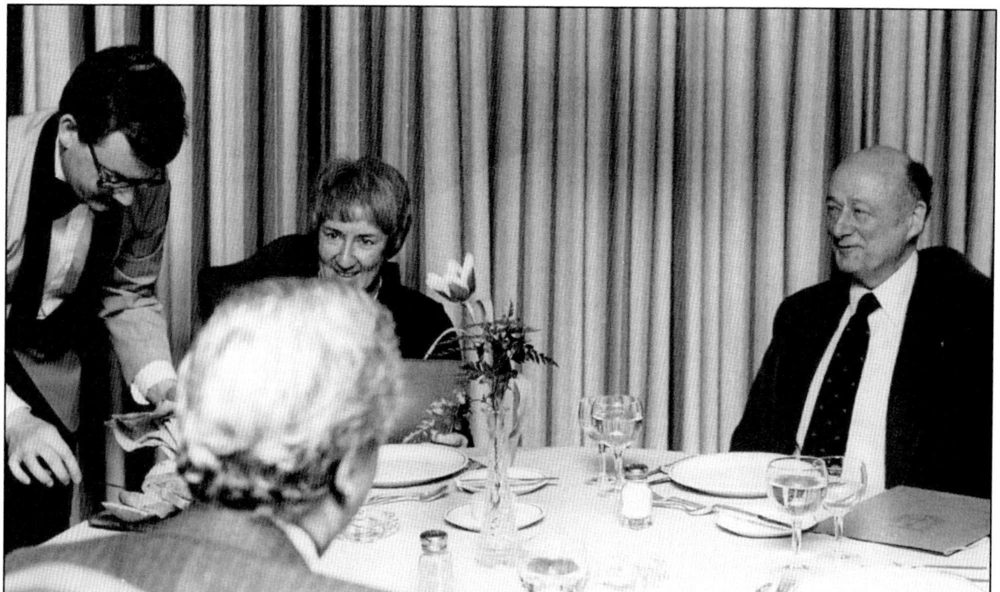

Former Mayor Ed Koch is seen here in the Janet Lefler dinning room. To the left of Mayor Koch is Pres. Ursula Schwerin. This picture dates to the 1980s.

The college in June 2006 completed its 66th commencement. This 34th commencement exercise took place in 1974 at the RKO Albee Theater in Flatbush, in central Brooklyn. The student in cap and gown is Angela Scarpa. Scarpa helped finance her education by teaching and performing the ancient art of belly dancing and by working at a day care center. Seen hugging her mother is her daughter, Nancy. In 1971, Angela was delighted to learn that the college had an open door for late bloomers. She decided to pursue studies in early childhood education, attending classes full time for two years and graduating with honors.

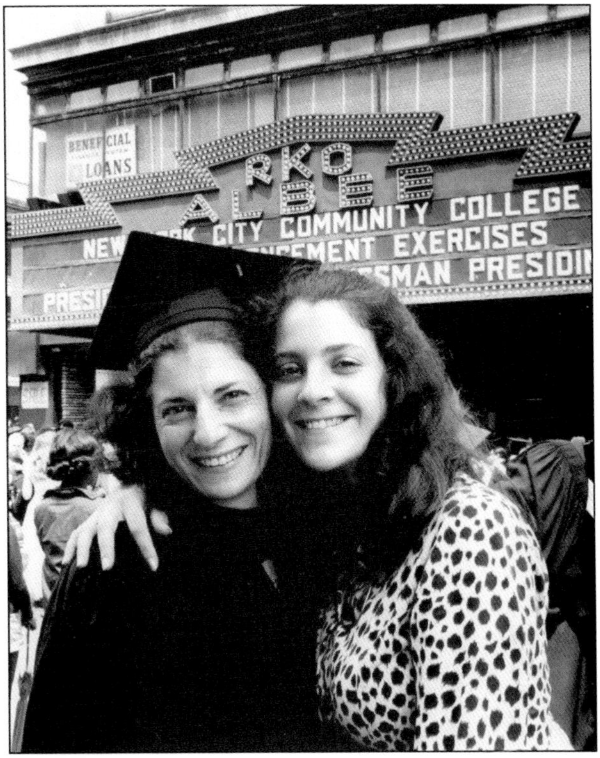

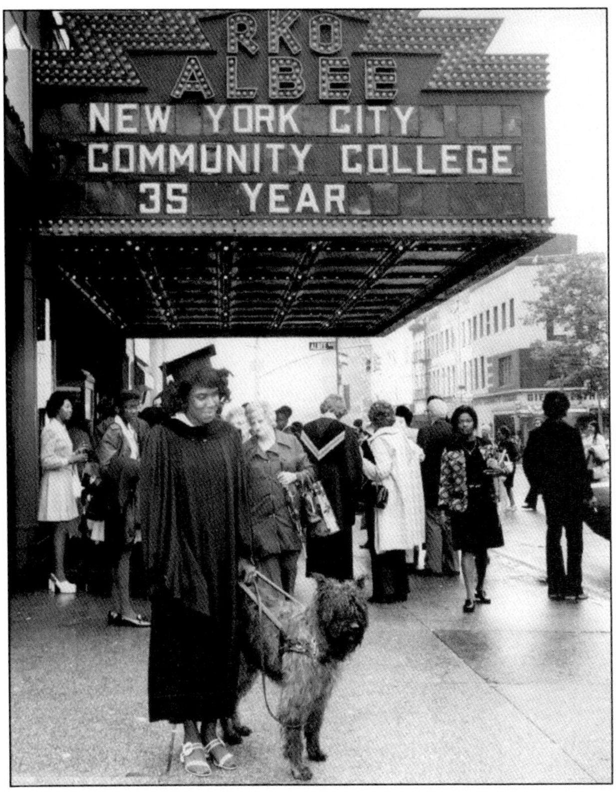

This 42nd graduation again took place in 1982 at the RKO Albee Theater, as this sign suggests. The college is especially proud of the achievements of students with disabilities. As the number of graduates has increased, graduations have been housed at large venues in Manhattan, first Carnegie Hall and later at the theater in Madison Square Garden.

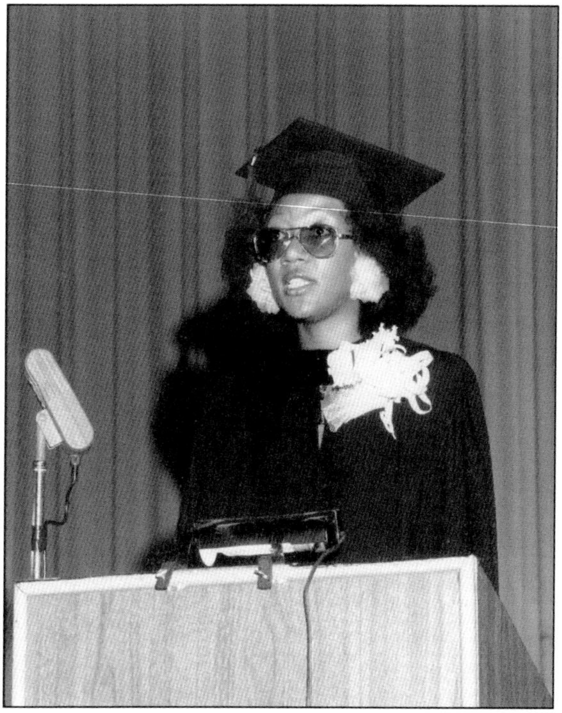

Another graduation ceremony is pictured with a proud speaker at the podium and proud parents and family in the audience.

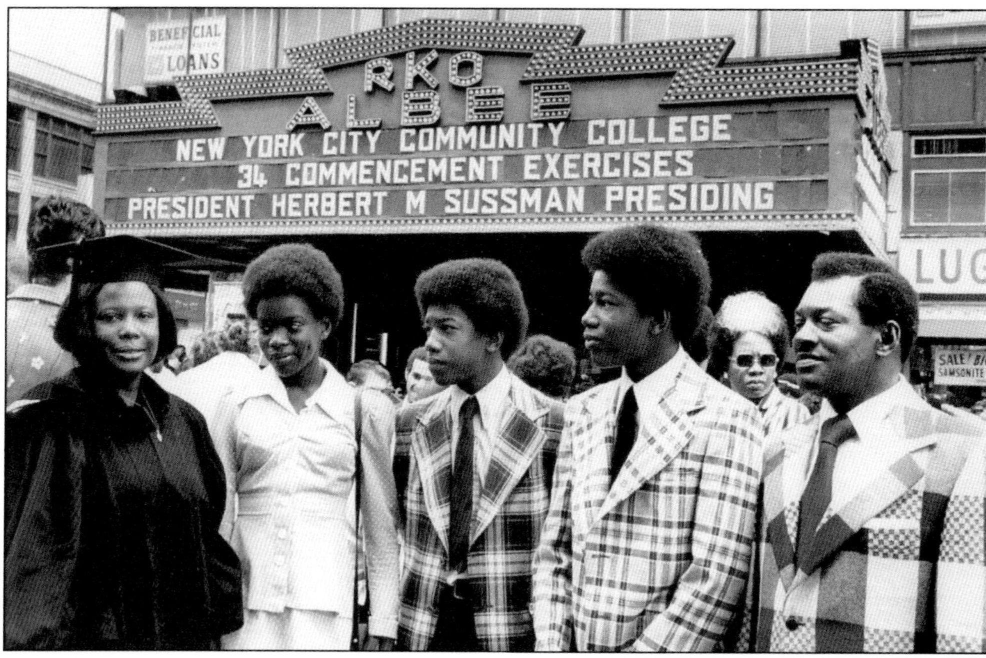

This graduation took place in 1981 at the RKO Albee Theater. The caption on the back reads, "Working nights as a nurse's aide at Flatbush General Hospital and attending day classes in nursing for two years at New York Community College earned Mrs. Mattie Alston an associate degree and eligibility to take the state exam for registered nurses, her lifelong goal." Sharing her joy on graduation day are her husband Henry, a machine operator; daughter Brenda, 11; and twin sons Derrick and Eric, 14.

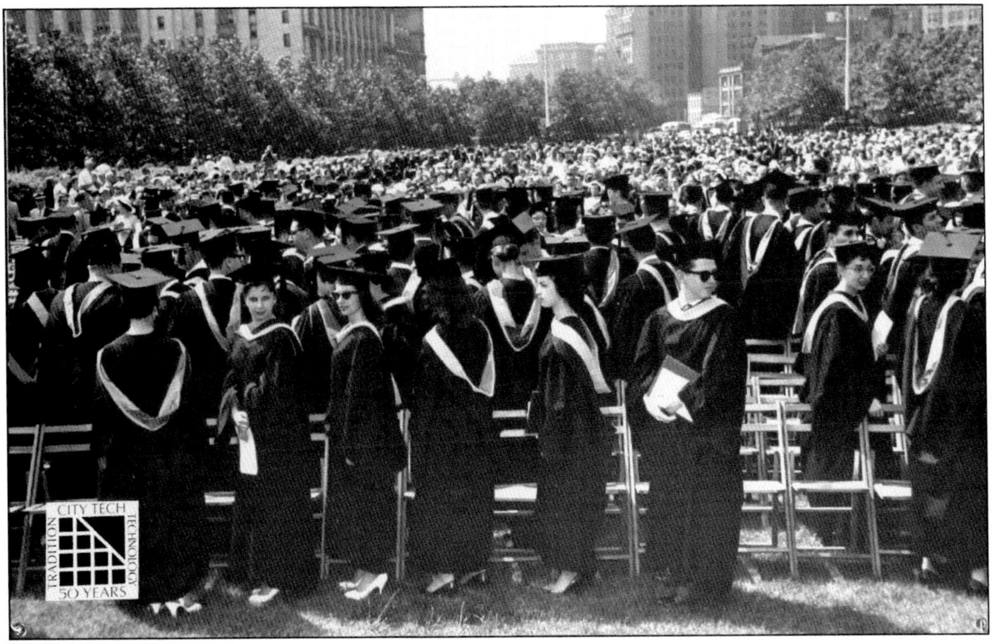

Some of the early commencement exercises took place outdoors at Brooklyn's Cadman Plaza. The most recent graduation at this venue was in the 1980s.

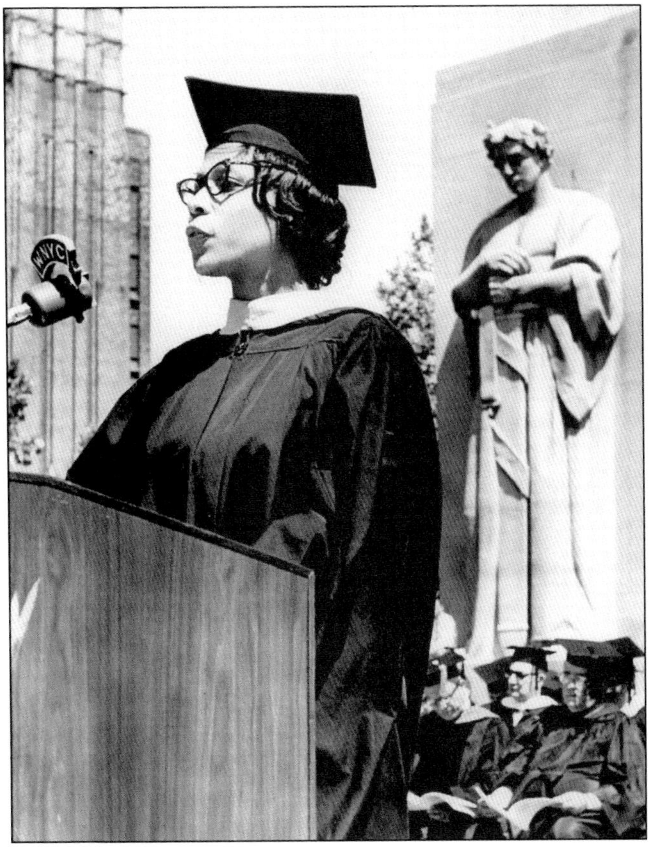

This commencement took place in 1964 at the Cadman Plaza's War Memorial. The class speaker was Barbara Gowan, who graduated from the Associate Degree Program in Secretarial Science.

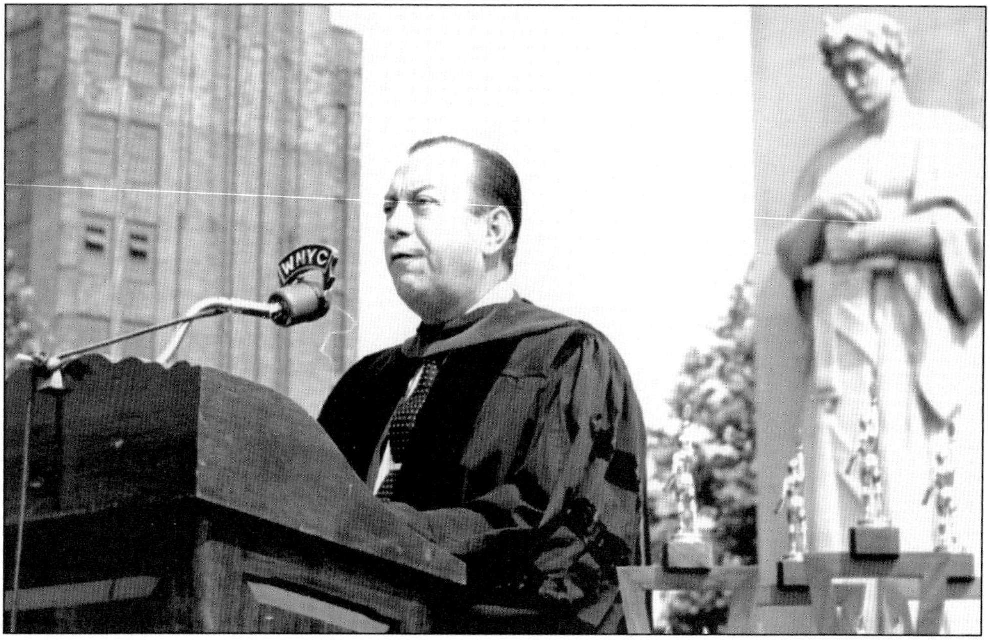

This commencement took place in 1957 at the Cadman Plaza's War Memorial. The keynote speaker was Mayor Robert Wagner, seen here at the podium. One can only guess what his message was to the graduates at that time.

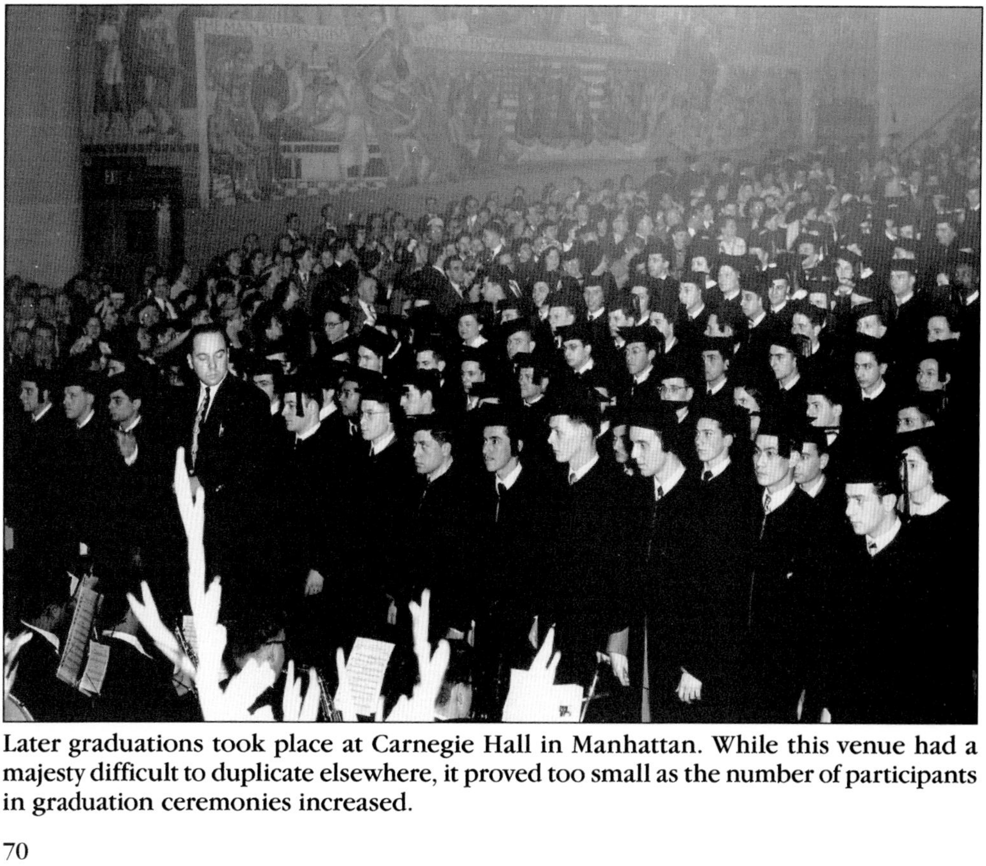

Later graduations took place at Carnegie Hall in Manhattan. While this venue had a majesty difficult to duplicate elsewhere, it proved too small as the number of participants in graduation ceremonies increased.

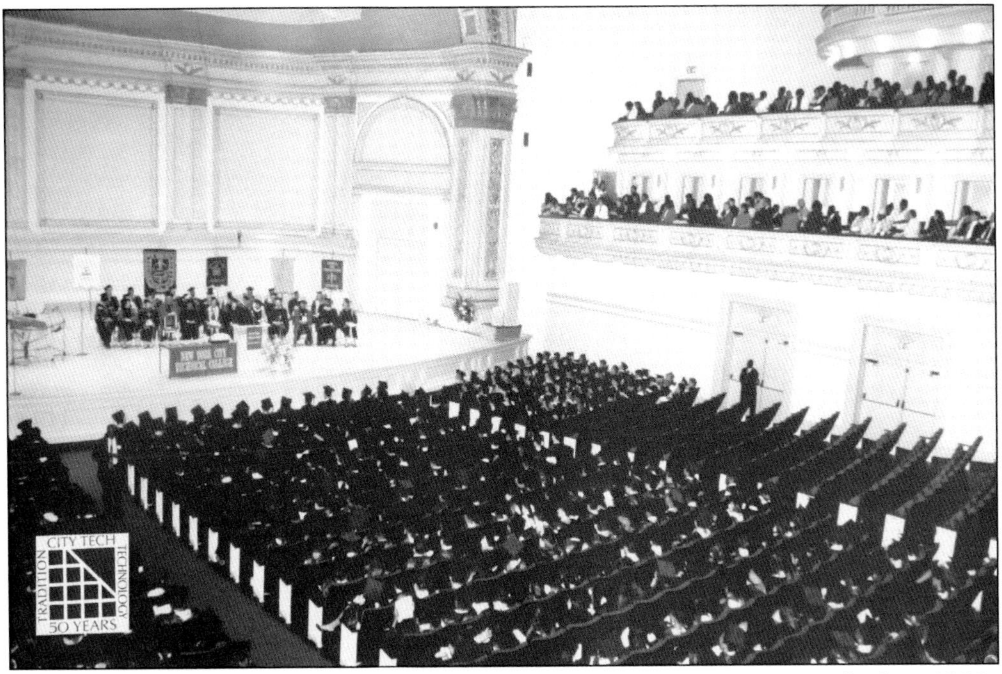

Another graduation takes place at Carnegie Hall in this image. Since the late 1990s graduation has taken place at the theater at Madison Square Garden.

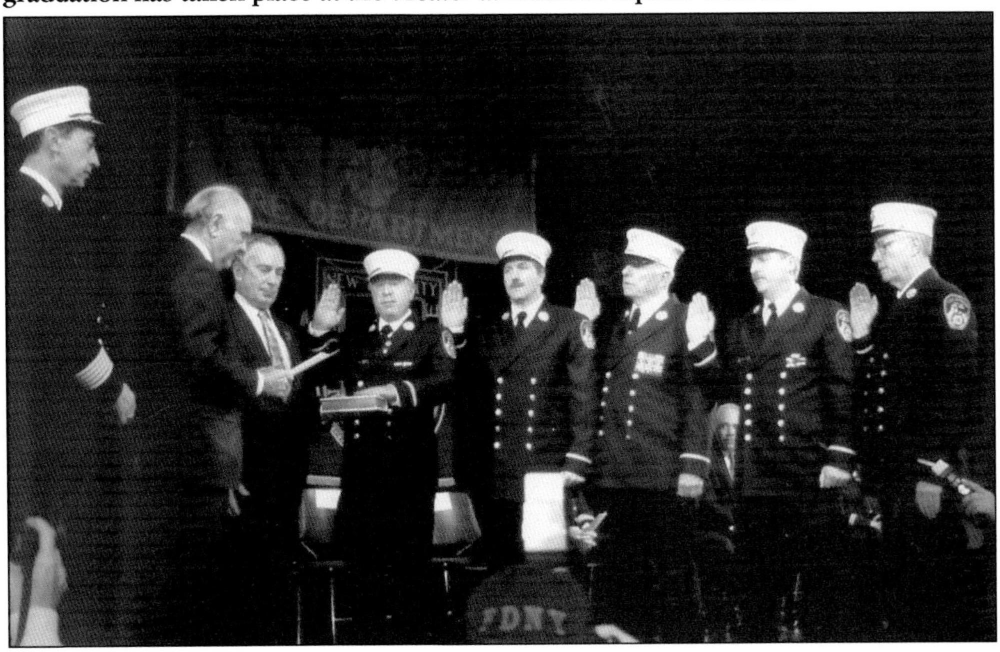

For years, the Fire Department of New York, one of the sources of civic pride, has conducted its graduation ceremonies at the college. The man doing the swearing in is none other than Mayor Michael Bloomberg. Mayor Bloomberg also took the stage at the New York City College of Technology on January 17, 2007, to deliver his sixth state-of-the-city address. Among those singled out for praise on that day was Feliberto Estevez, the mayor's chef and student of the New York City College of Technology.

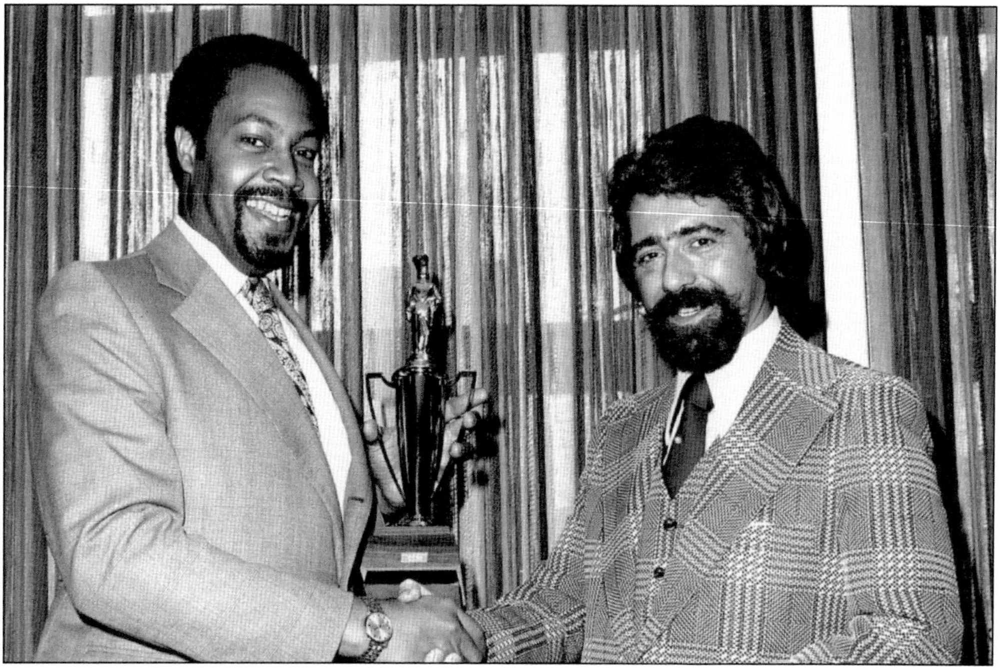

The caption on the back of this picture reads, "Alfred Capers, left, is all smiles as Gaston Gaudrey, of the Long Island Culinary Association, presents him with the industry group's annual trophy for exemplary achievement in the culinary arts." The presentation was made during the senior luncheon of the New York City Community College's Hotel and Restaurant Management Program. Capers was among 2,300 graduates at the college's 34th commencement on June 11, 1974.

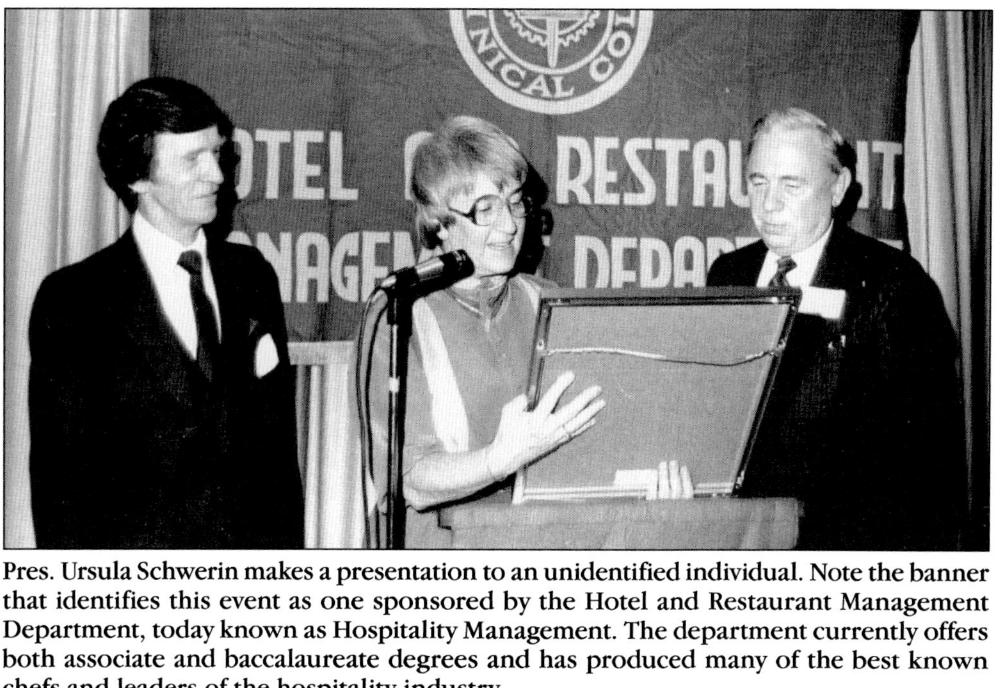

Pres. Ursula Schwerin makes a presentation to an unidentified individual. Note the banner that identifies this event as one sponsored by the Hotel and Restaurant Management Department, today known as Hospitality Management. The department currently offers both associate and baccalaureate degrees and has produced many of the best known chefs and leaders of the hospitality industry.

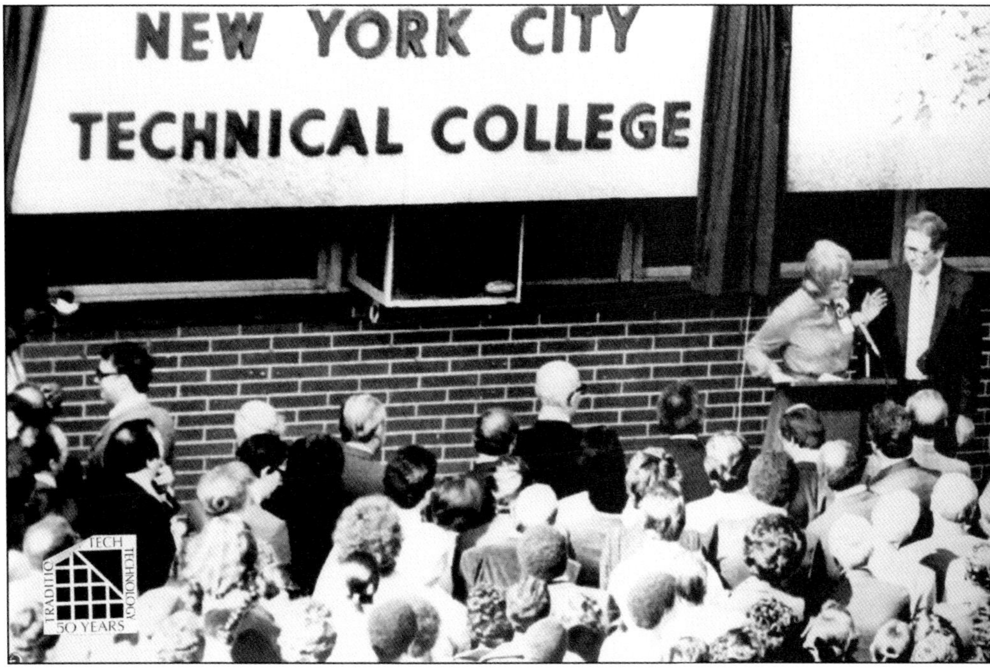

In July 1980, Gov. Hugh Carey signed a bill granting the college senior college status. The name was changed from New York Community College to New York City Technical College. President Schwerin is seen at the podium. In 2002, the name of the college changed again, to New York City College of Technology.

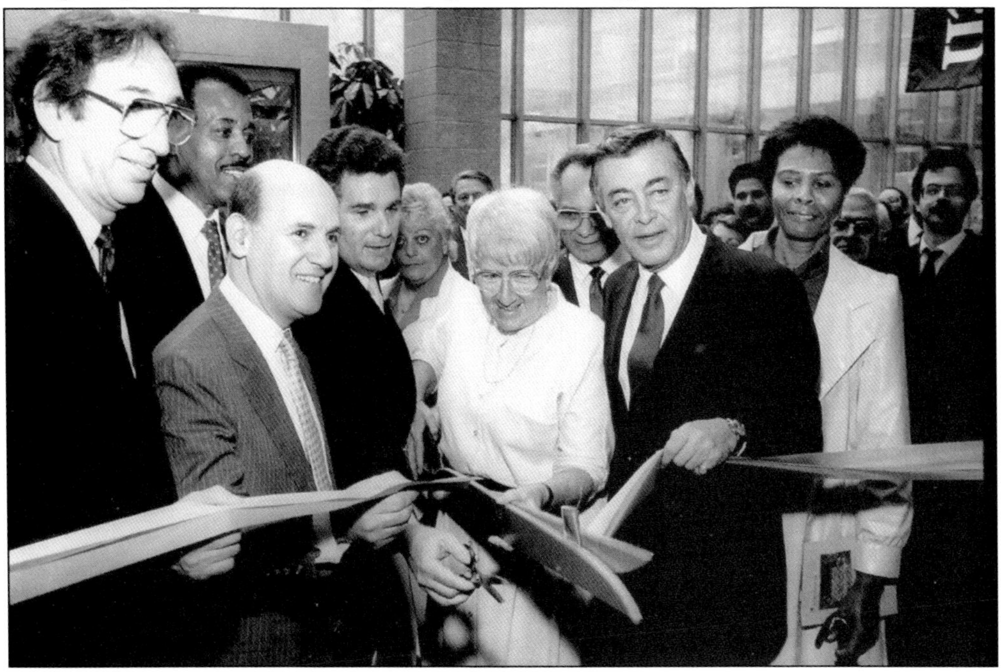

President Schwerin is seen here cutting a ribbon, officially opening the Atrium walkway in 1984. The man to the right of President Schwerin is longtime Brooklyn Borough president Howard Golden.

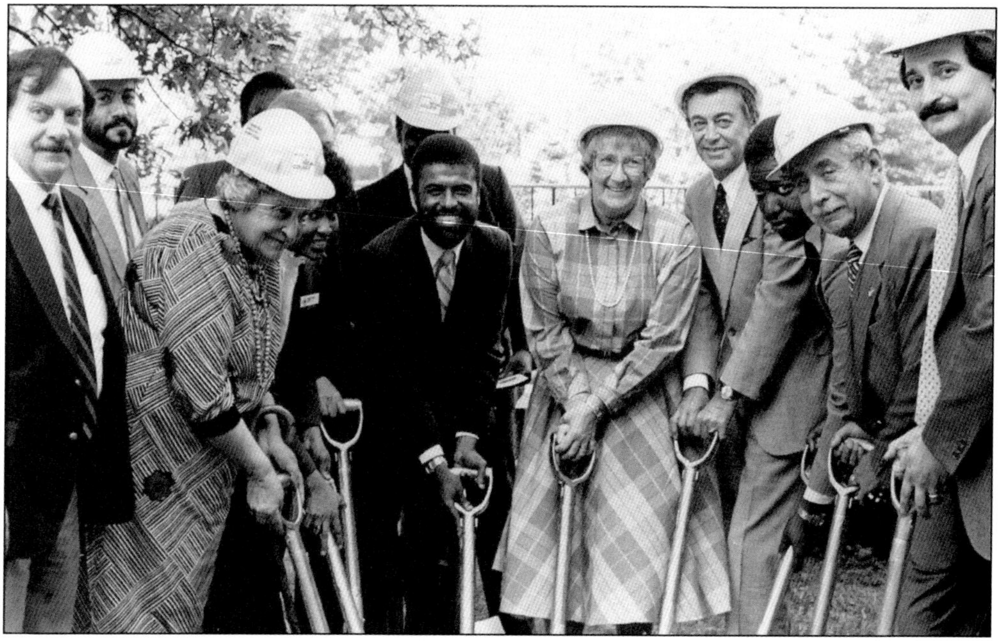

This picture was taken on May 14, 1985. This was the first step in a City Tech "Master Plan," the city university's long-term plan for the development of a college. President Schwerin is in the middle and to her left is Brooklyn Borough president Howard Golden.

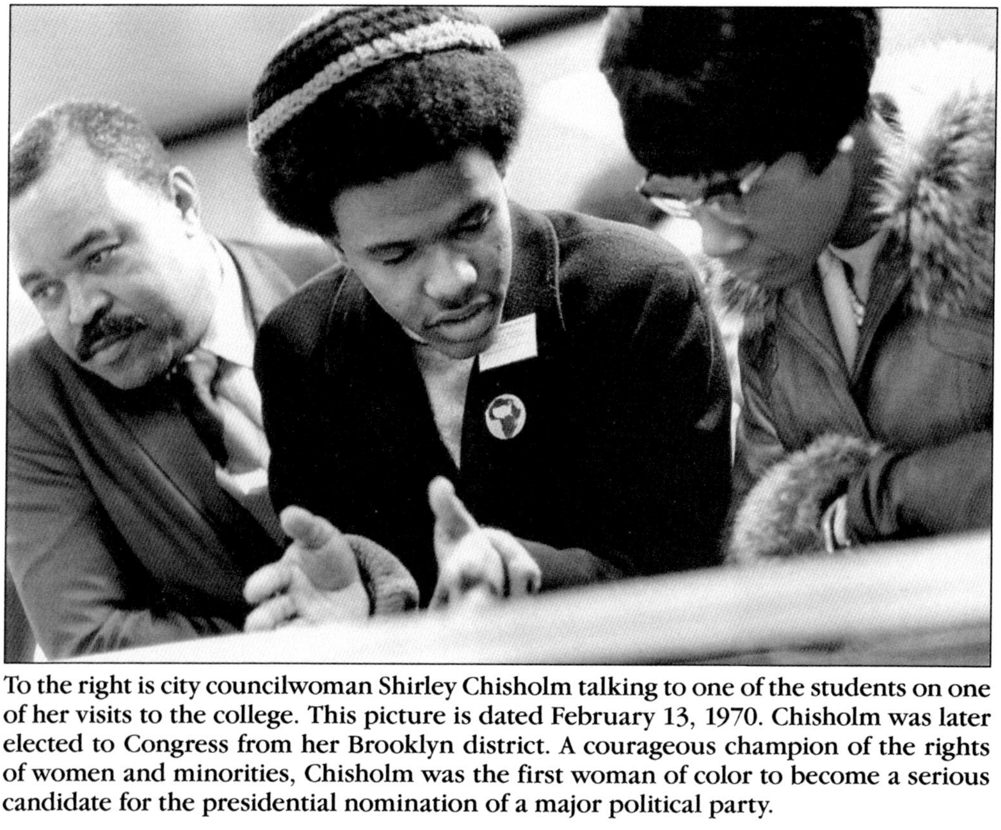

To the right is city councilwoman Shirley Chisholm talking to one of the students on one of her visits to the college. This picture is dated February 13, 1970. Chisholm was later elected to Congress from her Brooklyn district. A courageous champion of the rights of women and minorities, Chisholm was the first woman of color to become a serious candidate for the presidential nomination of a major political party.

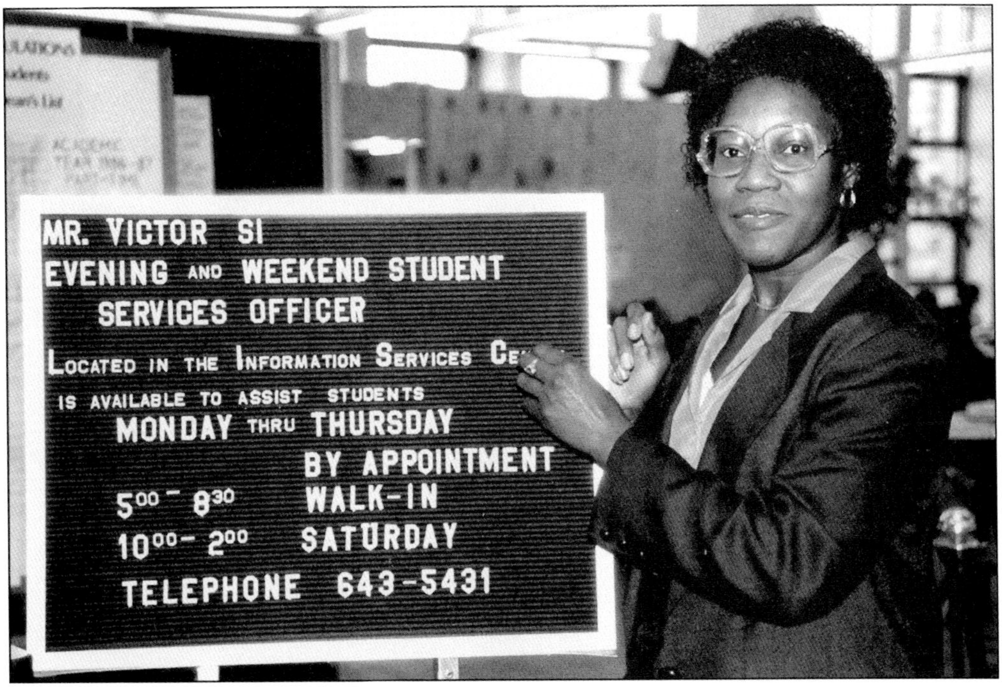

This *c.* 1980 sign announces Victor Si as the evening and weekend services officer.

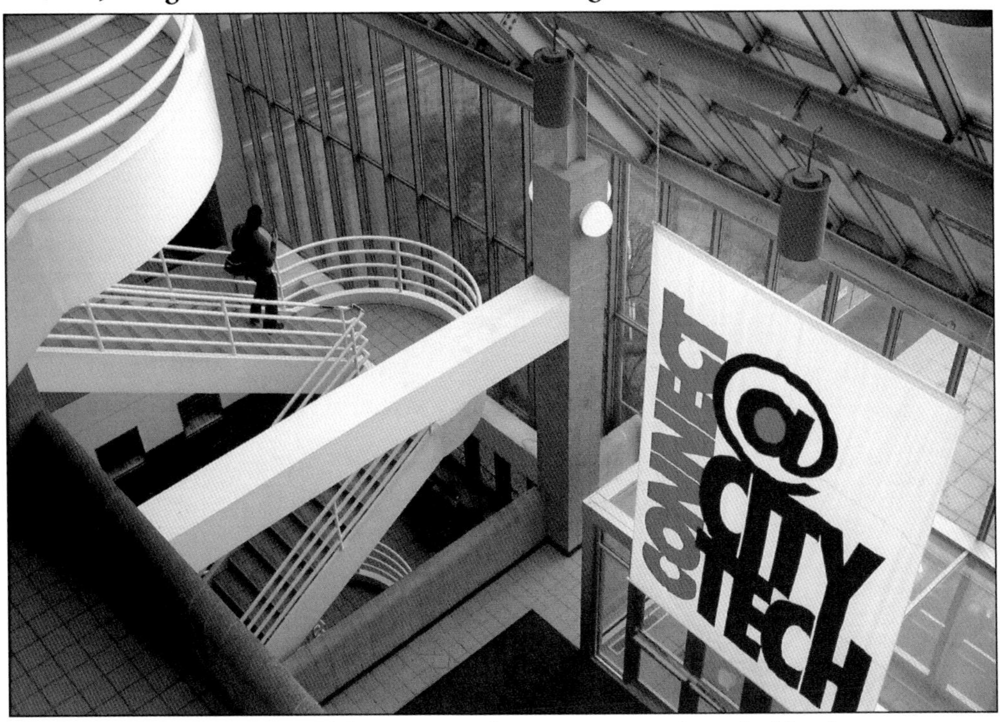

Shown here is the interior of the Atrium. The Atrium provides valuable classroom space and an airy, attractive environment filled with benches and other space for students to relax between classes. For student convenience, large parts of the Atrium provide Wi-Fi (wireless networking) access.

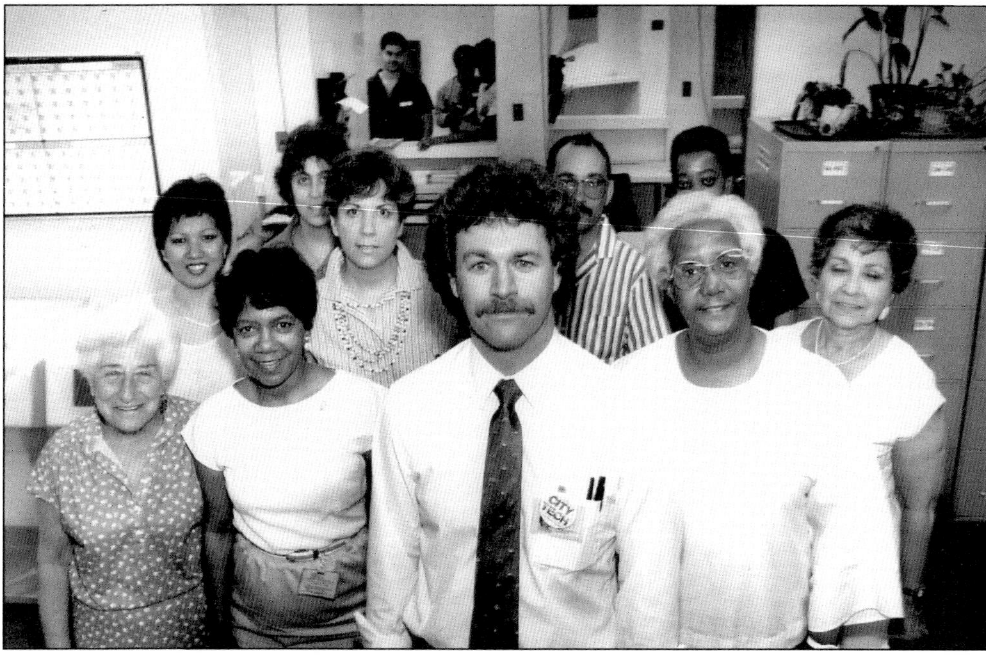

This is a picture of the College Registrar's Office staff. In the center is the registrar, Jerry Berrol, who has served in the post since 1985. In 1985, students stood in long lines to pick up punch cards to register and in other lines to see if they were eligible to graduate. Today these and other routine tasks are done via the Internet at any time.

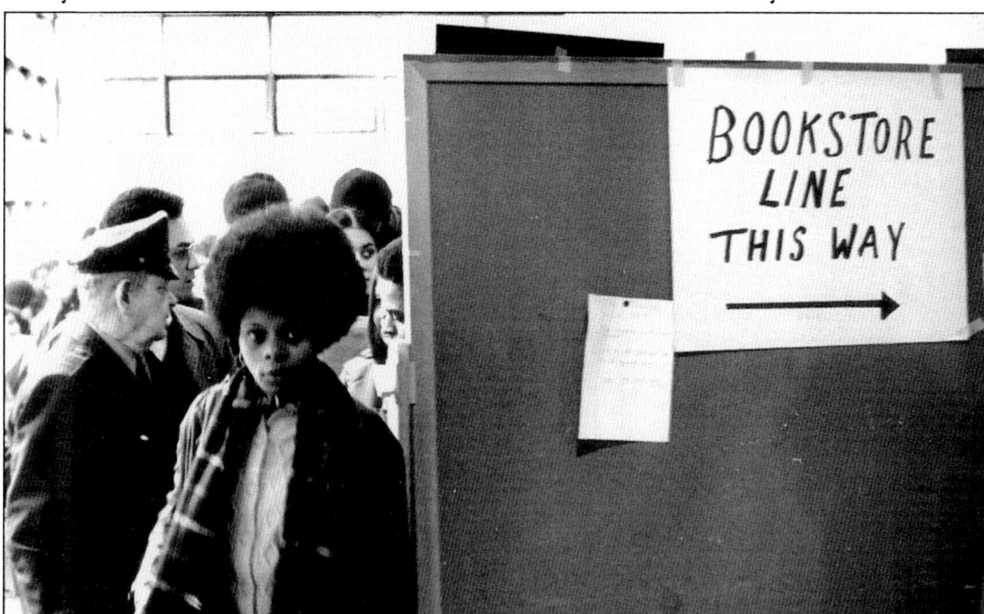

All students have memories of trying to purchase books during the first days of classes. The lines were huge and often necessitated a security guard present to maintain order. Hairdos and dress styles suggest that this picture is from the early 1980s. The college bookstore has finally hit the electronic age; students can today order books online and avoid scenes like this.

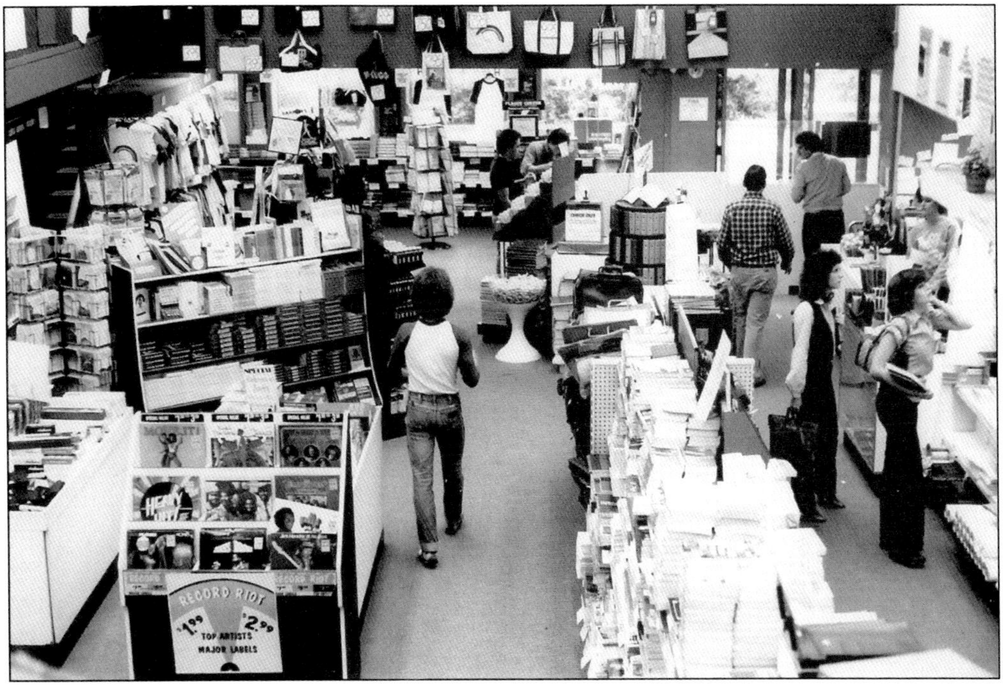

The college's bookstore is pictured during the 1970s or 1980s. When was the last time one could go to a bookstore and see old 78 rpm LP records for sale? By late 2007, students will be able to take advantage of a brand-new bookstore with a café and performance space.

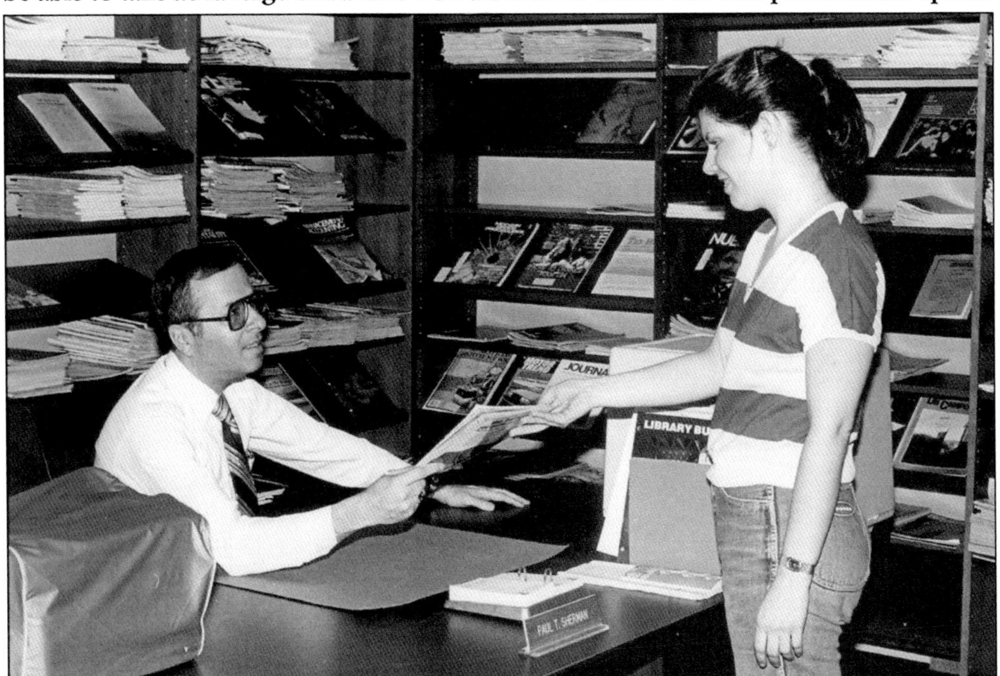

A student is helped by one of the librarians around 1980. There is probably a typewriter under the cover to the librarian's right. Today it would be a computer, accessing local, regional, and national databases.

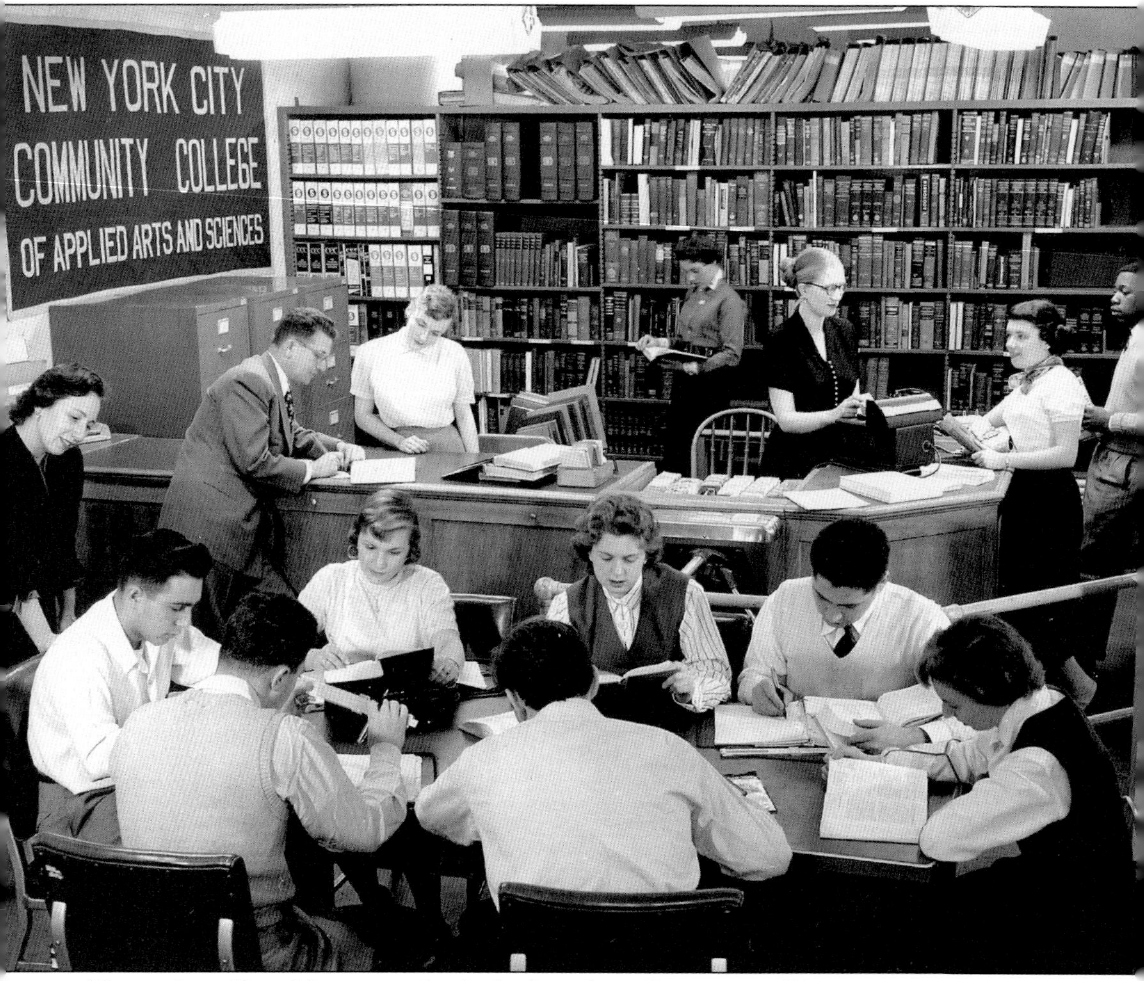

This is the college library as it looked when the college was still known as New York City Community College. Judging from the way students were dressed, this picture could be dated to the 1950s.

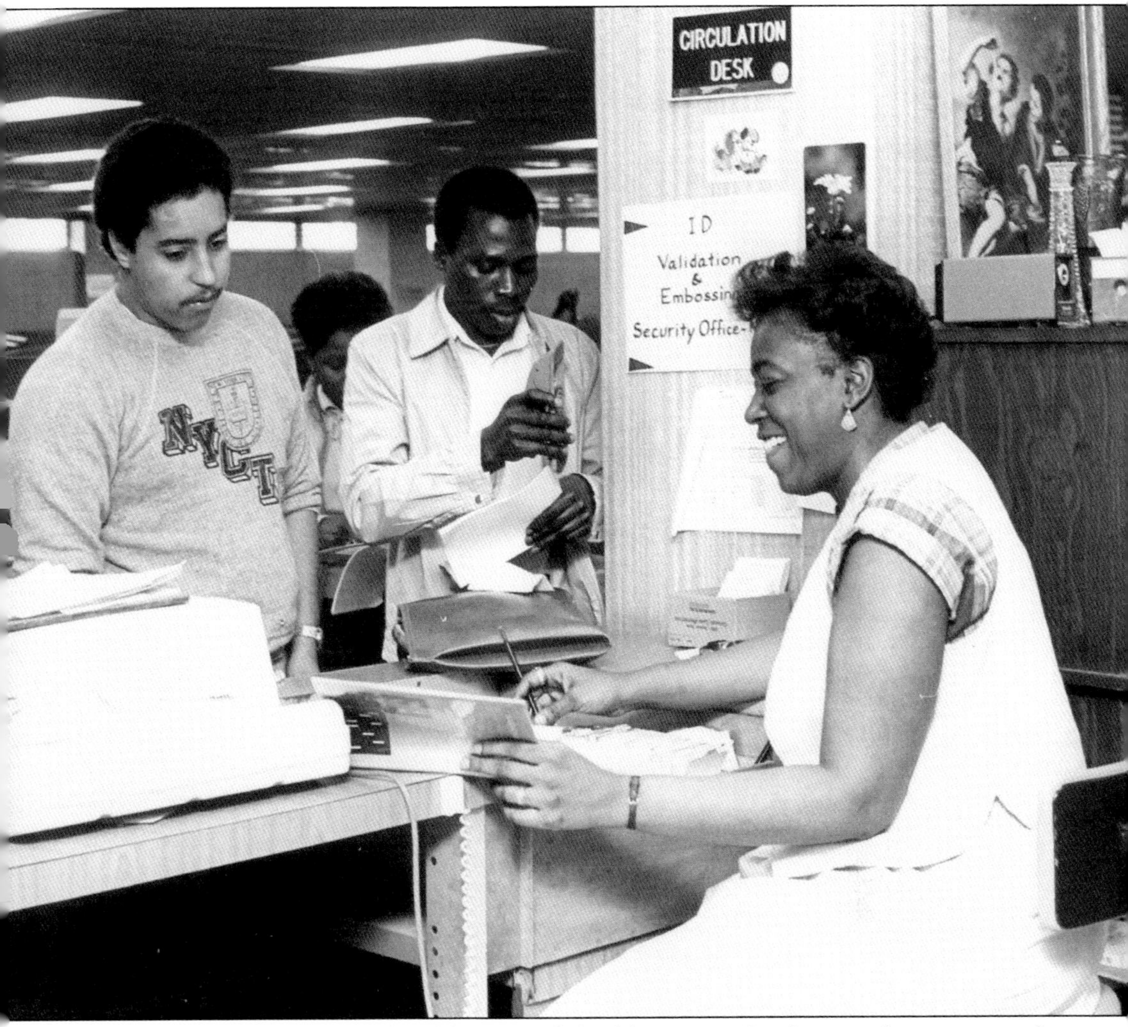

Students here are being helped by one of the librarians. Students today can search databases and catalogues around the globe from one of the many Internet-connected computers that fill the library.

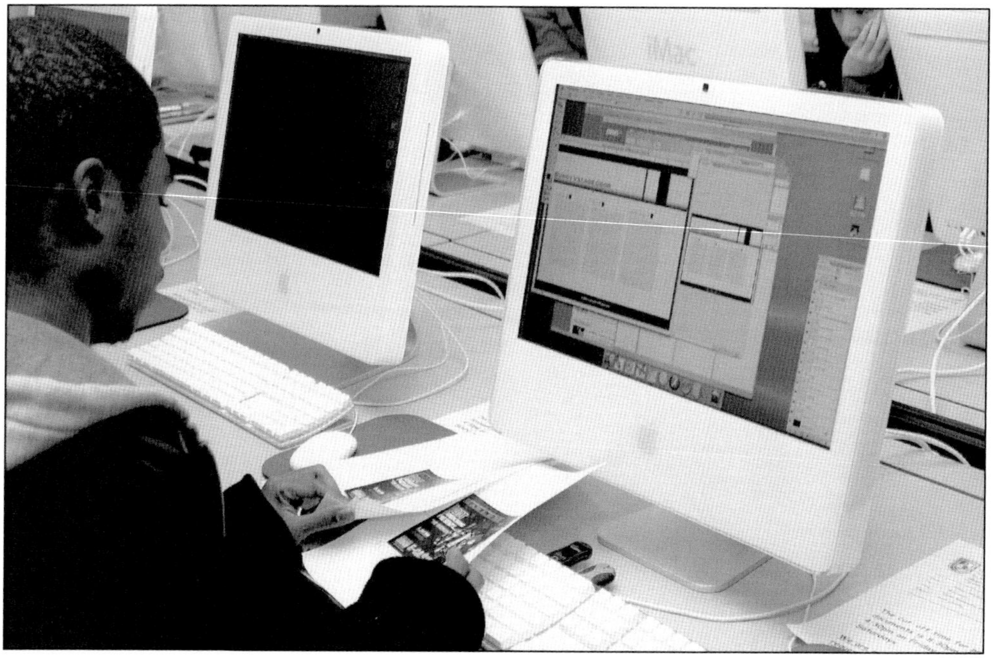

Over 4,500 students each semester visit the College Learning Centers, large facilities filled with computer labs, tutoring stations, and other tools to reinforce classroom instruction.

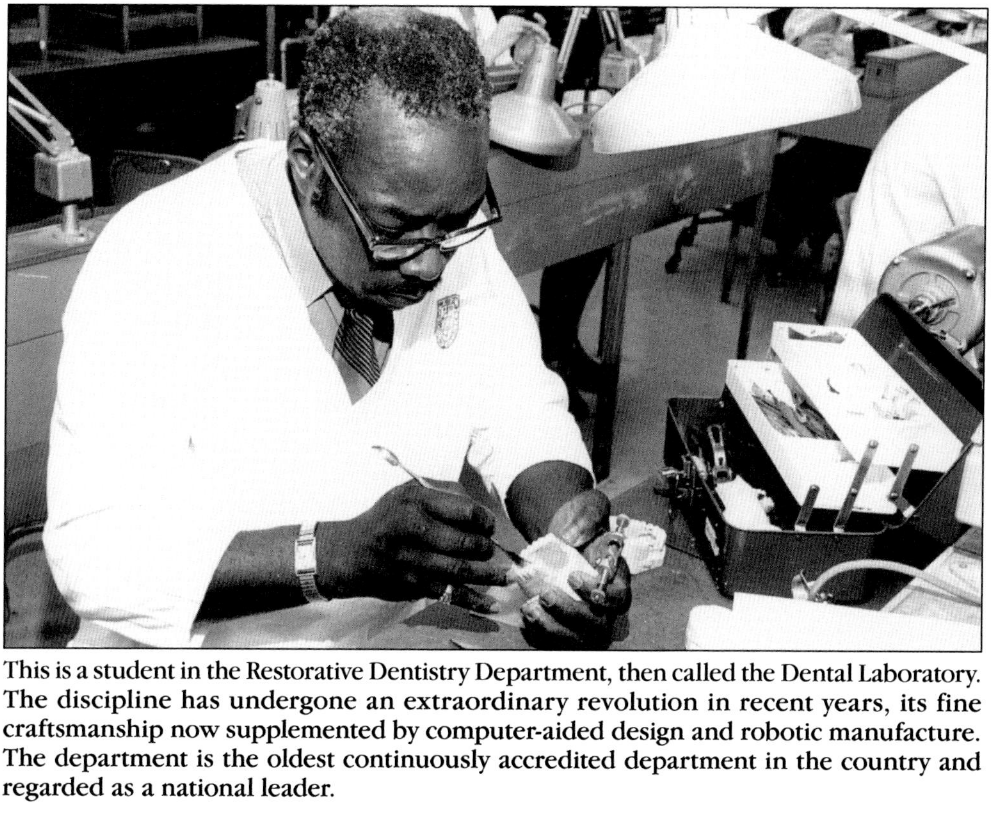

This is a student in the Restorative Dentistry Department, then called the Dental Laboratory. The discipline has undergone an extraordinary revolution in recent years, its fine craftsmanship now supplemented by computer-aided design and robotic manufacture. The department is the oldest continuously accredited department in the country and regarded as a national leader.

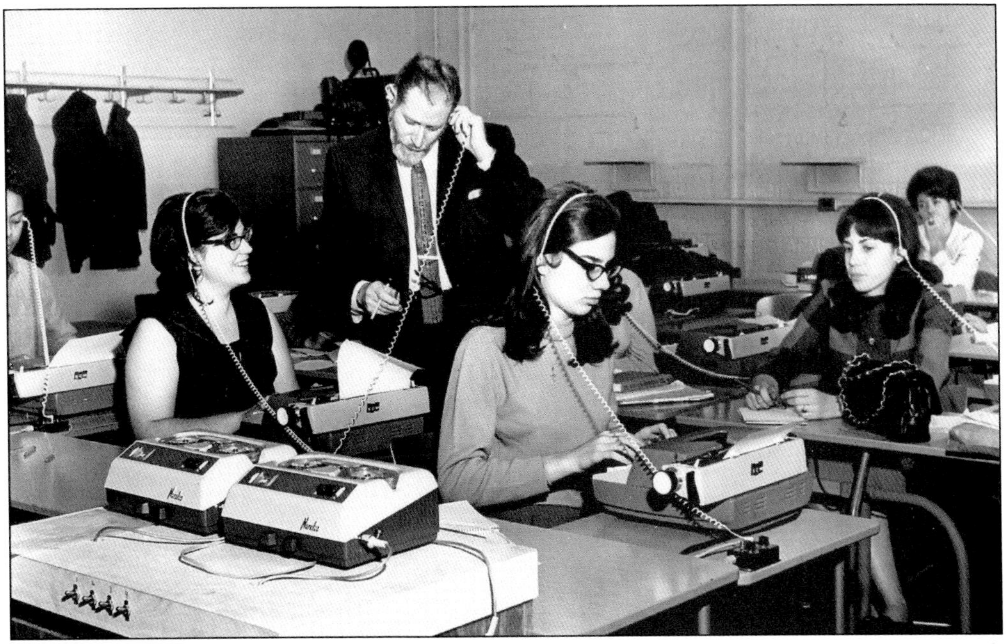

Students are seen in the Secretarial Science Program, which was discontinued in 1994. Note the old tape recorders on the side. Students would learn to transcribe what they heard on tape and type out a transcript. This class was probably conducted during the 1960s. The instructor is Prof. Bert Schwartz.

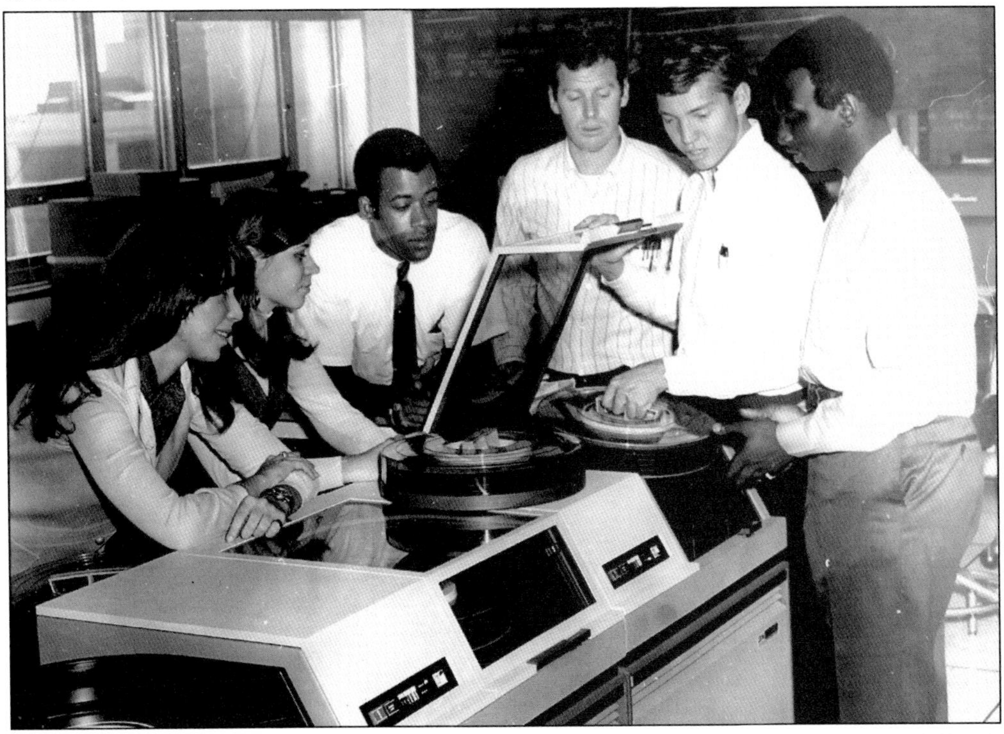

This picture dates back to the 1960s. Technology today is so advanced that it is difficult to recognize machines that stretch back to the distant past.

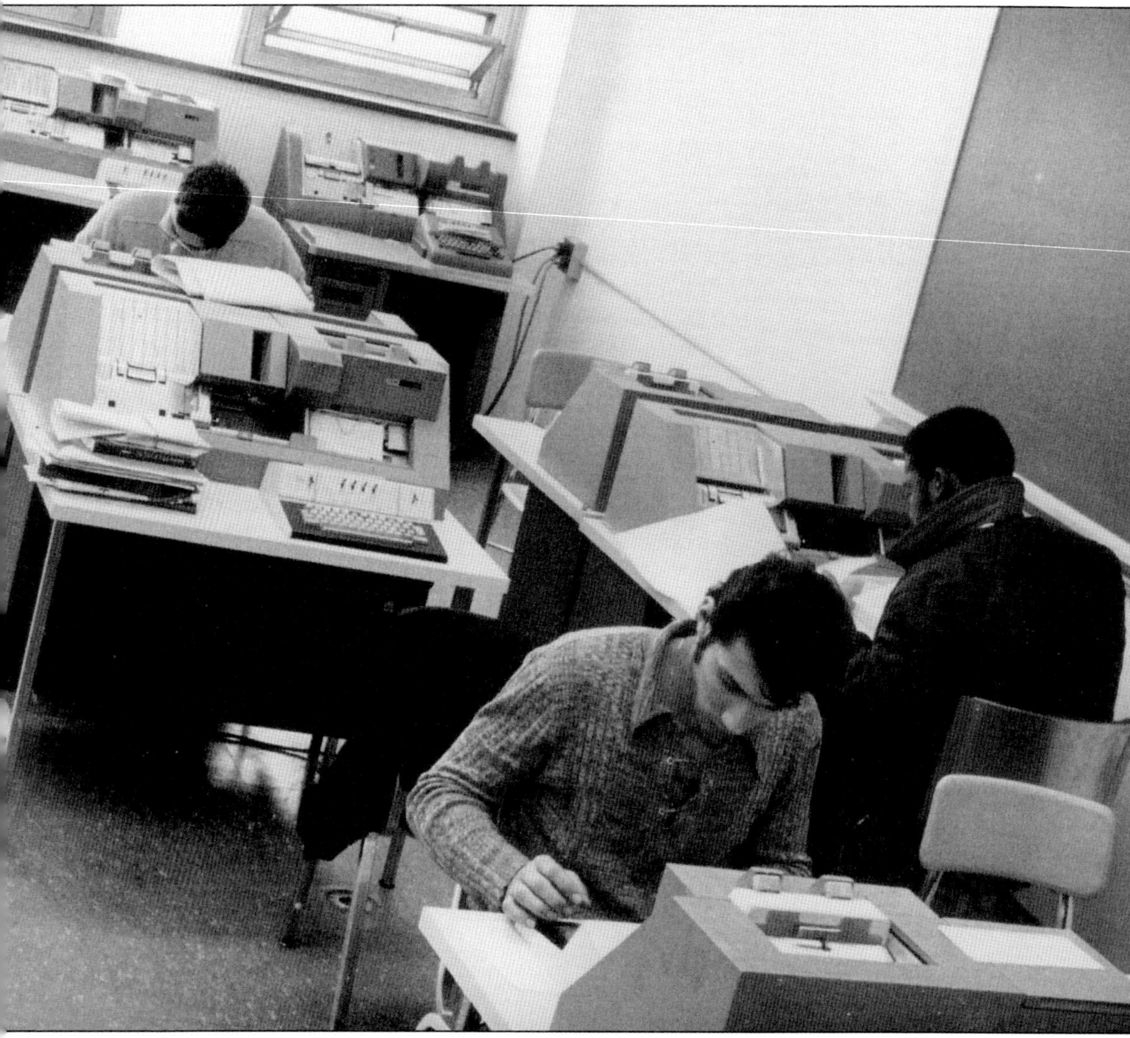

These students look like they are working on very early computers.

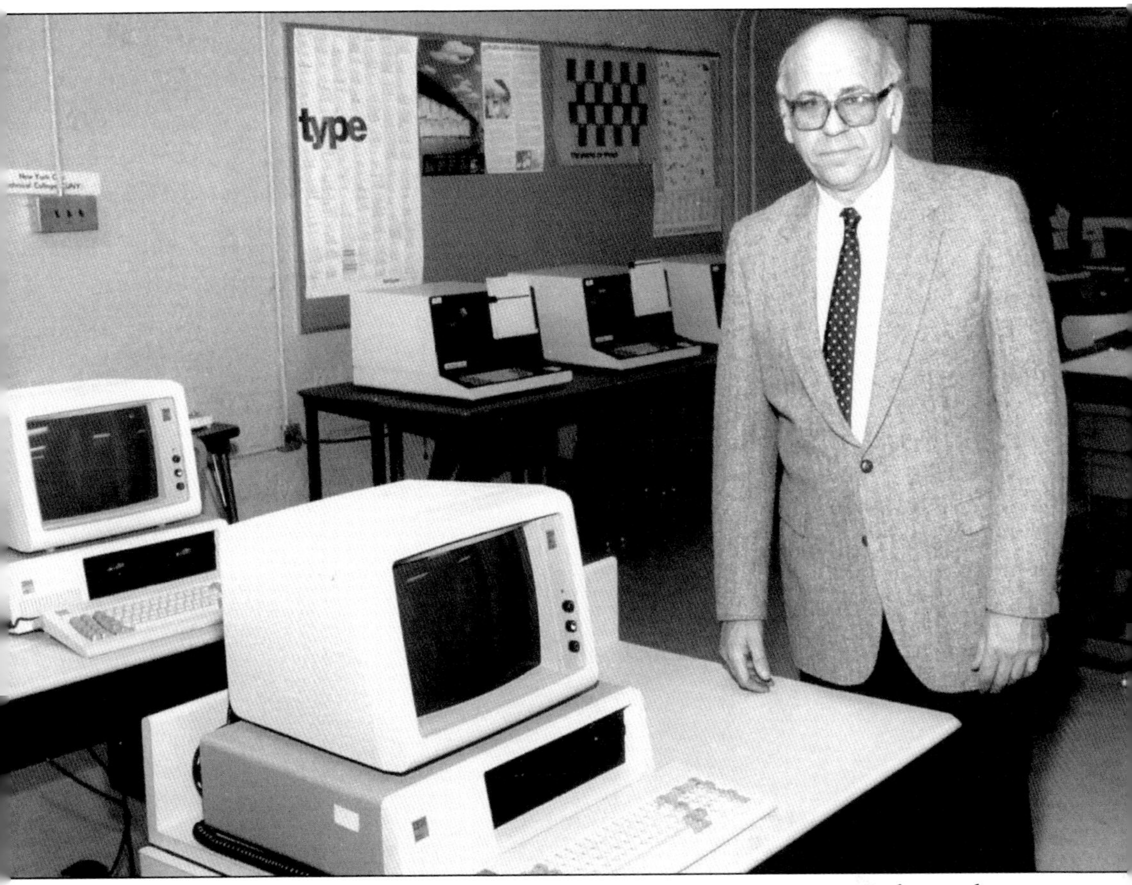

This is an early computer room. Standing by this computer is Dr. James Deluca, who was the chairperson for the Graphic Arts Department in the 1970s and 1980s.

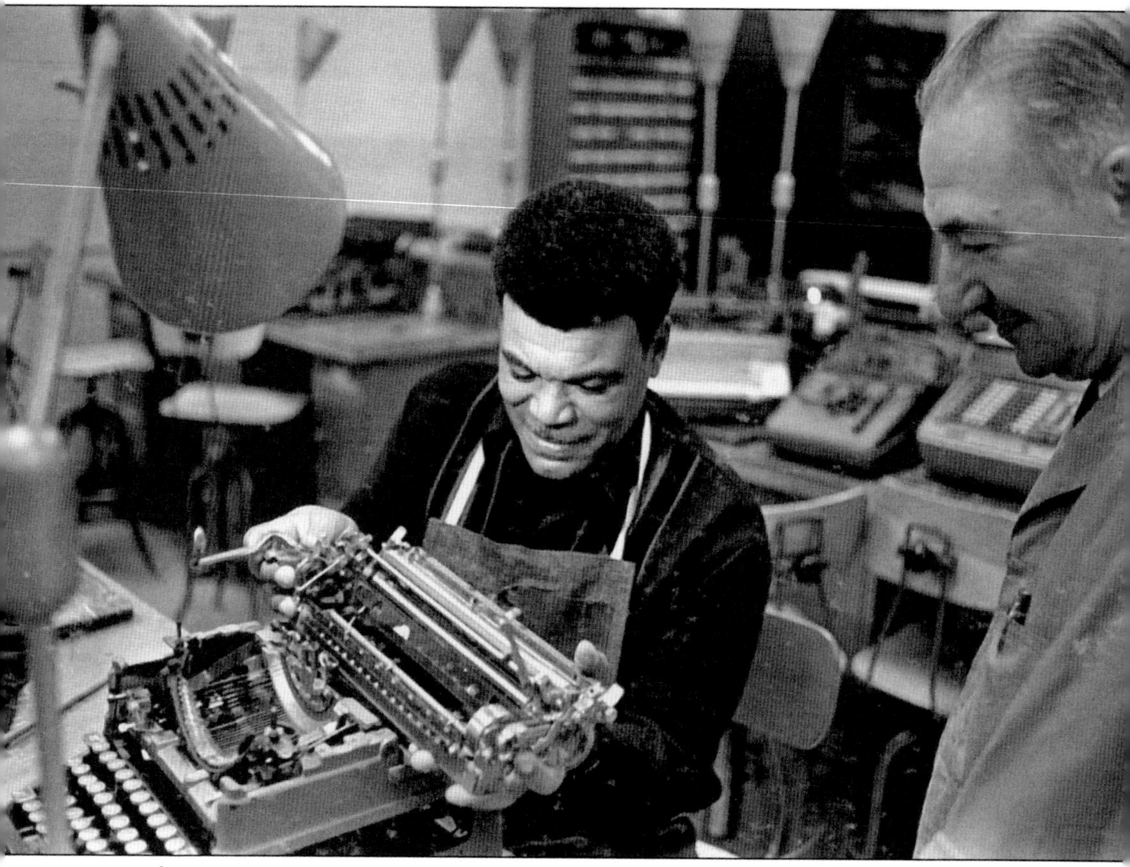

A student repairs an ancient typewriter. Today students in Computer Engineering can construct and repair sophisticated computers. There are not many typewriter repair people.

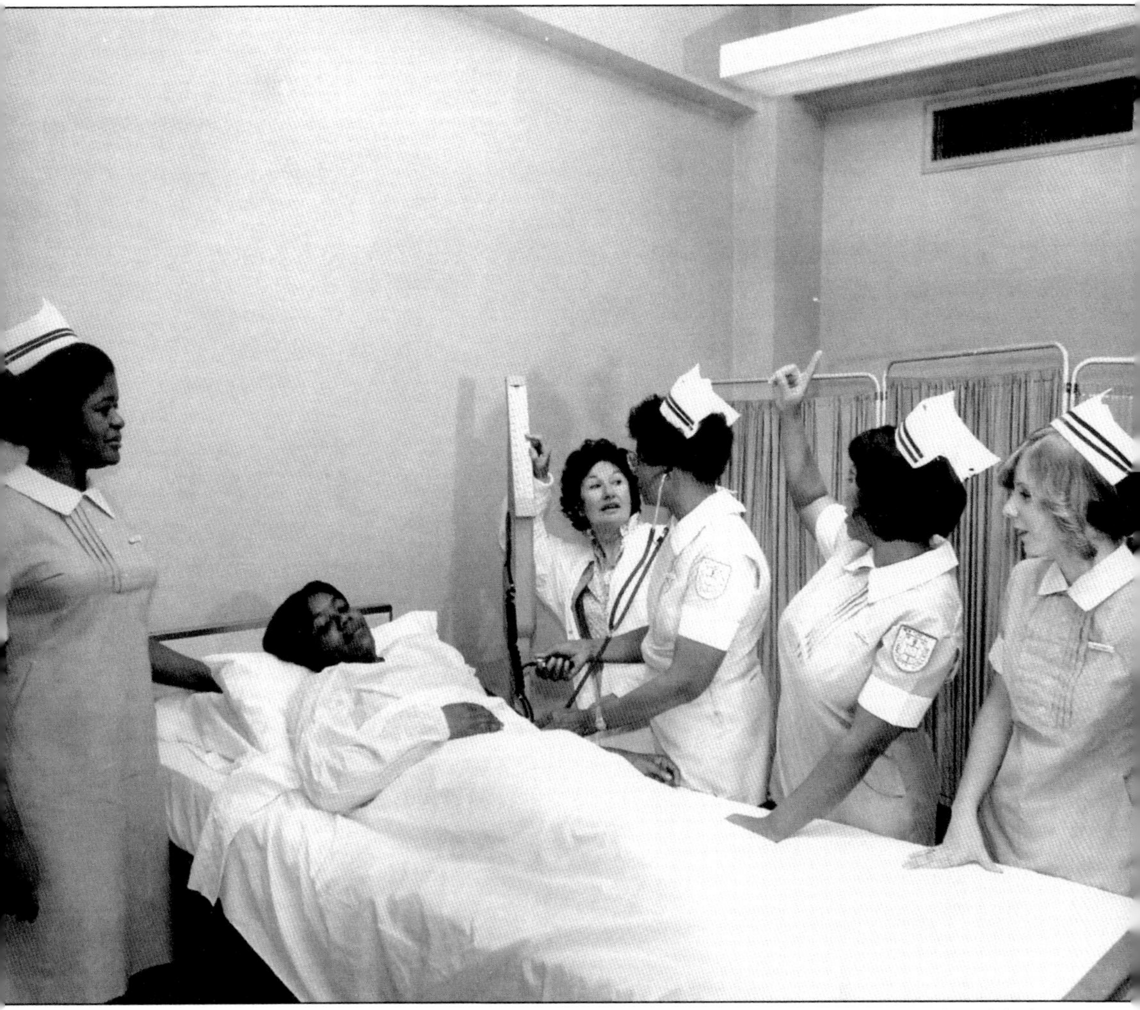

The Nursing Program at the New York City College of Technology has recently added a baccalaureate program to meet the urgent need for bachelor-level trained nurses. The clinical program has nearly doubled in size. The program includes a strong emphasis on community nursing, management skills, and research and critical thinking abilities.

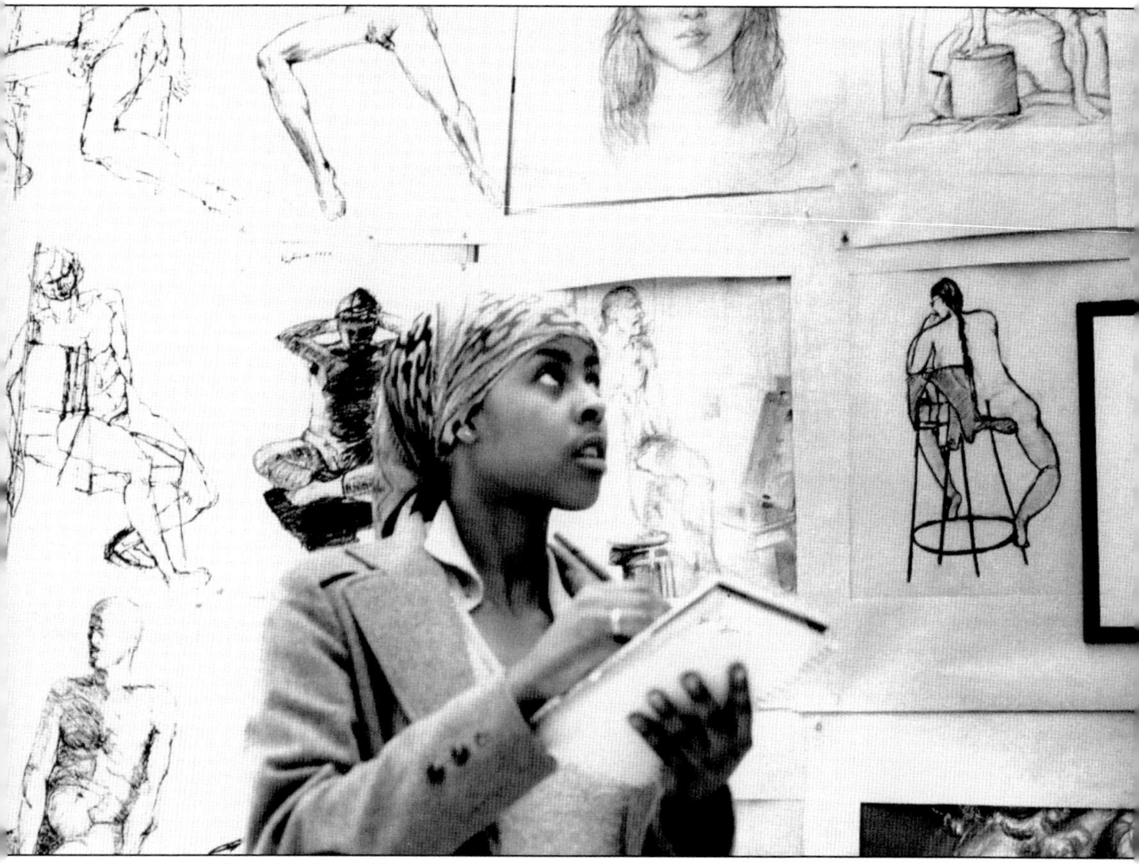

This is a student in the college's Advertising Design Program in the early 1970s. Students in this program take several courses in model drawing. Today the program emphasizes the most advanced computer-based design, but students continue to learn the basics that a skilled professional must know, including life drawing and other traditional skills.

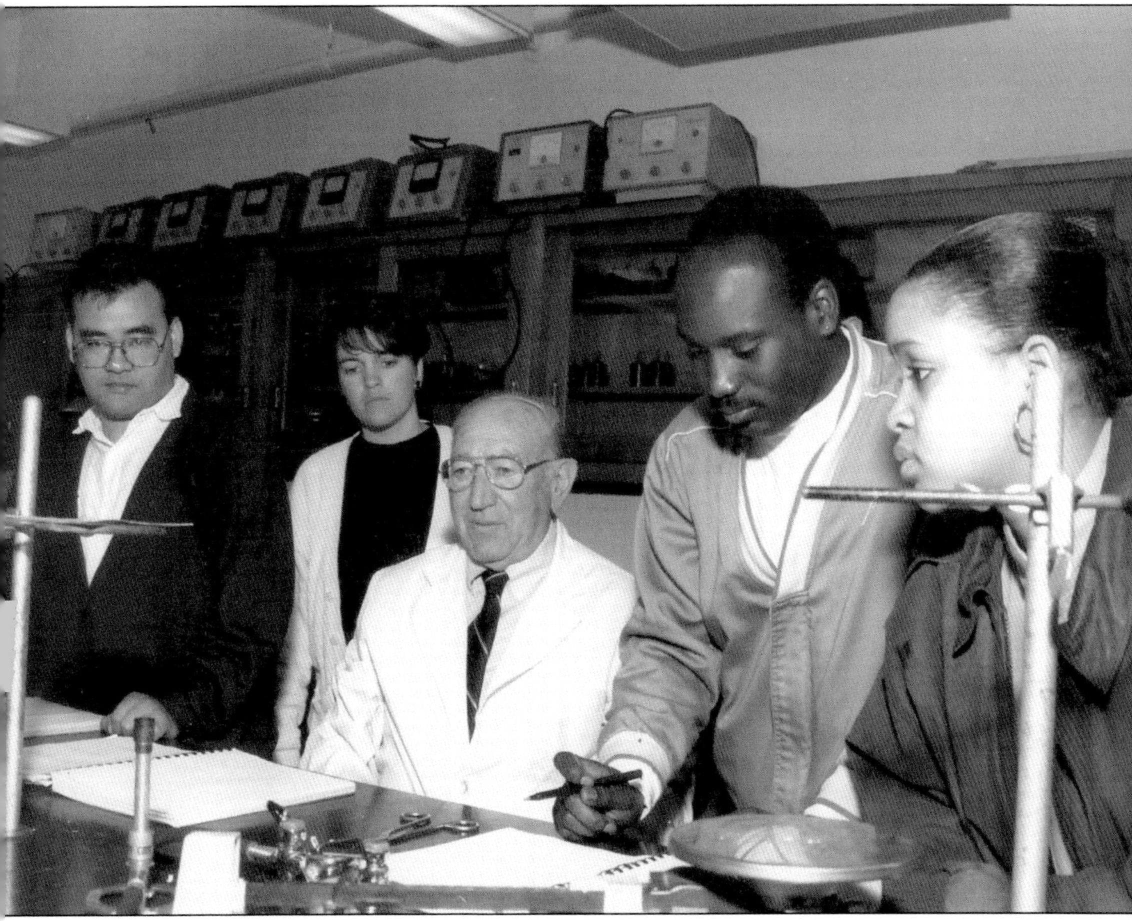

Seen here is a scene from a physics class. Students in the engineering technologies must take several physics classes and advanced mathematics in addition to the specialized requirements of their majors.

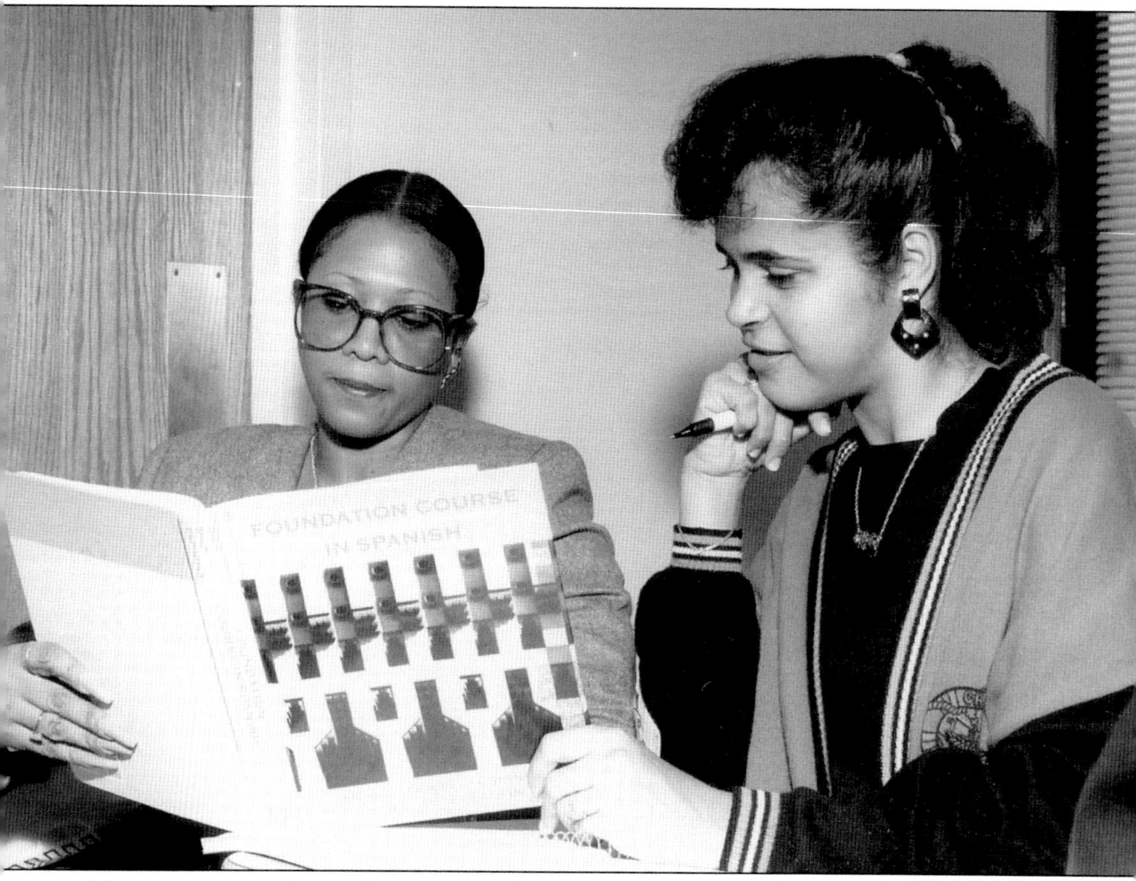

These are two students who appear to be studying for a Spanish exam. The text identifies this as an elementary Spanish course. Foreign language courses are still required for liberal arts majors. The college recently added courses in Mandarin, Arabic, and American Sign Language.

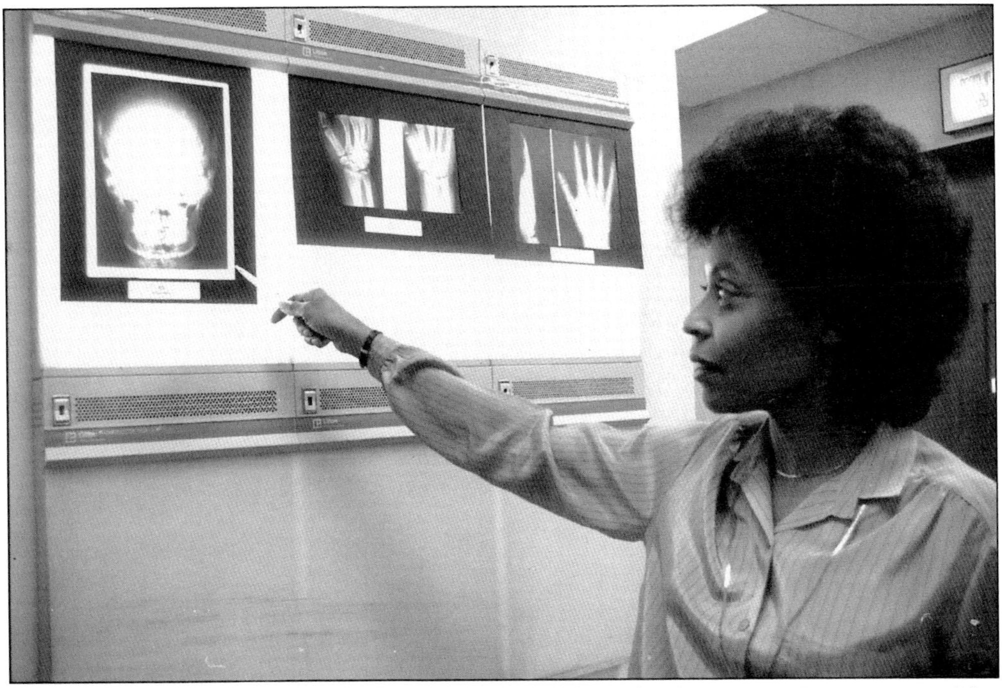

Pictured here is our Radiologic Technology and Medical Imaging Department. The instructor is identified as Prof. Mary Alice Brown, who is currently the chair of this department.

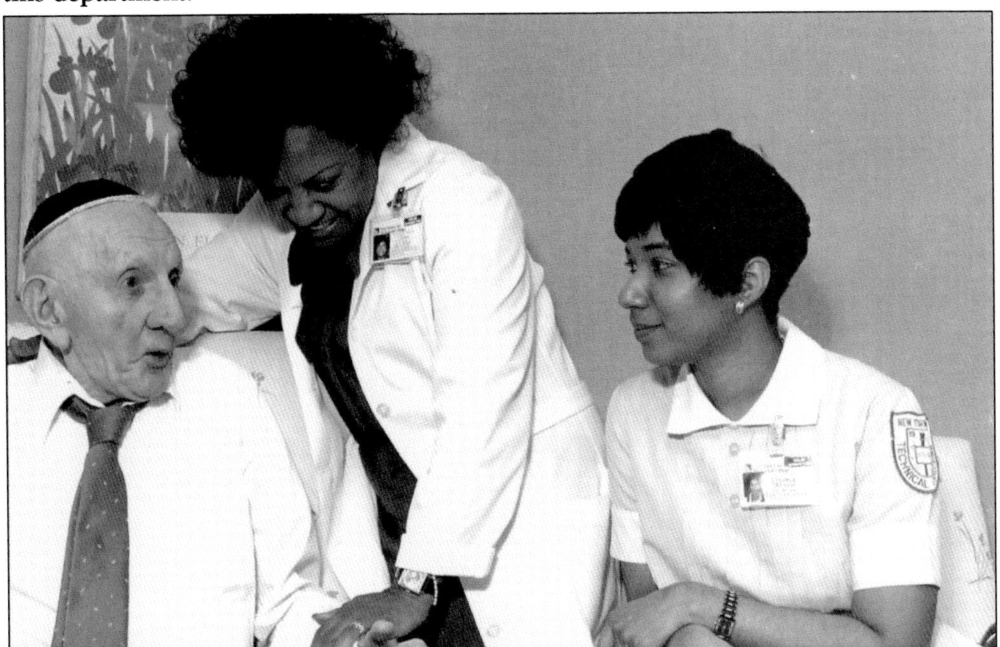

In this picture, New York City College of Technology nursing students care for an elderly Jewish gentleman who is in a residential care facility in Central Brooklyn. The 60th year of the college marks the 45th anniversary of the Nursing Department.

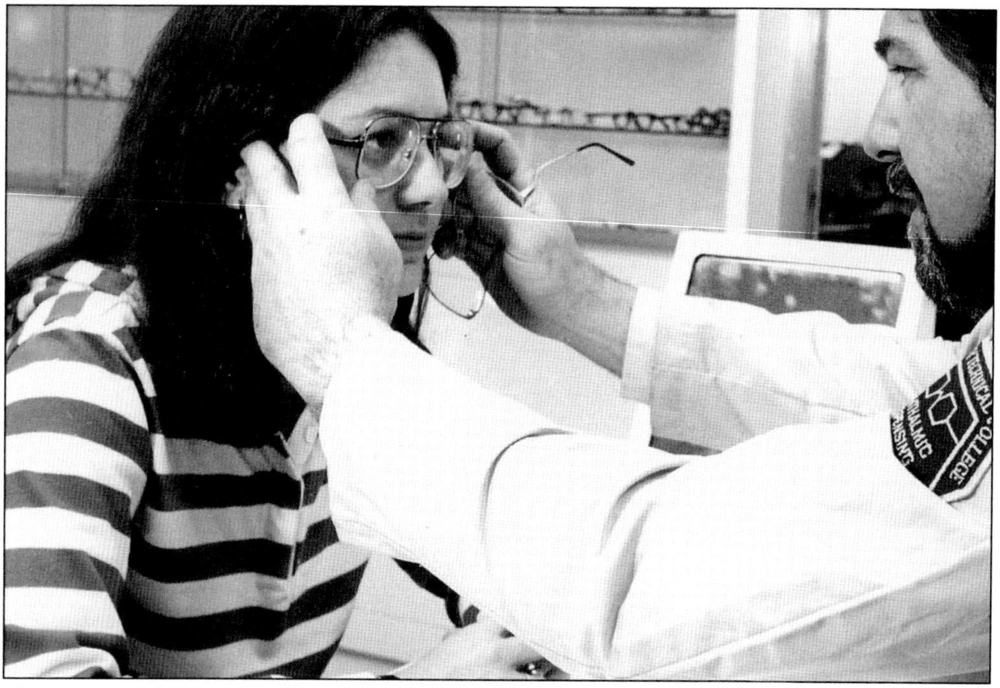

These are students in our Vision Care Department, enrolled in the Ophthalmic Dispensing Associate Degree program. Students under the supervision of faculty take care of their fellow students who are being fitted for a new pair of glasses. The Vision Care Clinic provides high-quality, low-cost service to the larger community.

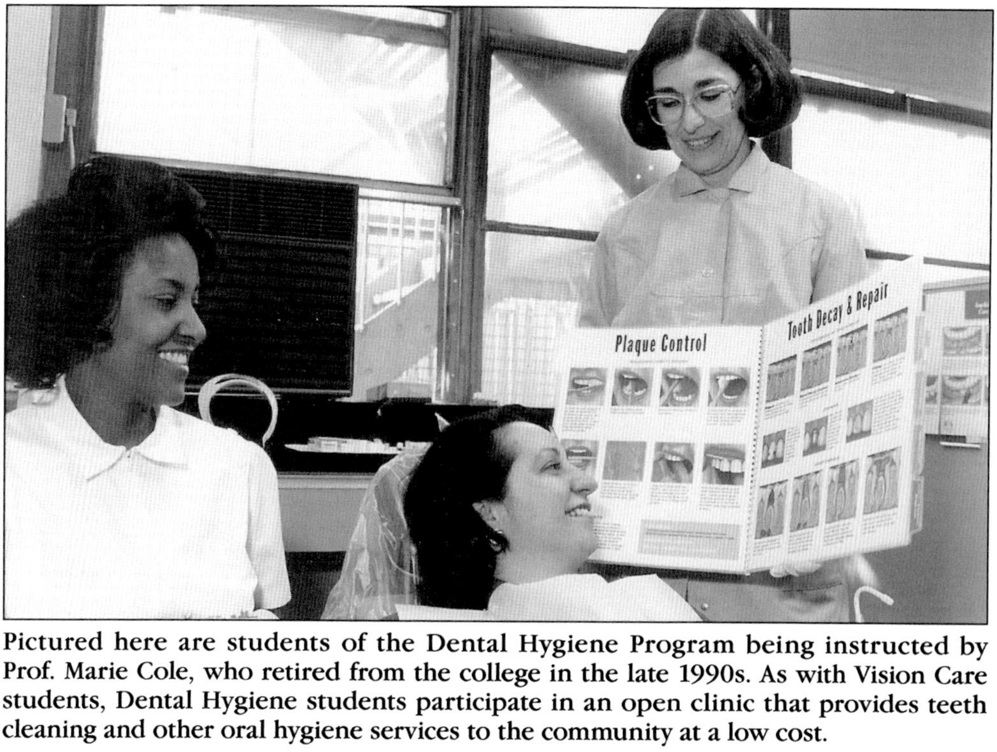

Pictured here are students of the Dental Hygiene Program being instructed by Prof. Marie Cole, who retired from the college in the late 1990s. As with Vision Care students, Dental Hygiene students participate in an open clinic that provides teeth cleaning and other oral hygiene services to the community at a low cost.

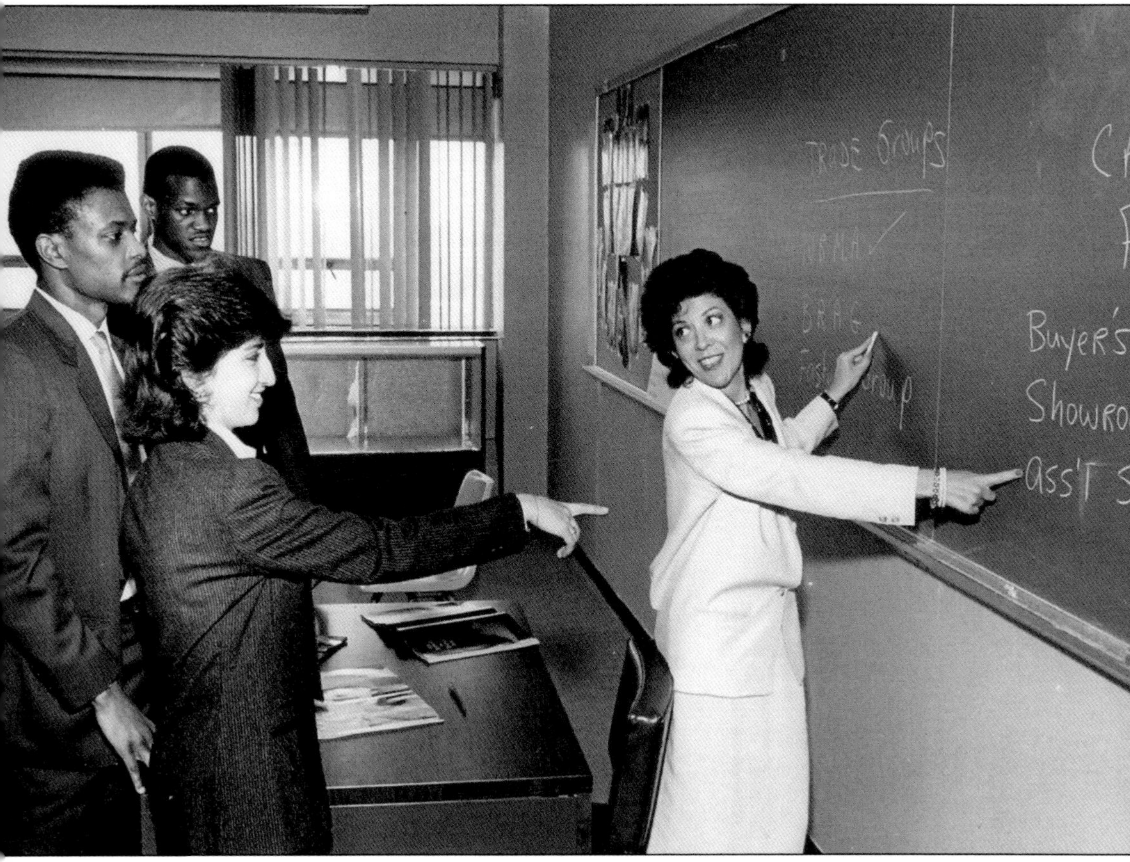

Prof. Anyse Winston is a marketing instructor in the Business Department. The Marketing and Accounting Programs serve over 1,000 degree students each year.

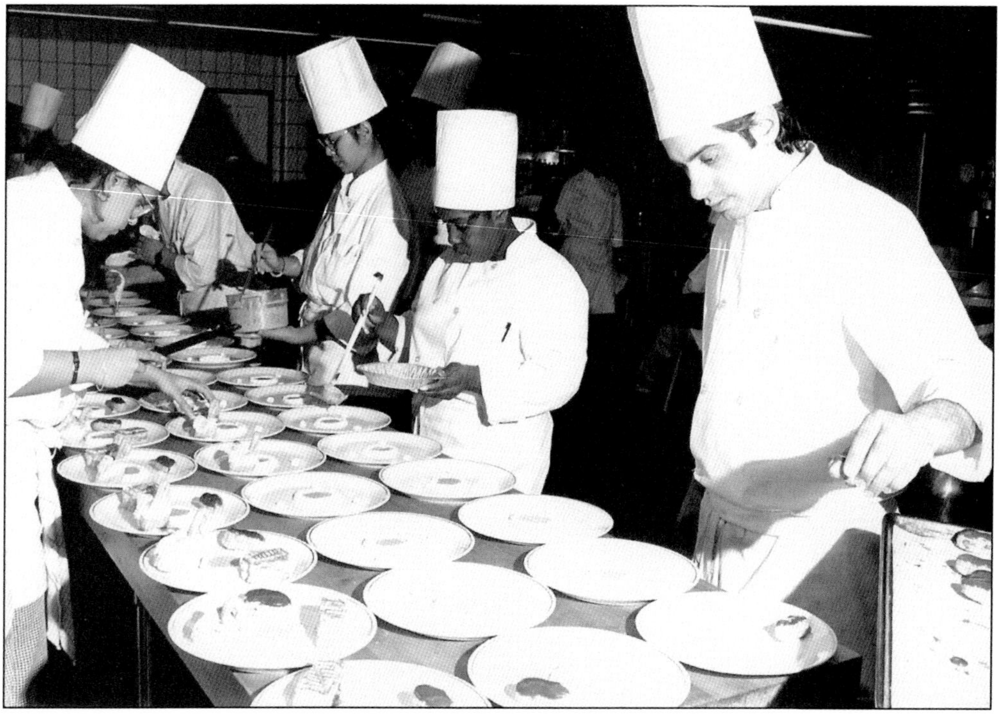

Seen here are students preparing a meal in the Hospitality Management Program. Students in this program go on to employment in the leading restaurants in New York and include some of the best-known names in American culinary arts.

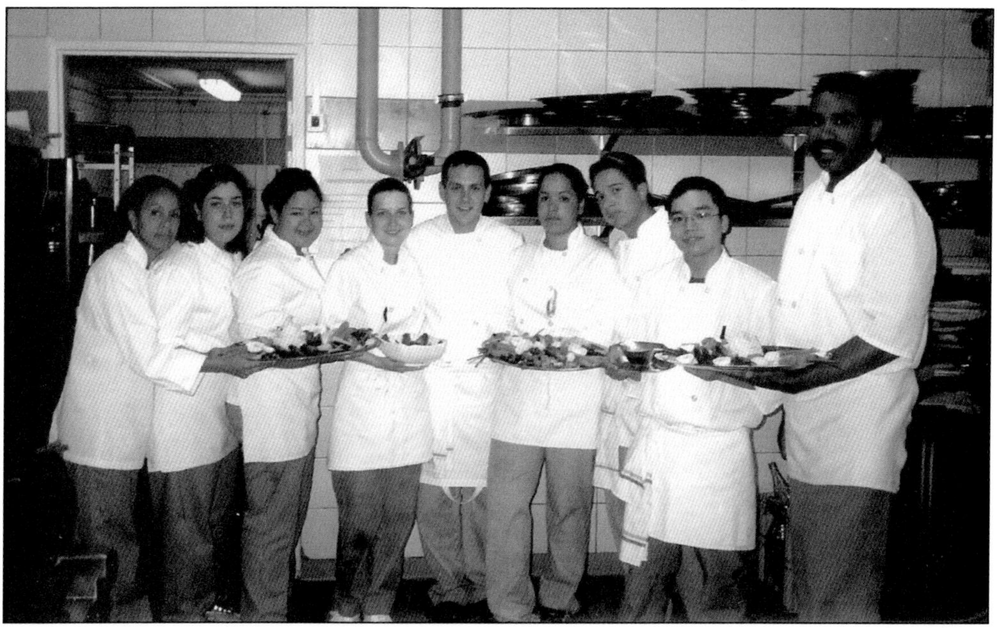

Culinary arts students proudly display their finished work for the camera here. Today culinary arts students from the Hospitality Management Program are regular award-winners in regional and national competitions, including the grand prize at the New York International Hotel, Motel, and Restaurant Show in two of the last three years.

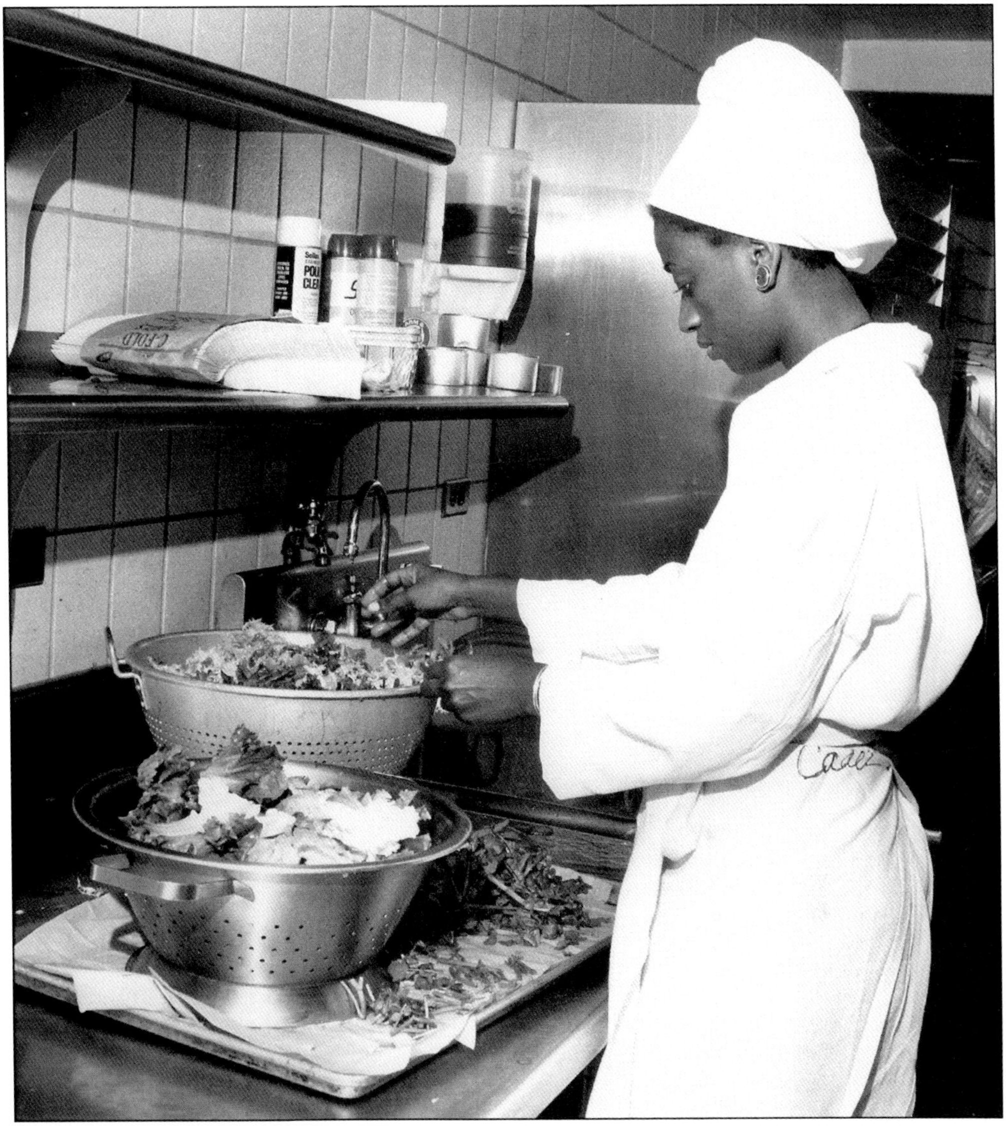

A New York City College of Technology student prepares a salad for the dining room. Students in the Hospitality Management Program assume many roles as part of their educational experience. They not only prepare the meals but are responsible for serving and cleaning up after they serve their guests. The approach of the program is that students must learn every aspect of their profession.

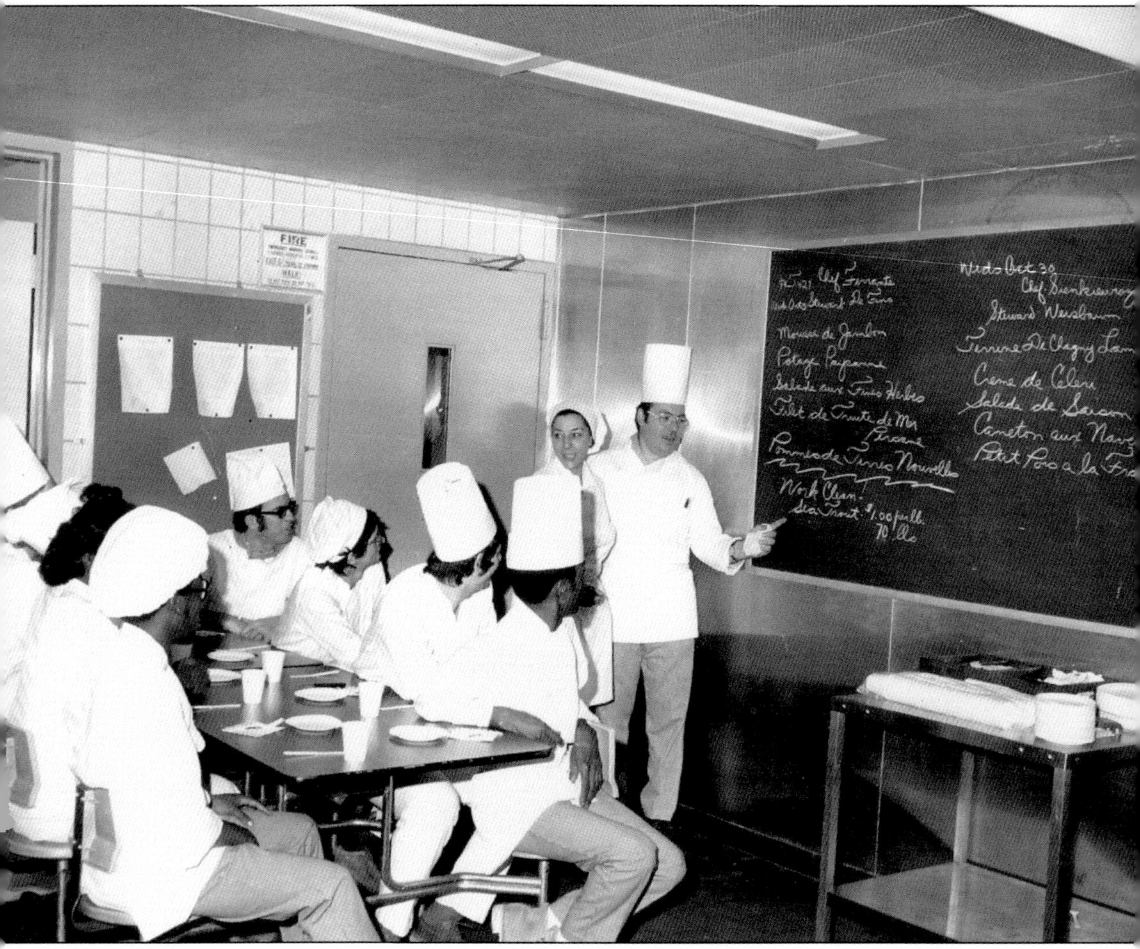

This is a classroom didactic in the Hospitality Management Program. Students are learning the art of cake making. Faculty in this department have been members of the U.S. Culinary Olympics team and one retired faculty member, Francis Lorenzini, was even knighted by the French government for his skills in the pastry arts. Work has begun on a total renovation of the main culinary laboratory.

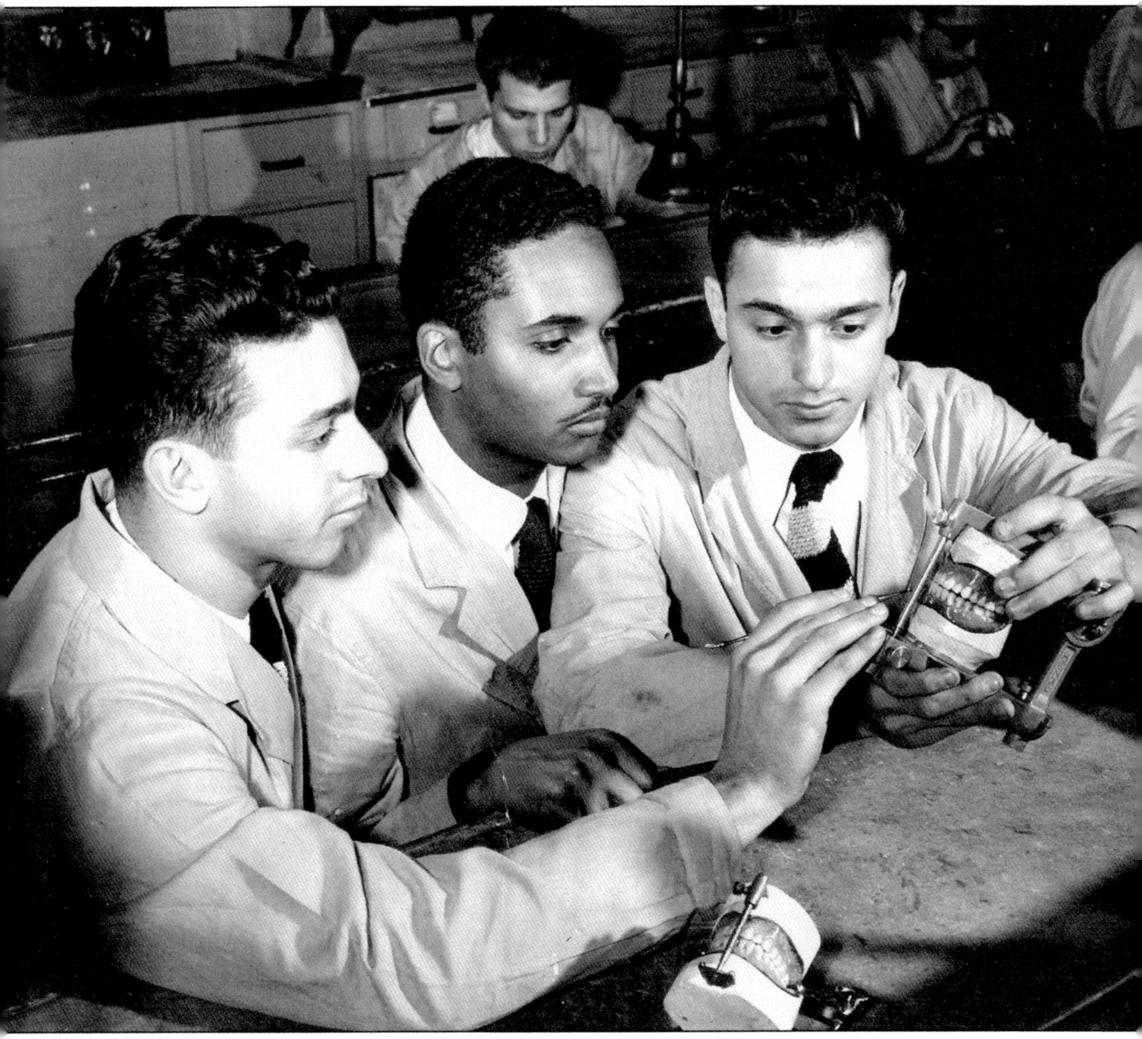

This picture was taken on June 25, 1953. The caption reads, "Dental Laboratory, critique on denture, the final assembly before casting." Although the work today employs more advanced technology, current students must still learn the manual skills required for casting and other basic restorative dentistry. The majority of technicians in restorative dentistry in New York City graduated from this flagship program.

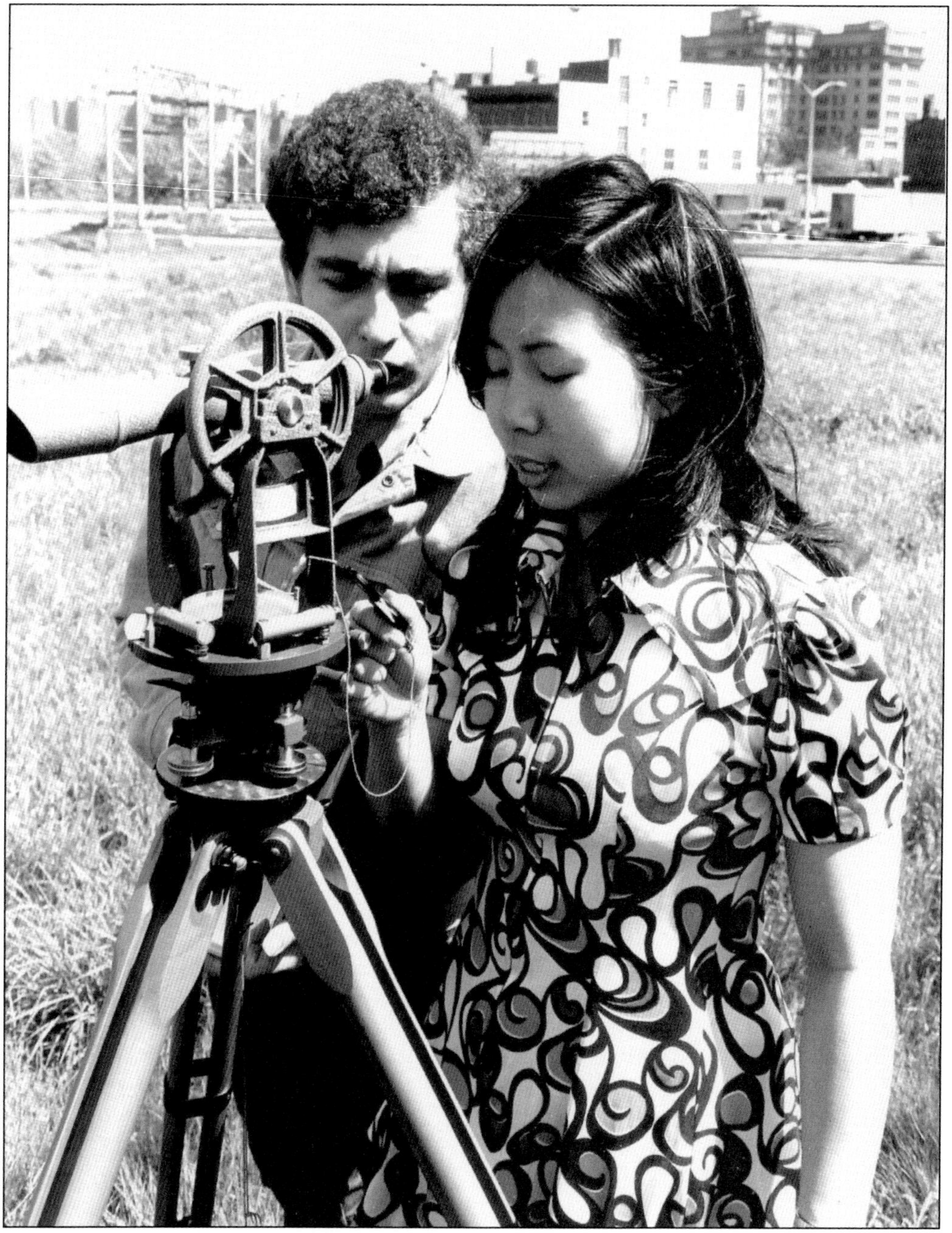

Students in the Construction and Civil Engineering Technology Department in the mid-1970s learn surveying skills. These skills remain important today but are augmented by the more advanced laser-based and other instruments of the digital age.

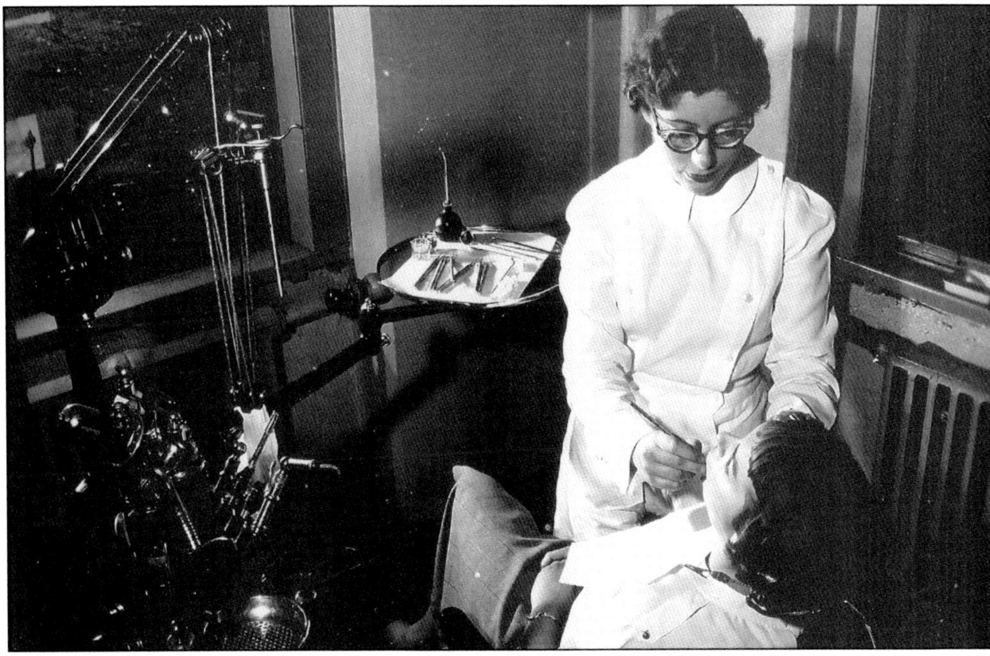

The Dental Hygiene Department dates back to the fall of 1947 with 40 women registered in this department. This picture shows early years of the department, probably in the late 1940s.

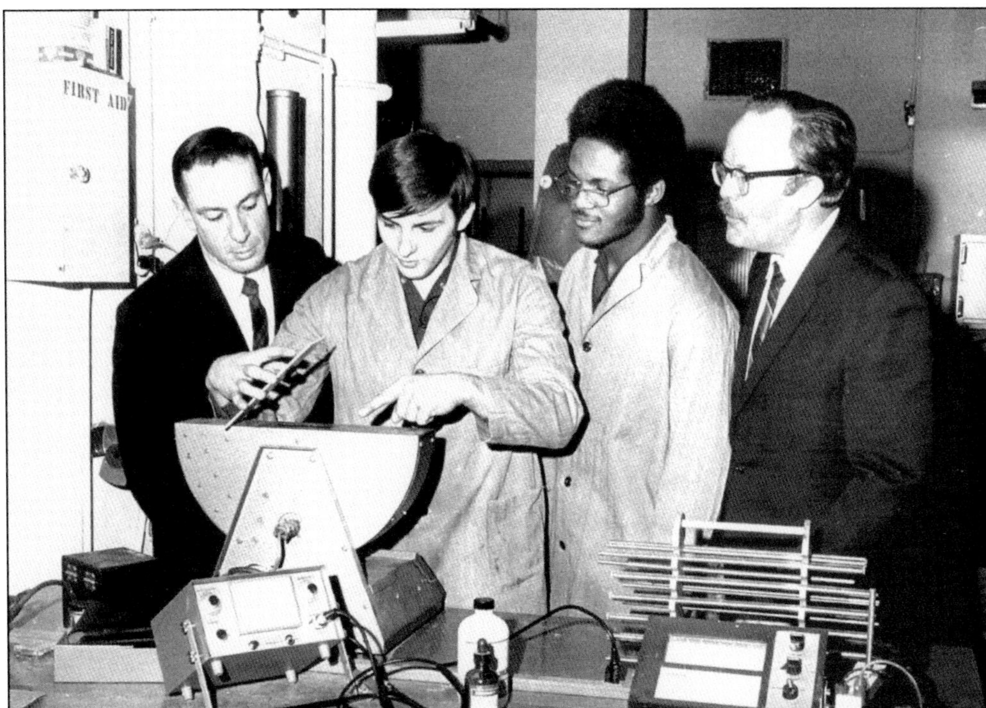

Judging from the laboratory coats this is a chemistry class, one can guess what type of experiments these students are performing. The picture dates back to the 1960s.

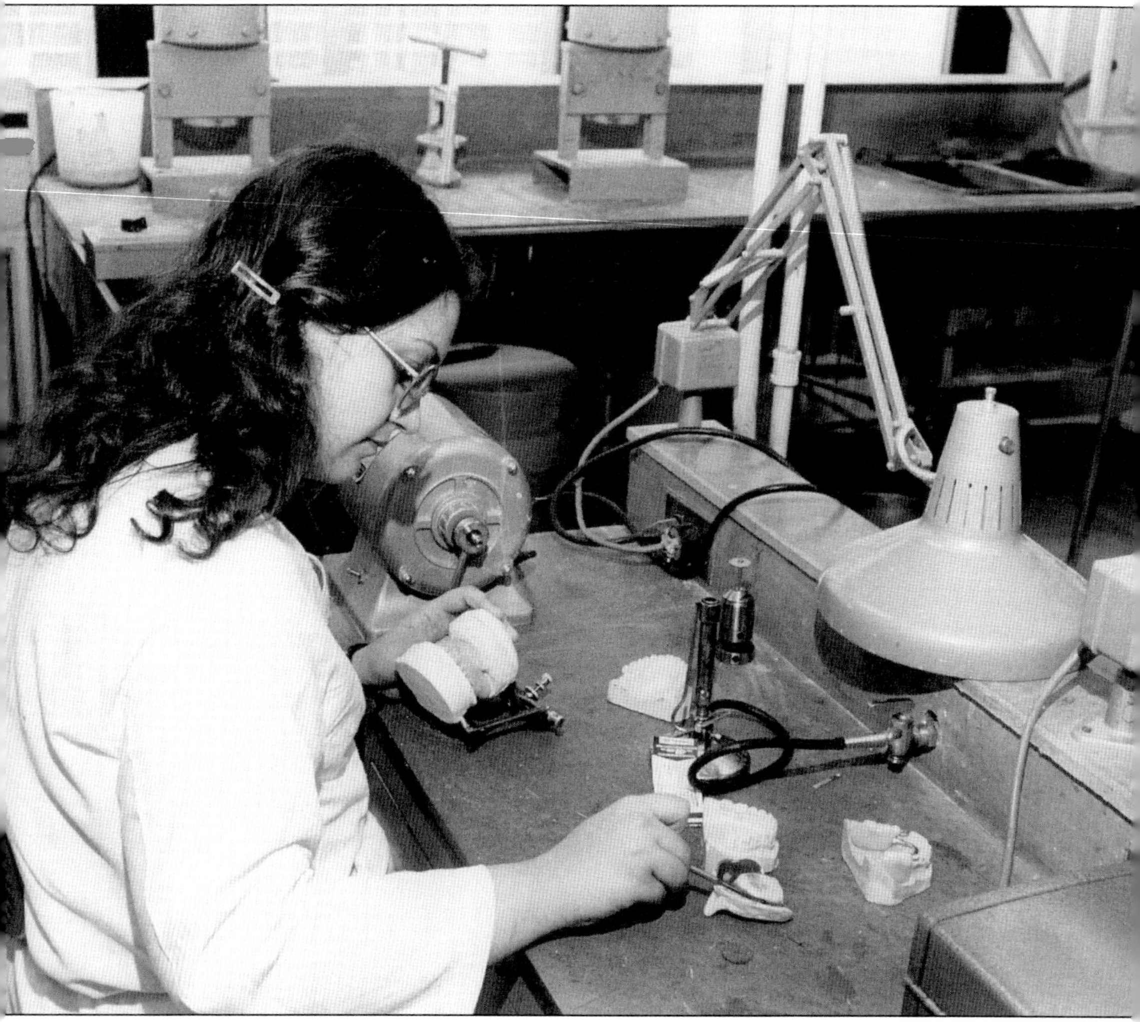

A female student works at creating dentures. Restorative Dentistry is part art, part technology. Students must be masters of both. Today this process is computer assisted and often relies on robotic manufacture, but the dual emphasis on art and technology remains.

Kenneth Rockensies, a professor in the Physics and General Science Department, is pictured here.

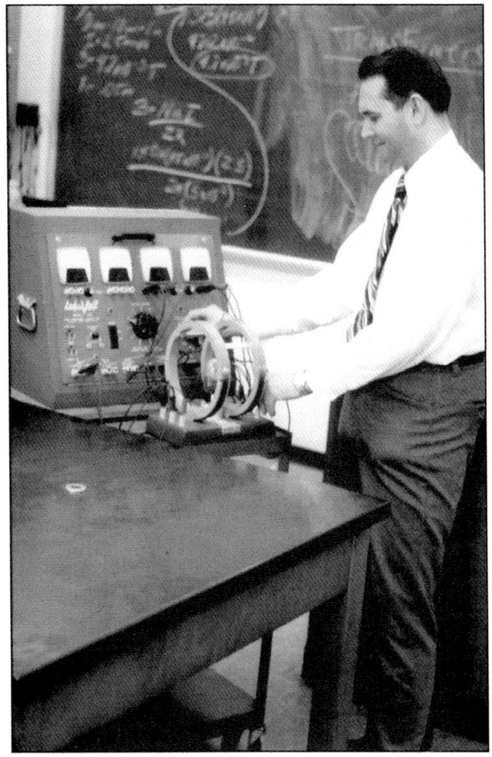

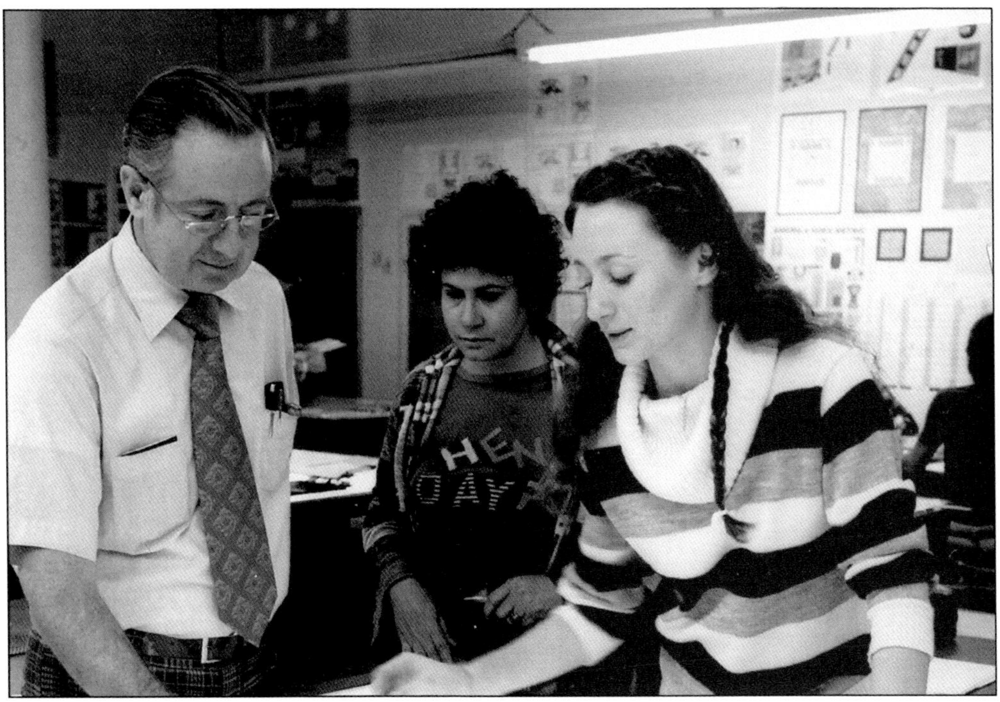

This picture reads, "The New York City Community College Voorhees Campus Section." Picture is from the early 1970s, after the college absorbed what remained of the Voorhees Institute of Technology. The man in the picture is identified as Professor Hanratty.

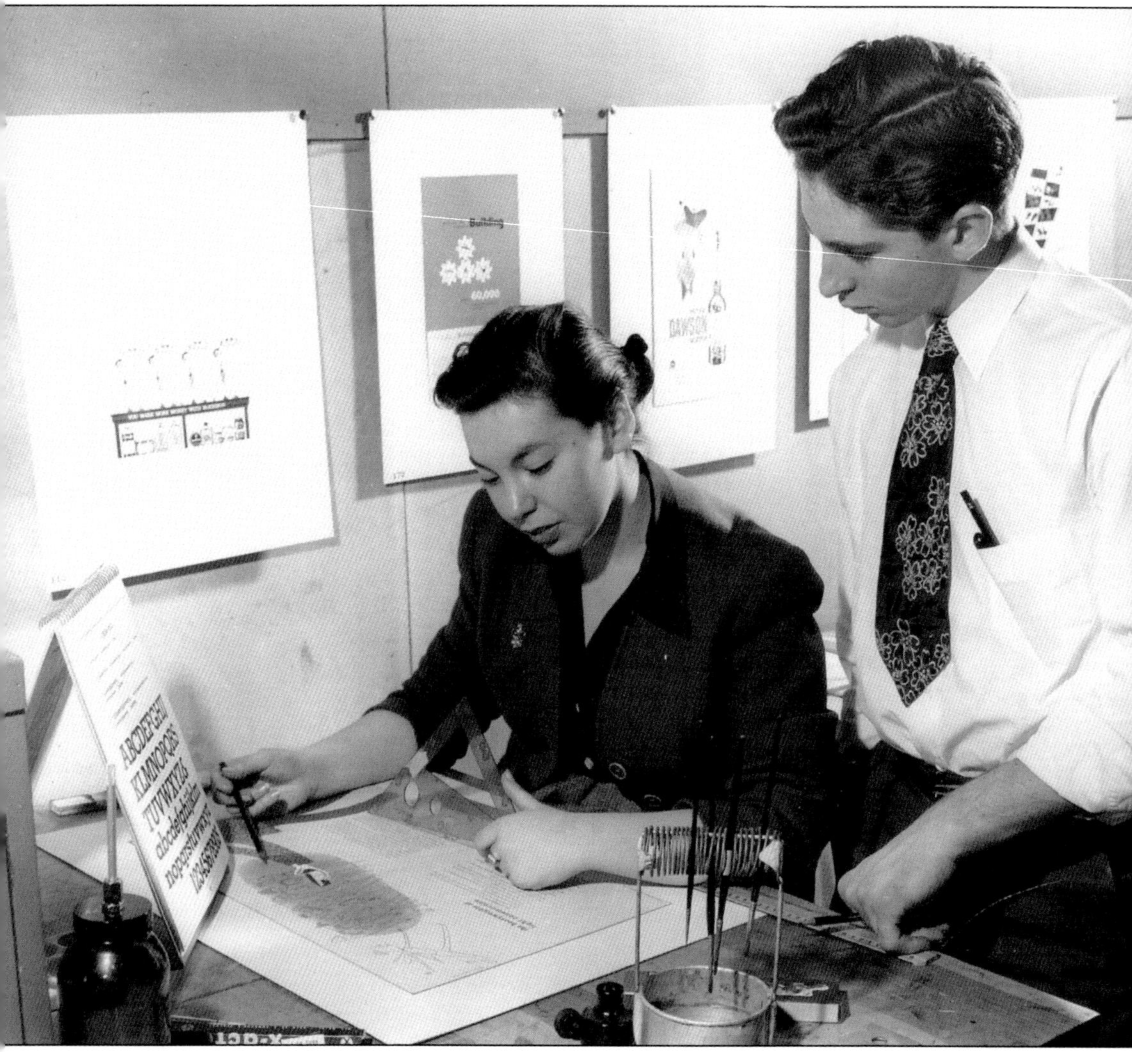

Seen here are Art and Advertising Design students, in a studio of the 1970s. The Advertising Design and Graphic Arts Department is today the largest department in the college.

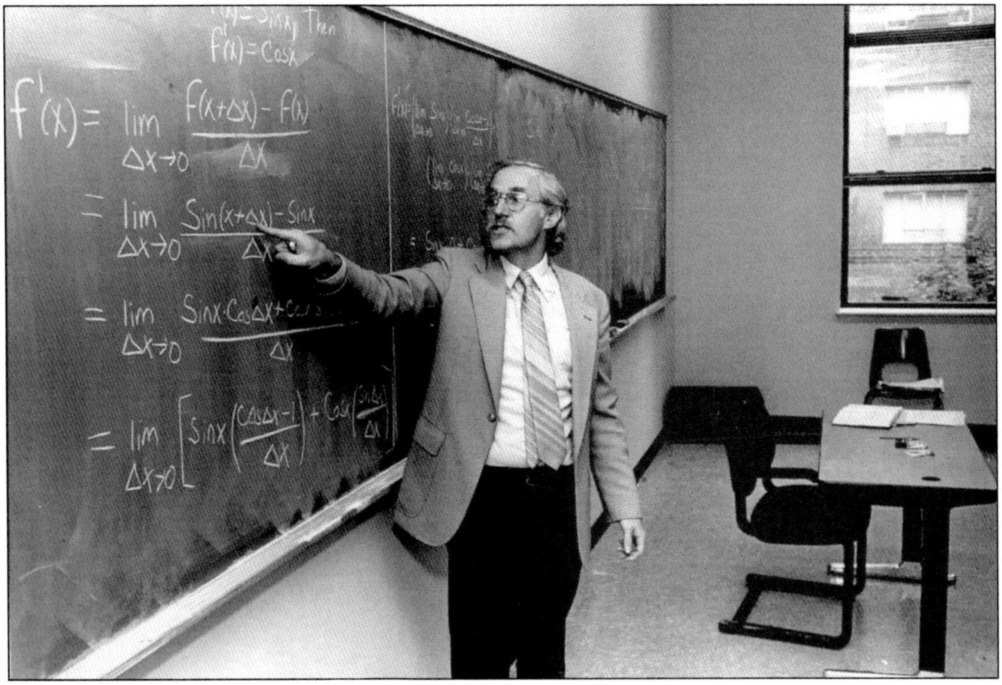

Pictured here is a math class in the 1960s. Every program at the college requires mathematical competency. In some departments, this may mean six or more semesters of college-level mathematics.

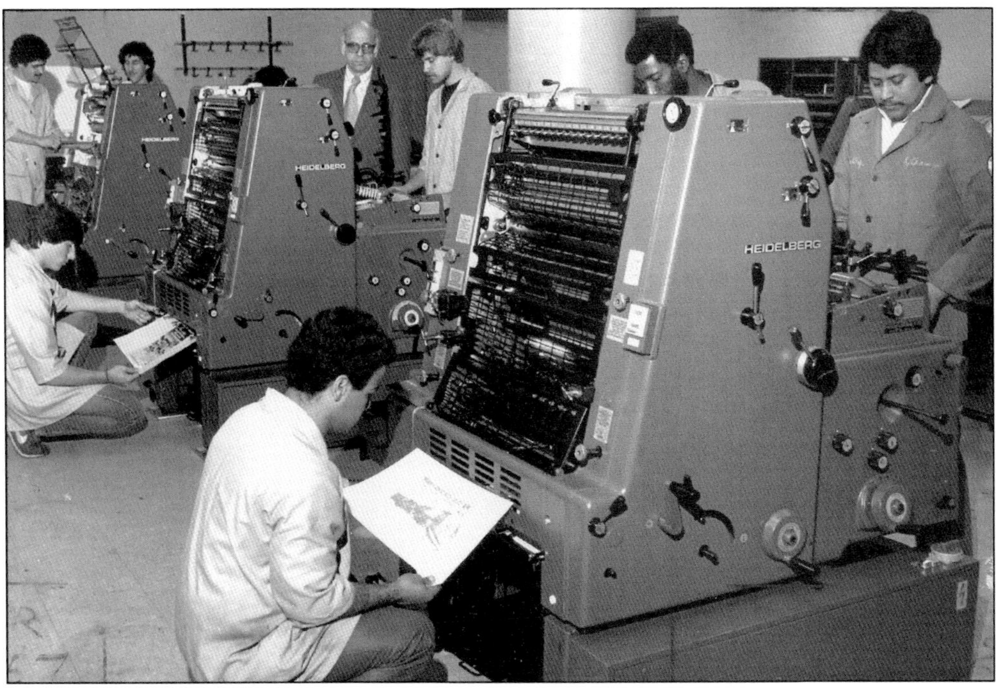

Students are pictured in the Graphic Arts Department. The man in the background dressed in a suit is Dr. James DeLuca, longtime chair of the department.

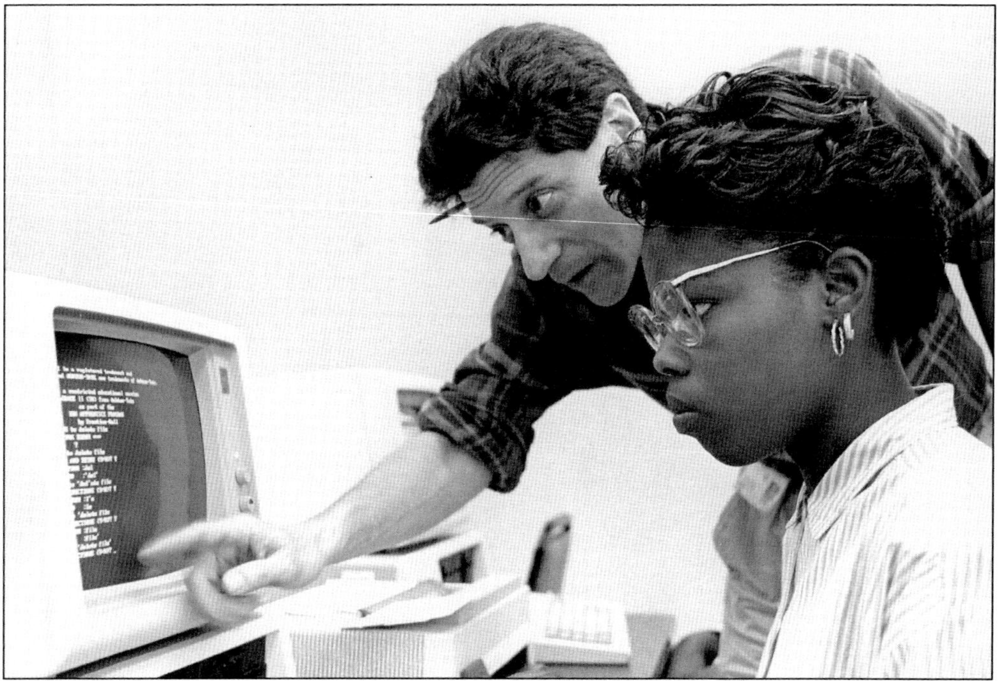

Seen here is Prof. Gary Popkin, working with a student on an early model IBM computer. Professor Popkin is a well-published author of a number of basic works on computer programming.

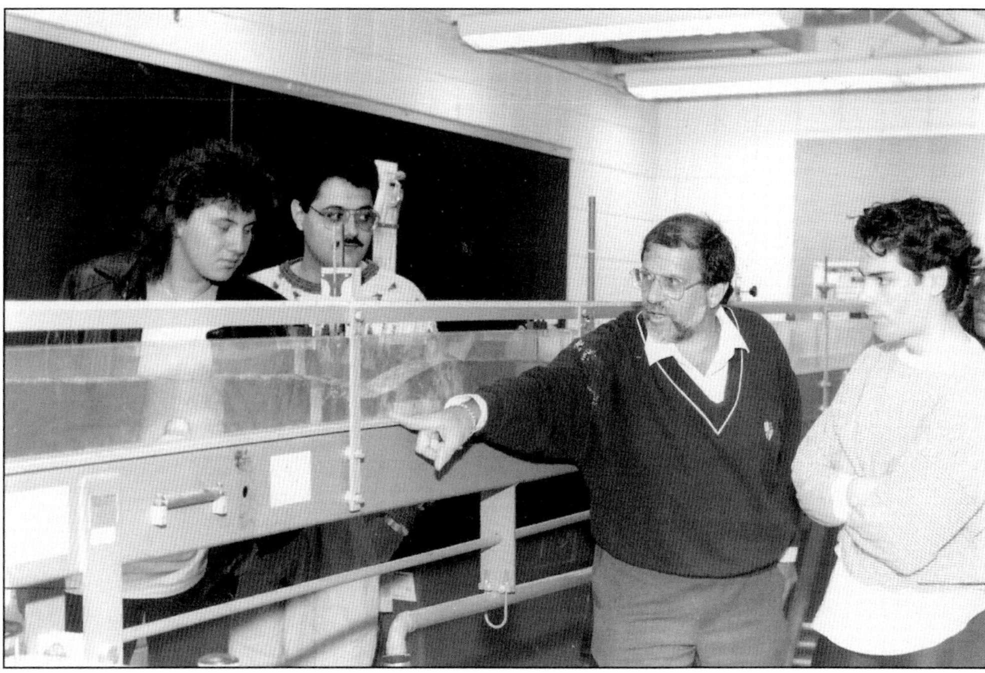

These are students from the Construction and Civil Engineering Technology Department, dating back to the 1970s. Prof. Elliot Colchamiro demonstrates basic properties of fluids.

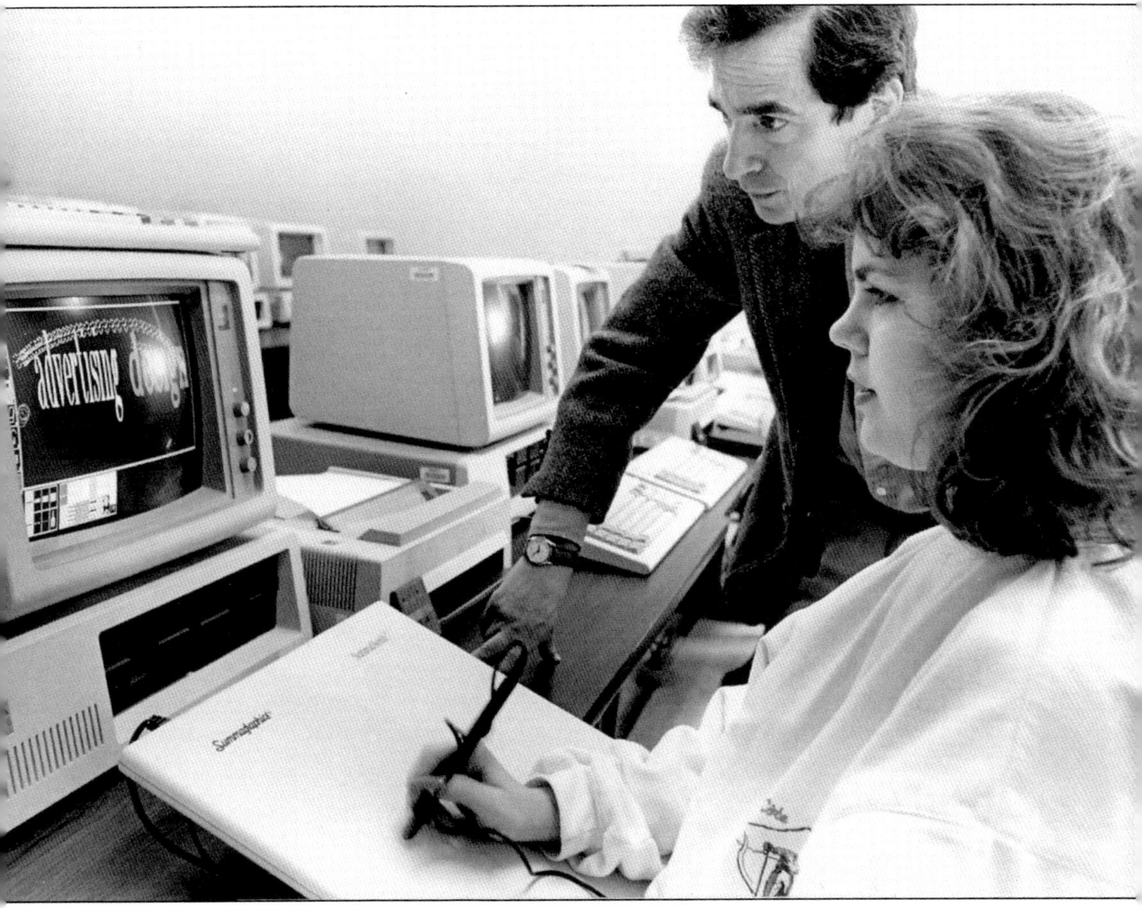

This computer identifies this as a student in the Advertising Design and Graphic Arts Department. Today the largest department at the college, it is the direct descendent of the Commercial Art Program, one of the earliest degree programs. The man in the picture is Prof. Joel Mason, currently the chair of the department..

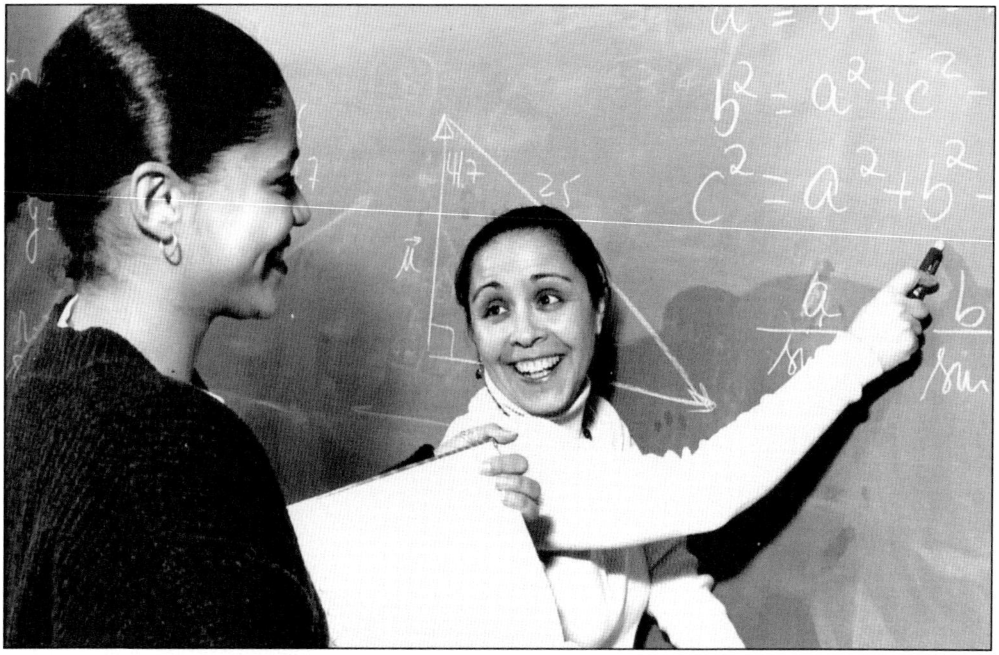

Pictured here is Dr. Estella Rojas from the Math Department teaching a class around the 1980s. Dr. Rojas was later to coordinate the creation of learning communities at the college and to provide smoother and more integrated entry of new students into the college, funded by a Federal Fund for the Improvement of Post-Secondary Education (FIPSE) grant.

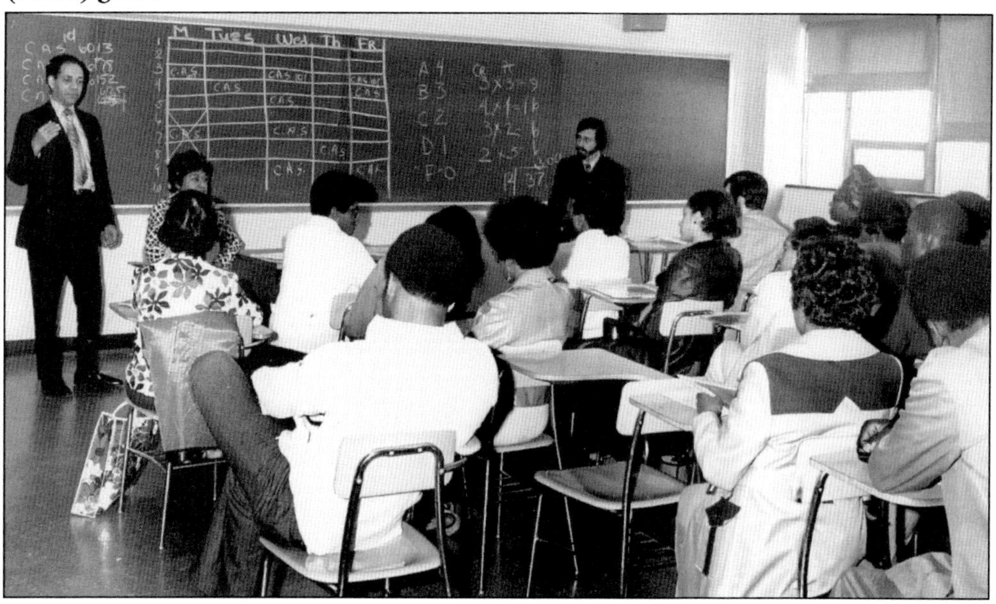

The caption on the back of this *c.* 1969 picture reads, "Making It to College-Dr. George Howard, director of Brooklyn Urban Center of State University of New York, describes college life to some 80 young men and women who upgraded their academic skills there during the past year and qualified for enrollment at New York City Community College in downtown Brooklyn."

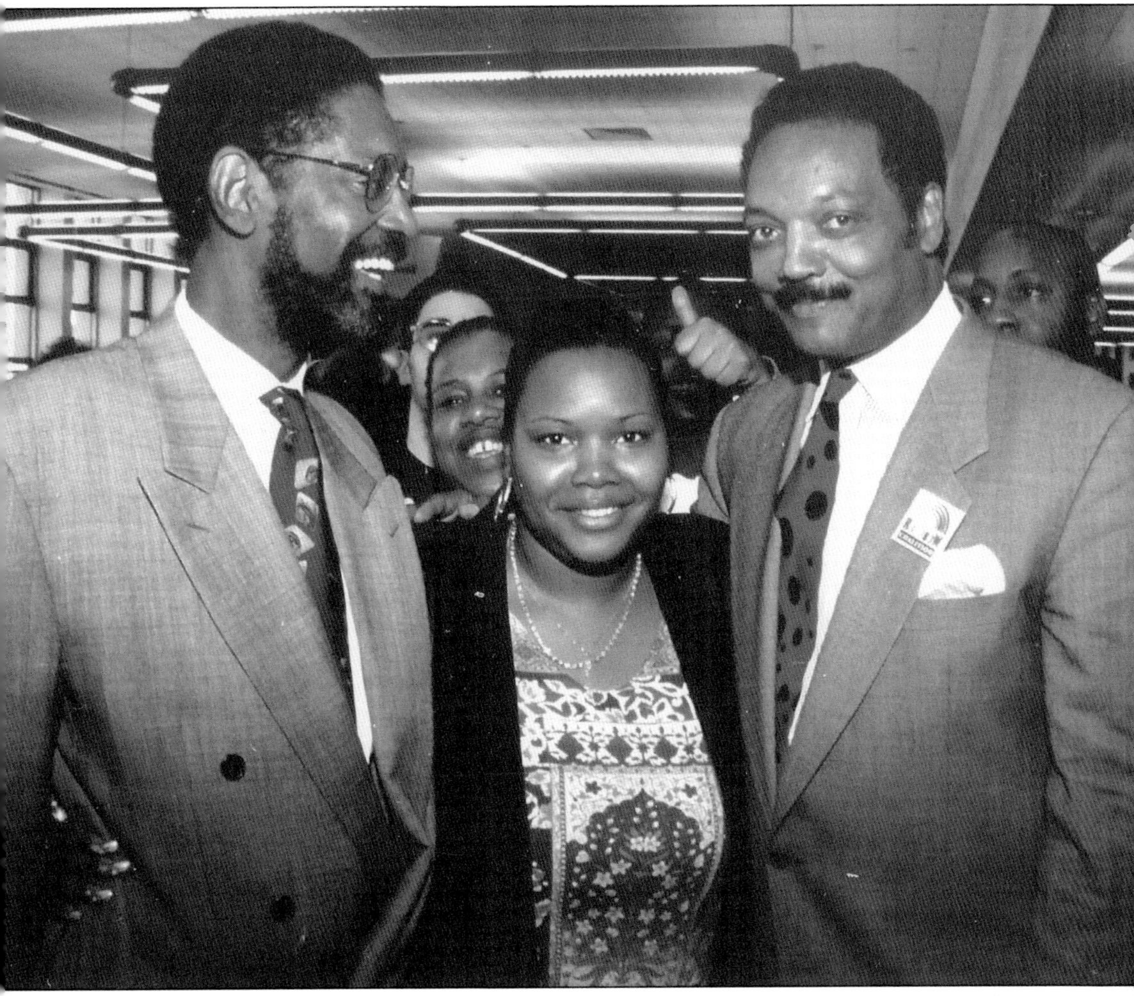

Pres. Charles Meredith is seen with the Reverend Jesse Jackson in one of his several visits to the New York City College of Technology.

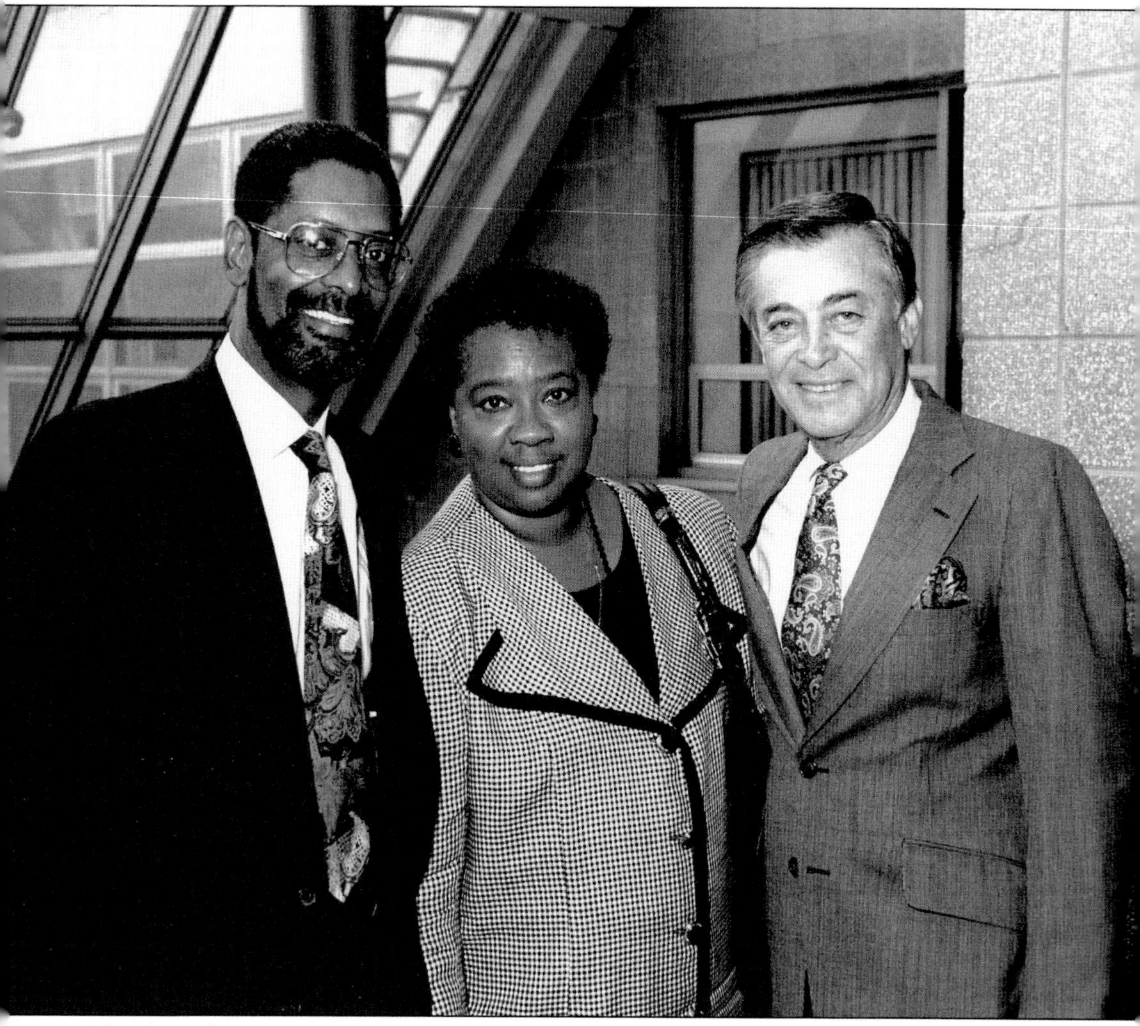

The first African American president of the college, Dr. Charles Merideth, is shown here with the former Brooklyn Borough president Howard Golden during the early 1990s.

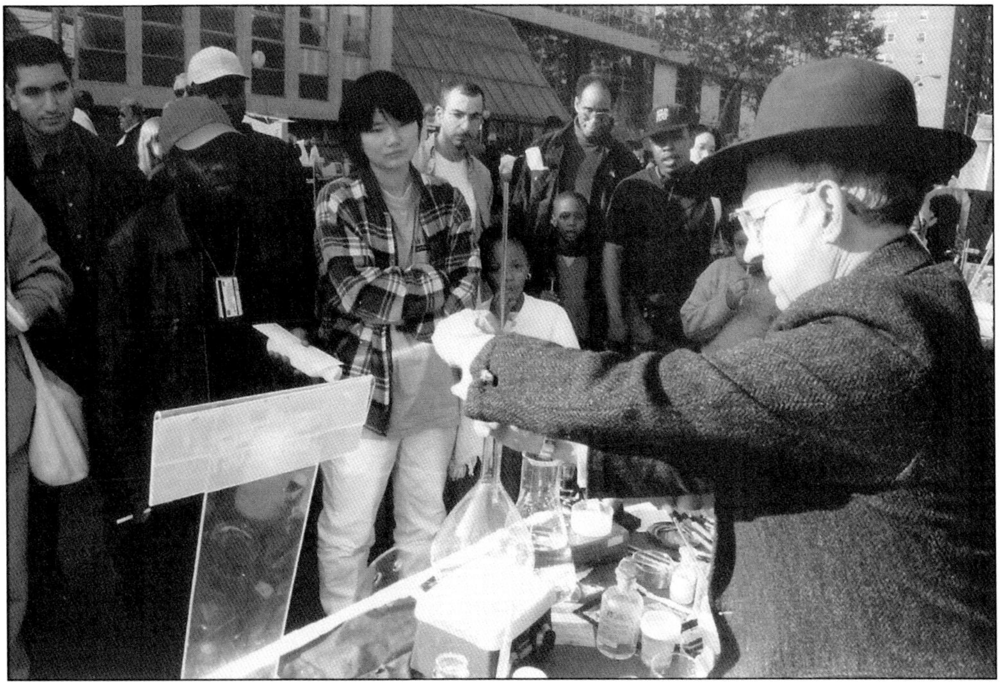

Seen here is a street scene from the 50th anniversary.

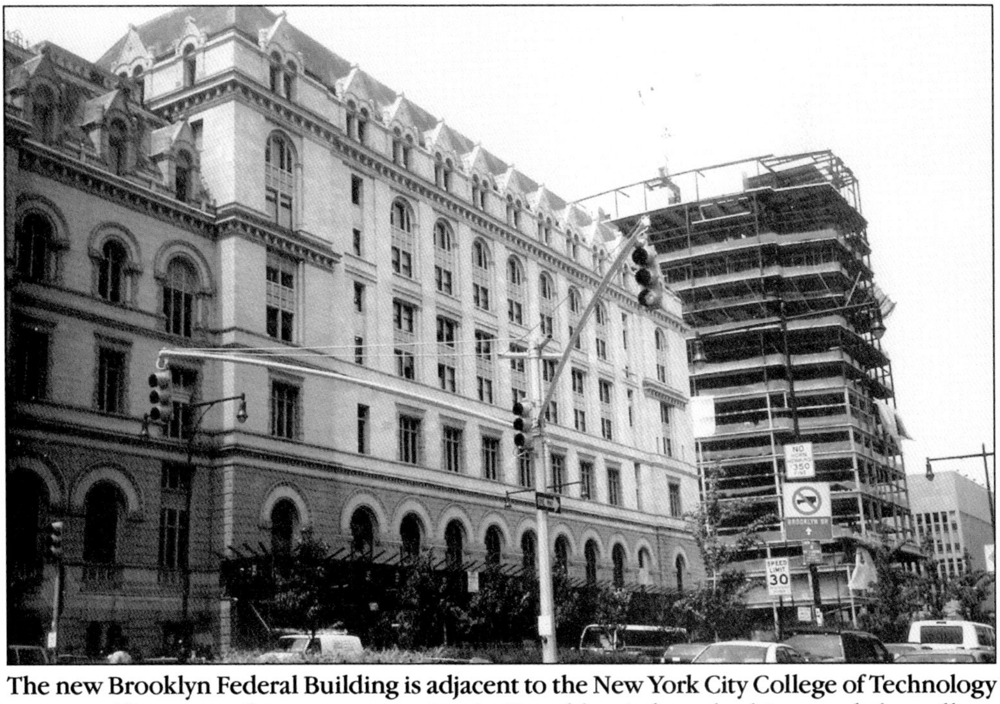

The new Brooklyn Federal Building is adjacent to the New York City College of Technology campus. The pace of new construction in Brooklyn is breathtaking, and the college is set to add to this momentum with the most significant construction project in its 60-year history.

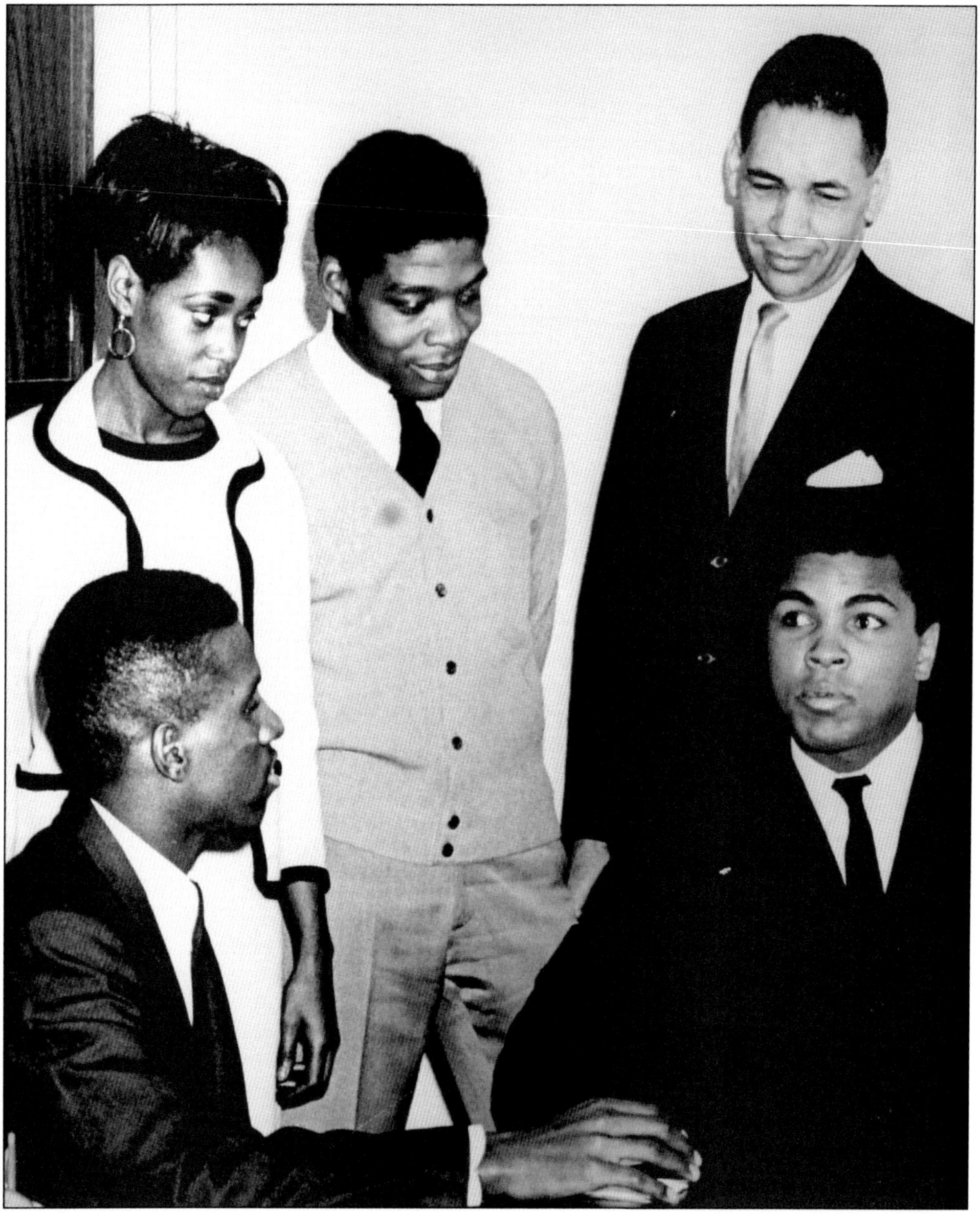

Mohammed Ali (right), former world heavyweight boxing champion visits the college in the 1980s. At the time of his visit, surveys described Ali as the best known athlete in the world.

A memorial was set up for the victims of September 11, 2001, by the promenade in Brooklyn Heights, located next to the college. Similar memorials were set up across the city, especially in places from which one would, in happier times, have seen the World Trade Center.

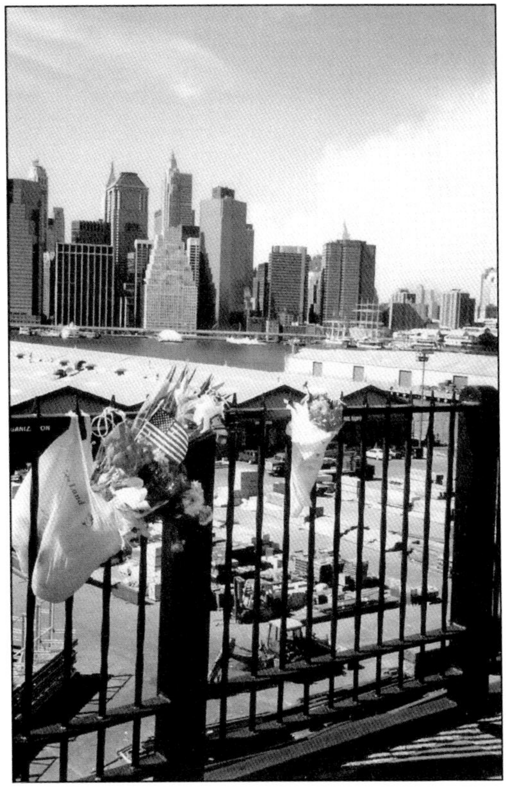

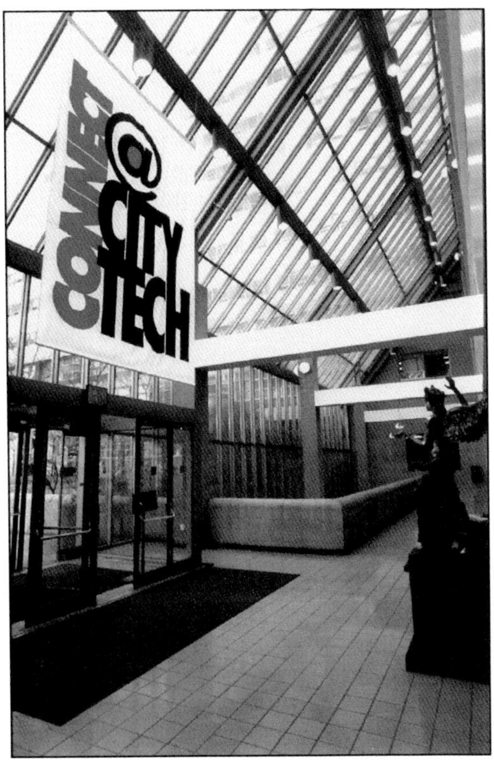

The Atrium entrance serves as a welcome to the college.

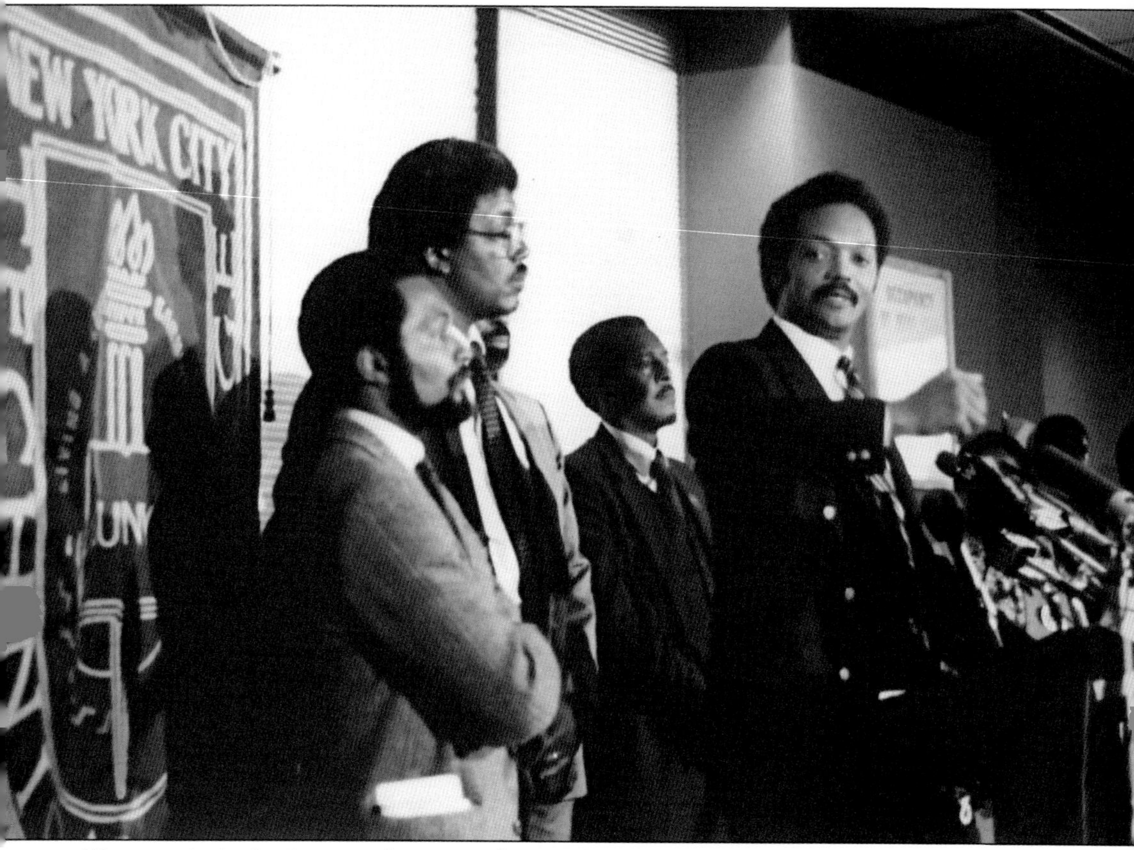

Here again is the Reverend Jesse Jackson when he spoke at the college. The banner in the background obviously reads, "New York City Technical College."

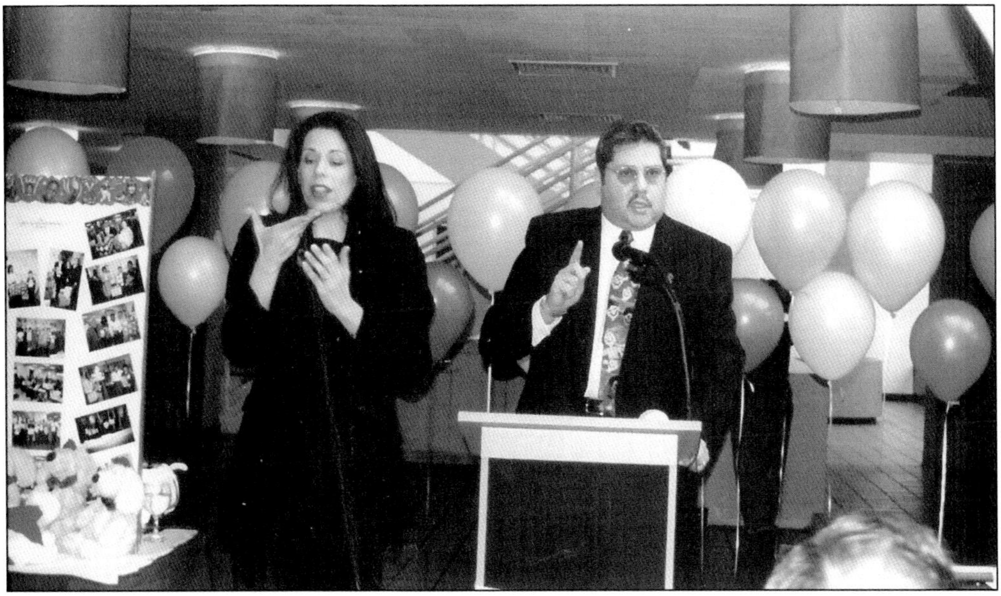

Here is the ceremonial conclusion of the Gifts for Special Children program, sponsored jointly by the Human Service and Hospitality Management Departments. Every December before Christmas, the college would sponsor this wonderful event that benefited children living with HIV and AIDS. Over the 18 years of this program, nearly 35,000 gifts were distributed and funding of over $75,000 was provided for libraries, hospices, and other agencies serving the needs of the children. On the right is Prof. Francisco Betancourt, former chair of the Hospitality Management Department, and on the left is Janice Rimler, who would sign at these and many other college events.

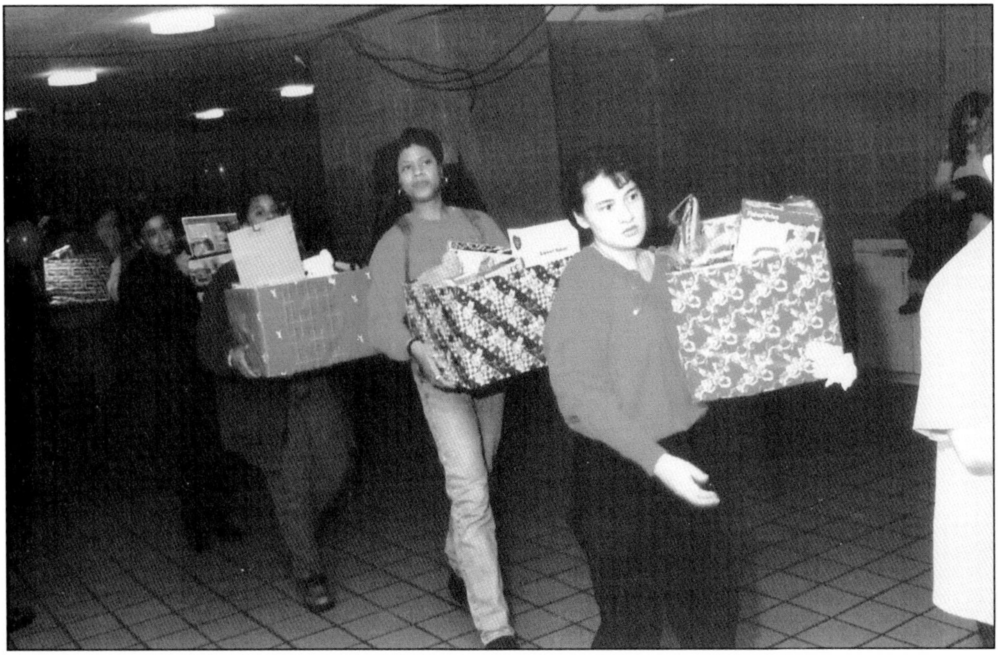

Pictured here are volunteers taking gifts for these kids to the various agencies that were part of the Gifts for Special Children program.

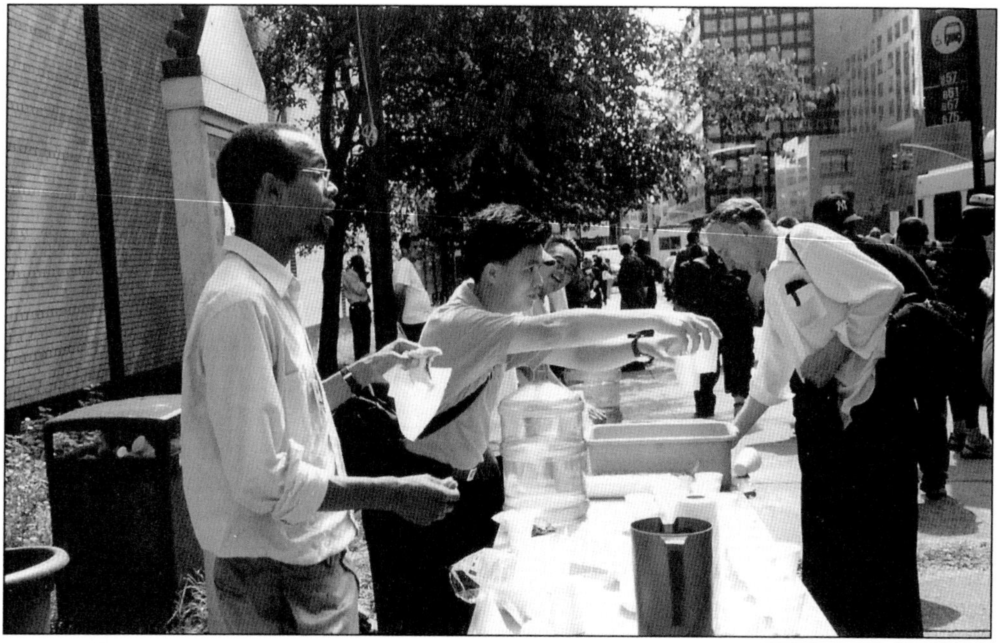

The world will not forget the events of September 11, 2001. The college is located just a short distance away from the Twin Towers, and across the street from the Brooklyn side of the Brooklyn Bridge. As people streamed across the Brooklyn Bridge by foot, the college opened its doors to all in need. Nursing faculty and students provided emergency care, and faculty and counselors did crisis intervention for individuals who needed it. Pictured here are students and staff offering water to those in need on September 11, 2001.

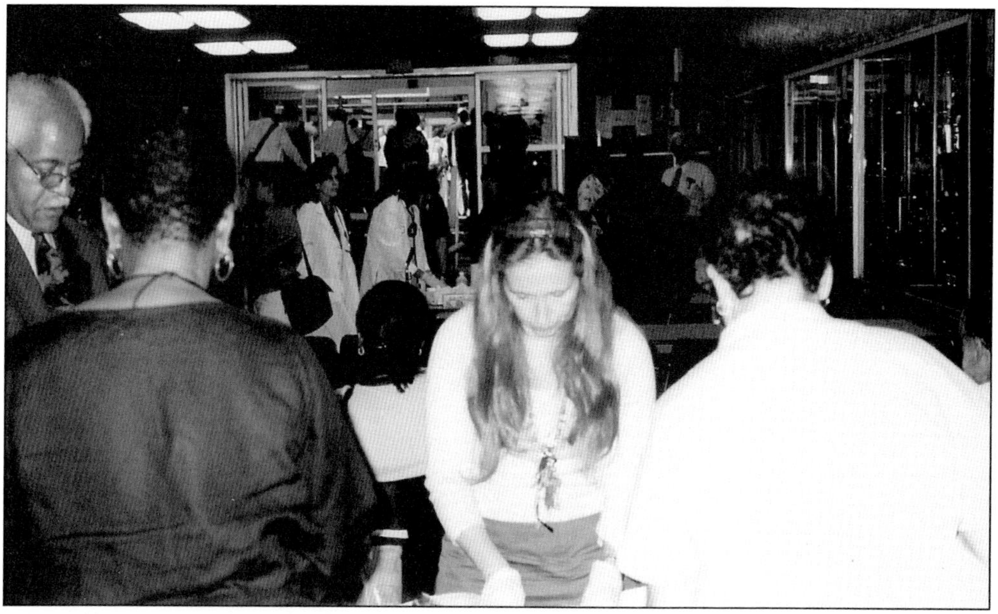

Pictured here are students, faculty and college personnel assisting those in need on September 11, 2001. The college spontaneously responded to the urgent needs, purchasing every loaf of bread, jar of peanut butter, and jar of jelly in the nearby market. Sandwiches and water were given to the tired and confused people streaming across the Brooklyn Bridge.

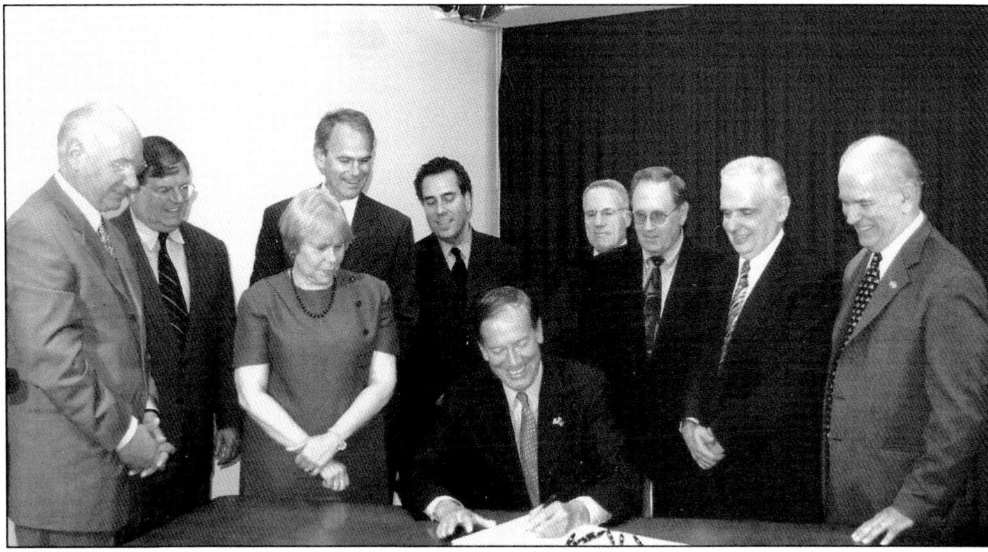

On July 12, 2002, Pres. Fred W. Beaufait, accompanied by alumni and staff of the college and supportive legislators, gathered for the ceremonial signing of the legislation that changed the name of the college to New York City College of Technology. Dr. Matthew Goldstein, Chancellor of the University, is seen on the left, with Dr. Benno Schmidt, chairman of the board of trustees, next to him. President Beaufait is standaing third from right, looking over the shoulder of Gov. George Pataki.

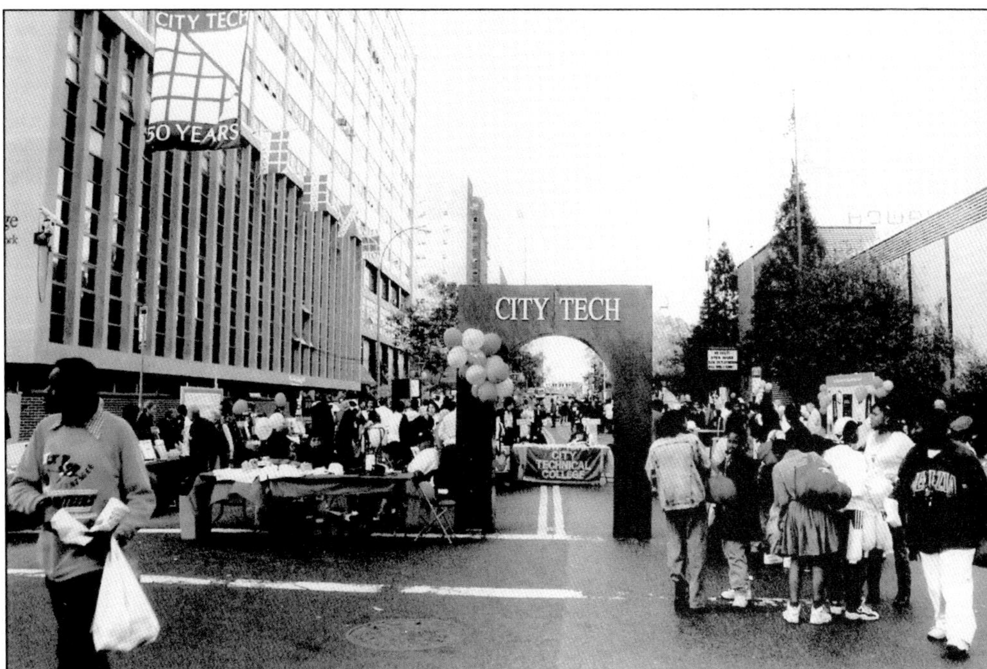

On its 50th anniversary, the college staged a street fair open to the entire community, stretching several blocks from the front of the college. Timed to coincide with a scheduled open house for prospective students, it attracted thousands of people from all over New York.

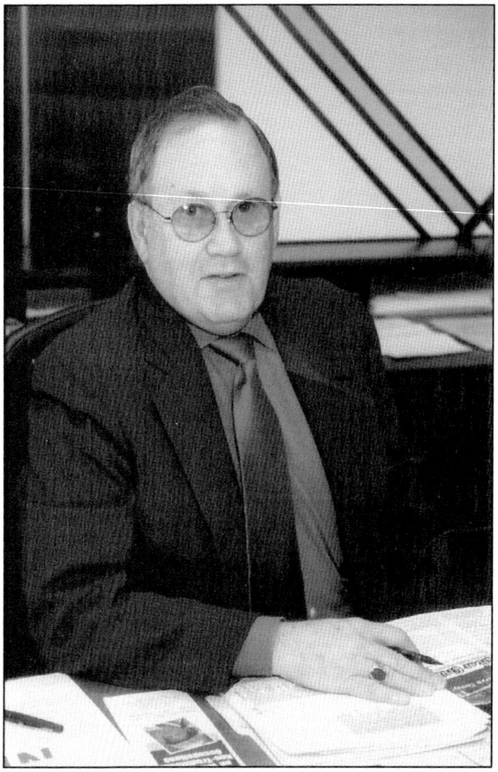

Pictured here is the seventh president of the college, Dr. Fred W. Beaufait. An engineer by training, Dr. Beaufait came to the college after helping to establish Project Hope, a Detroit-based program that facilitated the entry of educationally disadvantaged students into programs in automotive engineering.

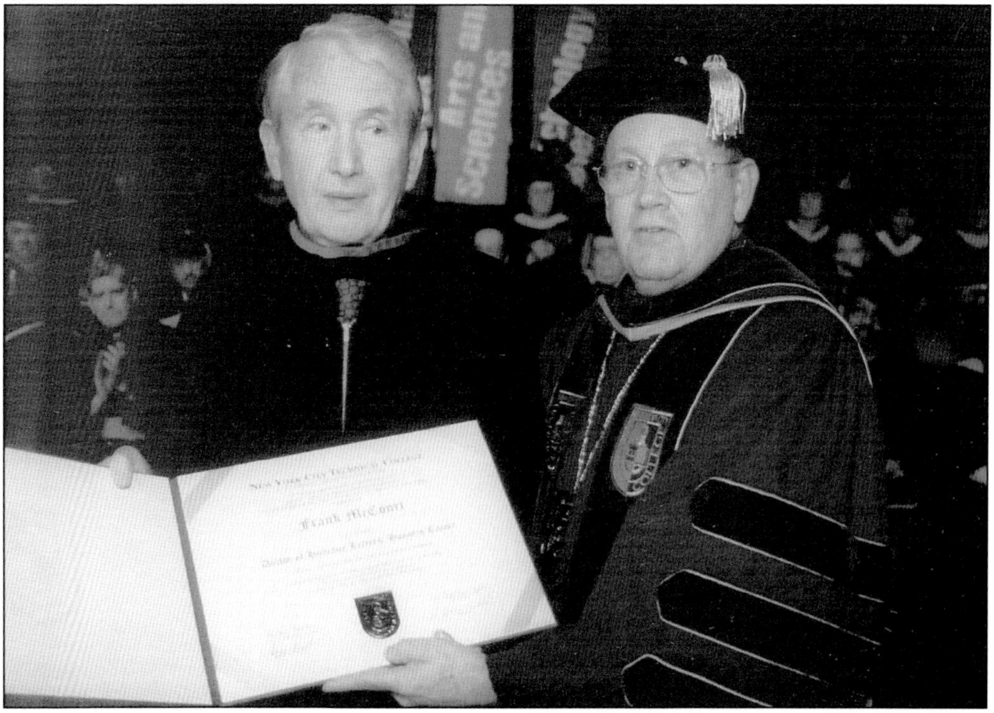

President Beaufait awards an honorary degree to Charles Gargano, a graduate of the college and the CEO of the Empire State Development Corporation.

Five

City Tech Today and Tomorrow
2007 and Beyond

As has been the case throughout its long history, the New York City College of Technology stands at the forefront of the nation in preparing a high-tech workforce for our future. This can be seen in a number of ways. First its academic offerings continue to evolve to meet new and emerging workforce needs.

Sometimes this means the development of new majors. For example, the vibrant entertainment industry in New York urgently needs a cadre of workers trained in the most sophisticated technologies to create the technology-infused stagecraft that is at the center of trade shows, expositions, and live performances of all sorts. Out of this need grew New York City College of Technology's program in Entertainment Technology, a bachelor's degree program that brings together the best practices of traditional stagecraft with the powerful tools made possible by laser physics, computer simulations, and the other technology-based miracles of the information age. It is the only program of its kind east of the Mississippi River and arguably the most sophisticated program of its kind in the United States.

The college is expanding its programs to meet the current and future needs of the nation's workforce. One example is the several health care areas at the college. For example, New York City College of Technology's Nursing Program has doubled the number of students in the pipeline. A graying population of nurses and a missing generation caused by short-term changes in health care hiring practices and stagnant wages in the 1980s and early 1990s contribute to a serious shortfall in registered nurses across the United States. One estimate suggested a shortage of over 17,000 registered nurses and LPNs in New York by the year 2010. Although it has not been easy for the college to address this problem, given the cost of nursing education and the equally serious shortage of nurse educators, the college has made enormous strides. It has relied on partnerships with health care unions and hospital consortia and has adopted new technology such as computer-simulated patients to facilitate this expansion. With a success rate on nursing licensure exams that would be the envy of many expensive private schools, the New York City College of Technology has done its part in producing the diverse, highly qualified cadre of health care professionals that this society demands.

New York City College of Technology is a national leader in its extraordinary diversity. Every study done in the private sector suggests that it is crucial to have a skilled workforce that reflects the enormous and growing diversity of our population. The late 20th century has amplified the historical mission of the United States as a melting pot, nowhere more than in New York. The New York City College of Technology reflects the role of New York City as a crossroads of the world. In 2006, for the fourth year in a row, *U.S. News* and *World Reports* listed the New York City College of Technology as the most diverse college of its type in the northern United States. Nowhere else can match the New York City College of Technology's ability to produce the diverse workforce that our society demands.

For all of these reasons, the college has grown and evolved. In 1992, 15 years ago, fewer than 400 of the approximately 10,000 students registered at the college were in bachelor's degree programs. Today baccalaureate students are about 4,000 of the more than 13,300 students enrolled in the fall of 2006. New faculty, trained in the era for which the college is preparing its students, have been added or have replaced baby boomer retirees. And a campus that was at near capacity a decade ago is inadequate to meet the needs of an expanding population. Expansion of the campus is crucial, and it is underway.

The New York City College of Technology will soon be the home to what is sure to be the architectural landmark of Brooklyn. Standing at the corner of Tillary and Jay Streets, directly across from the Namm Building, will soon be the most original piece of architecture since the Brooklyn Bridge, a masterpiece conceived by the celebrated architect Renzo Piano. It will be CUNY's first public-private partnership to develop academic facilities, creating over a 250,000 square feet of new teaching space. It will also be the first new building for the college in over 30 years where space is designed and constructed specifically for the high-tech programs that will occupy it.

At the same time, the college's Voorhees Building, the center for the engineering technologies, will receive a makeover changing it from a drab representation of the Industrial Era into a sleek icon of the Information Age. The new face of the building will make it clear to everyone who sees it that it is a place where one can create the future and can learn the technological skills necessary to thrive in it. The proposed new face of Voorhees will be seen in the pictures that follow.

In all of these areas the college will be ably led by Pres. Russell Hotzler, who took over the reins of the college in 2004, and the forward-looking senior management team he has assembled. President Hotzler summarizes yesterday, today, and tomorrow at the New York City College of Technology:

> While technologies have changed and professions have been transformed, what is at the heart of City Tech has remained constant—our basic educational approach. City Tech is a place where dedicated faculty, many joining us after successful professional careers in their chosen fields, work side-by-side with students in laboratory settings. The college was founded as a beacon of opportunity available to those who might not otherwise have access to higher education and it still performs this function today. And just as was true on the chilly morning in February of 1947, when the college opened its doors, we have one foot in the present and one in the future, keeping our programs aligned with the high-tech workforce needs of tomorrow.

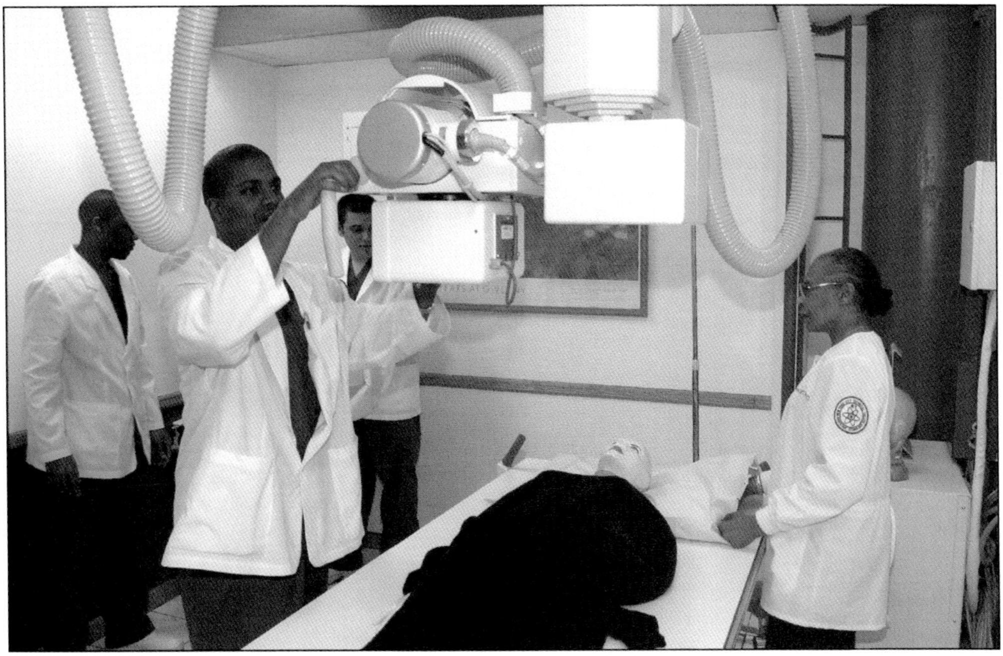

Radiologic Technology and Medical Imaging trains people for one of the fastest growing professions in health care. Digital radiography is the current state of the art and the college is now equipped to train students in this cutting-edge technology. Virtually all of the students in this program gain licensure immediately upon graduation and almost all are employed before graduation.

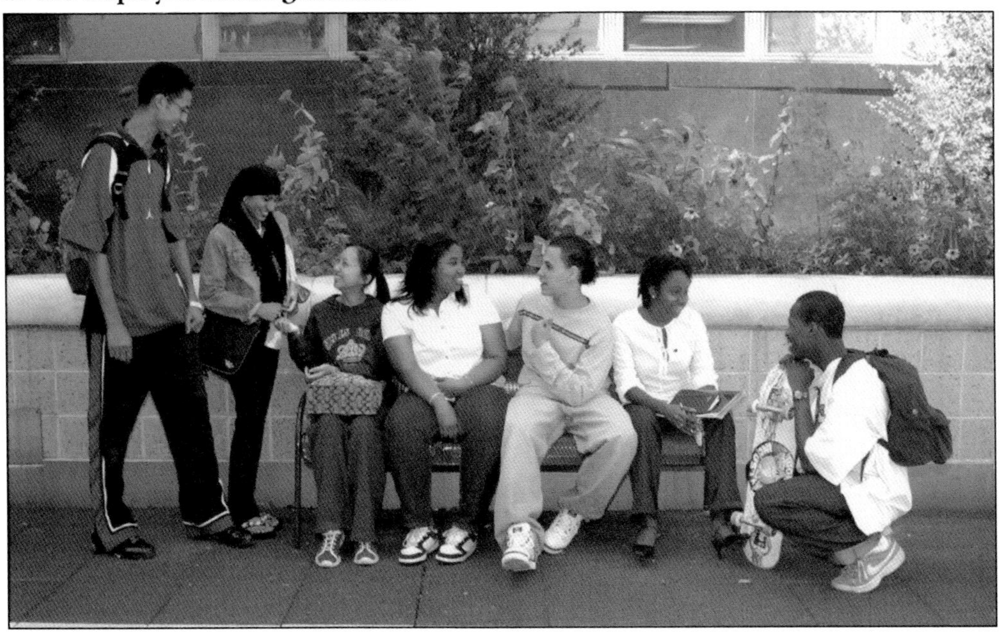

In 2006, for the fourth consecutive year, *U.S. News* and *World Report* cited the New York City College of Technology as the most diverse college of its type in the northern United States. It is unique in its ability to produce the diverse workforce that will be needed by the city, the state, and the country in the 21st century.

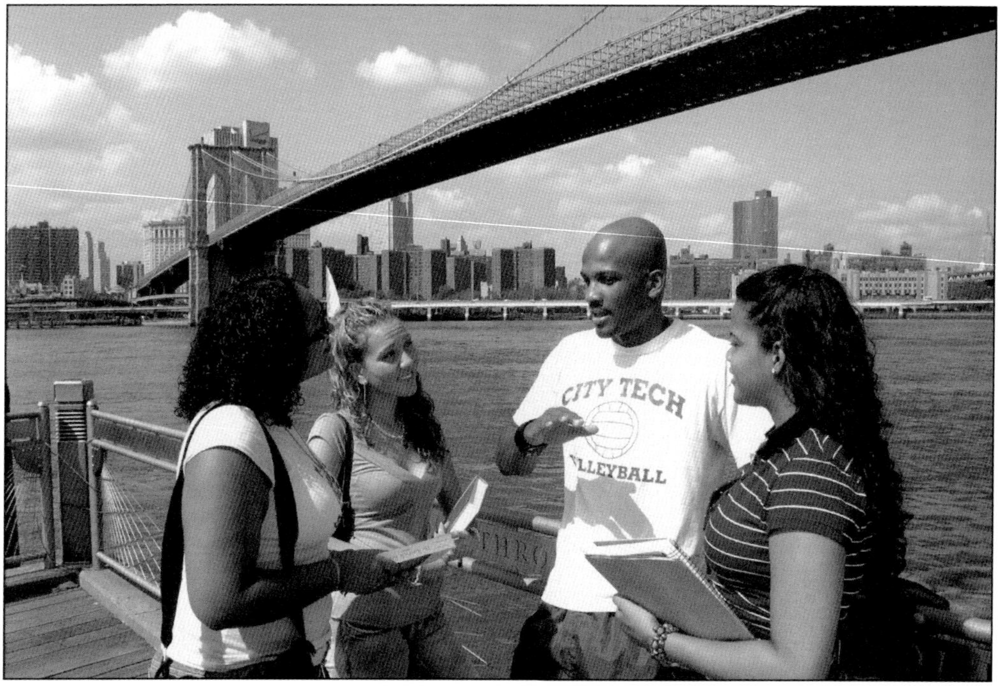

The Brooklyn Bridge, one of the better known architectural icons in the United States, begins literally steps from the college. On warm days, staff and students can be seen walking or jogging across the Brooklyn Bridge, or just hanging out.

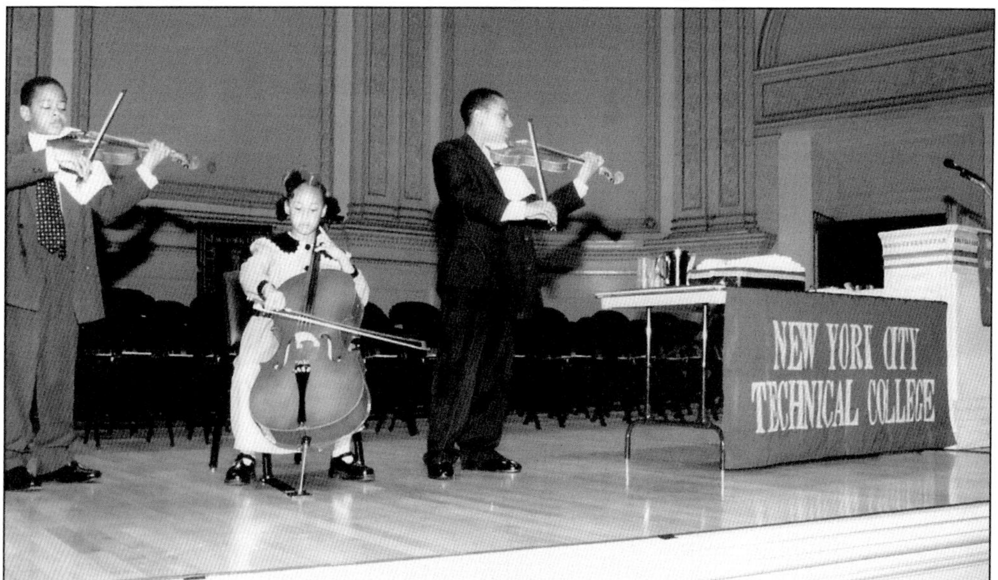

No graduation would be complete without the Constant family, who have performed at a number of commencements. The three performers, Pierre, Daniel, and Jessica are musical prodigies, children of a Haitian immigrant family. Home-schooled, these children began to attend college at an age that their peers were in elementary or middle school. All three received college degrees before most of their age mates were old enough for college.

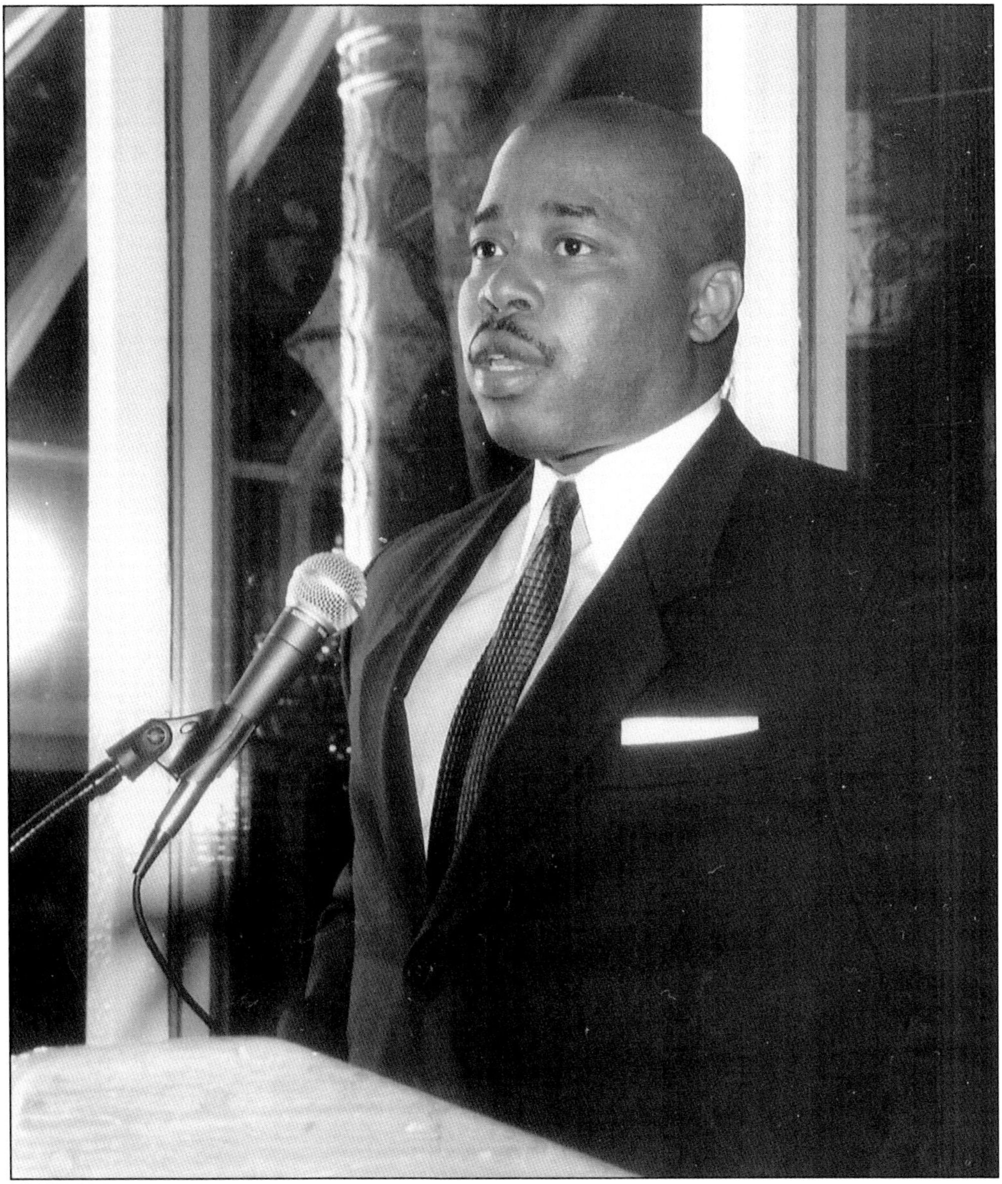

Eric Adams, a graduate of the college, was honored as Alumnus of the Year at the 2002 Best of New York dinner. The founder of 100 Blacks in Law Enforcement Who Care, Adams was elected to the New York State Senate in November 2006.

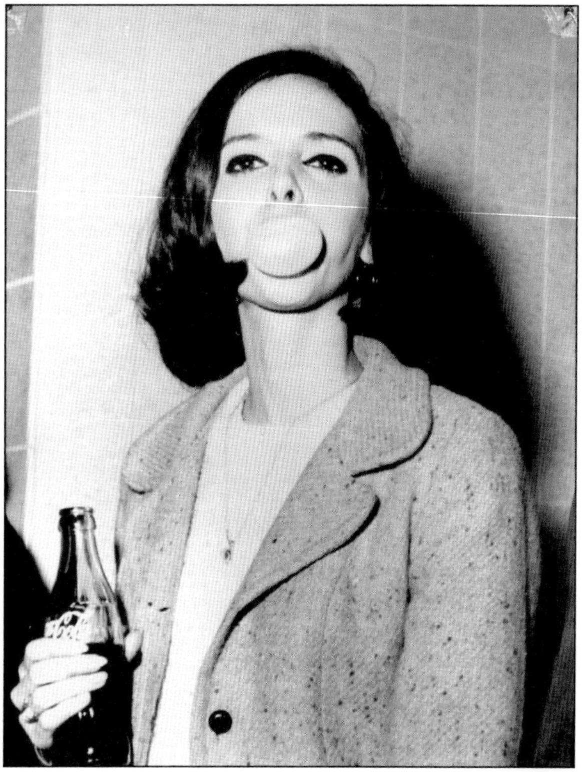

The date is irrelevant; whatever the age, when students relax they seek comfort food. The student here holds a bottle of Coke, as well as chewing bubble gum.

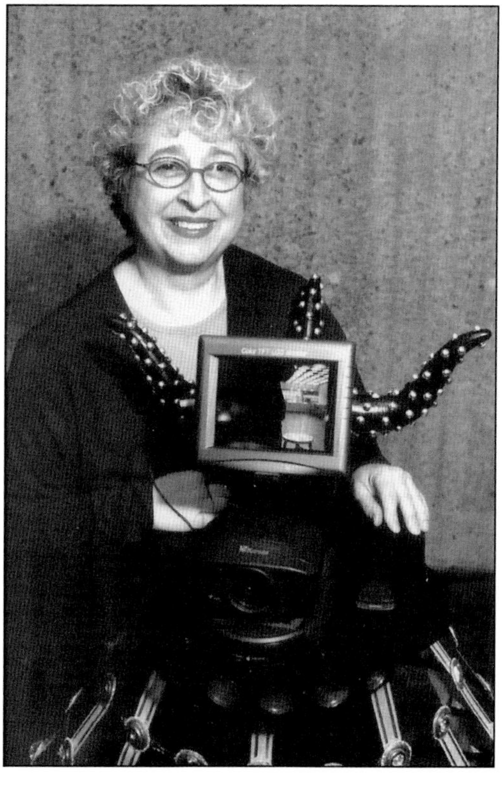

Prof. Adrianne Wortzel of the Advertising Design and Graphic Arts is a pioneer. Her interactive robots have roamed the floor of a museum and have offered visitors Internet-based psychoanalysis.

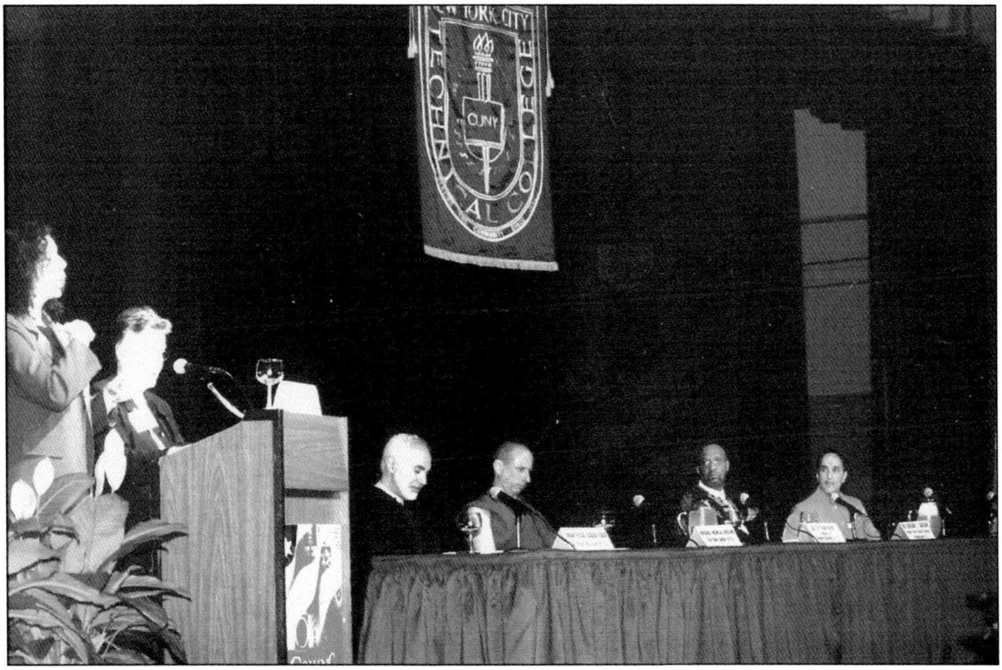

After September 11, 2001, to promote dialogue and healing, the college invited religious leaders from the major faiths to talk about faith and healing. It was an emotional event and one discussed for months afterward.

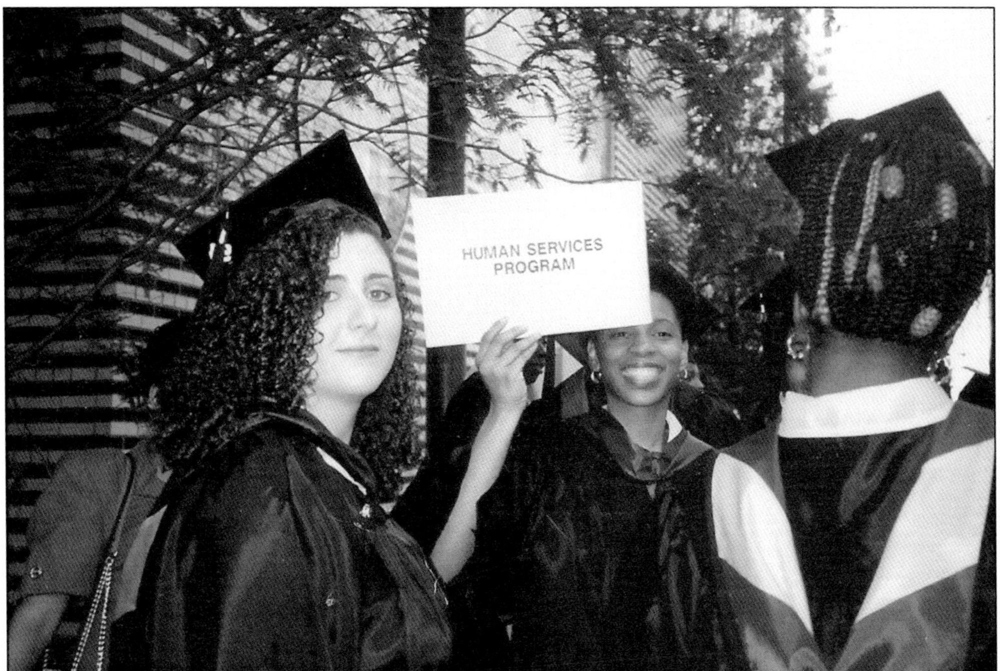

Several days before graduation, students with exceptional academic records gather for the annual Honors Convocation. Here are Human Services students gathered waiting to march into the 2002 Honors Convocation.

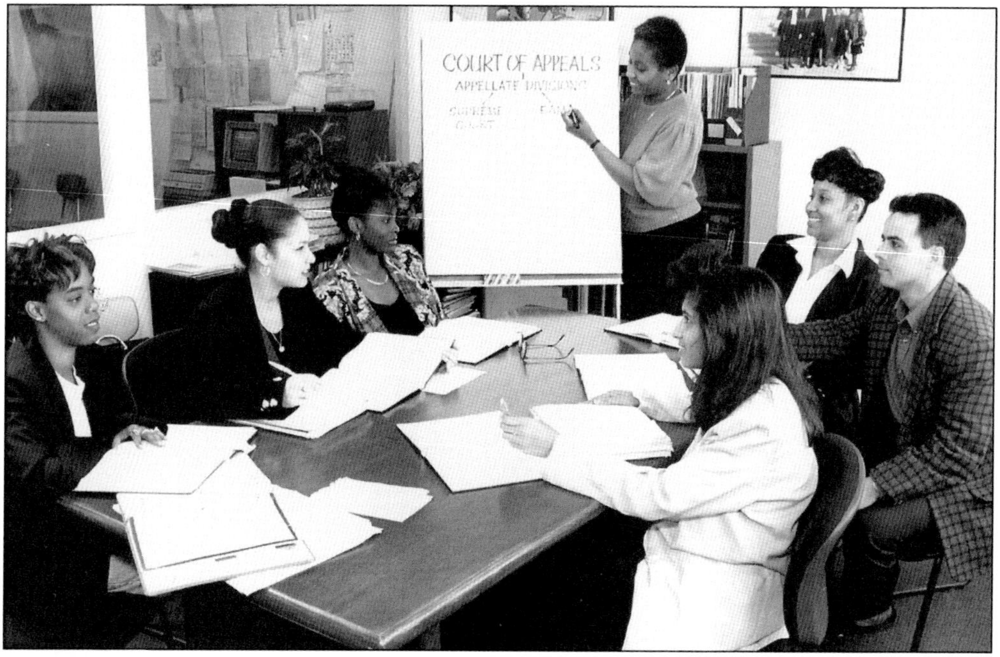

Students in Law and Paralegal Studies are shown in a seminar conducted by Prof. Lise Hunter.

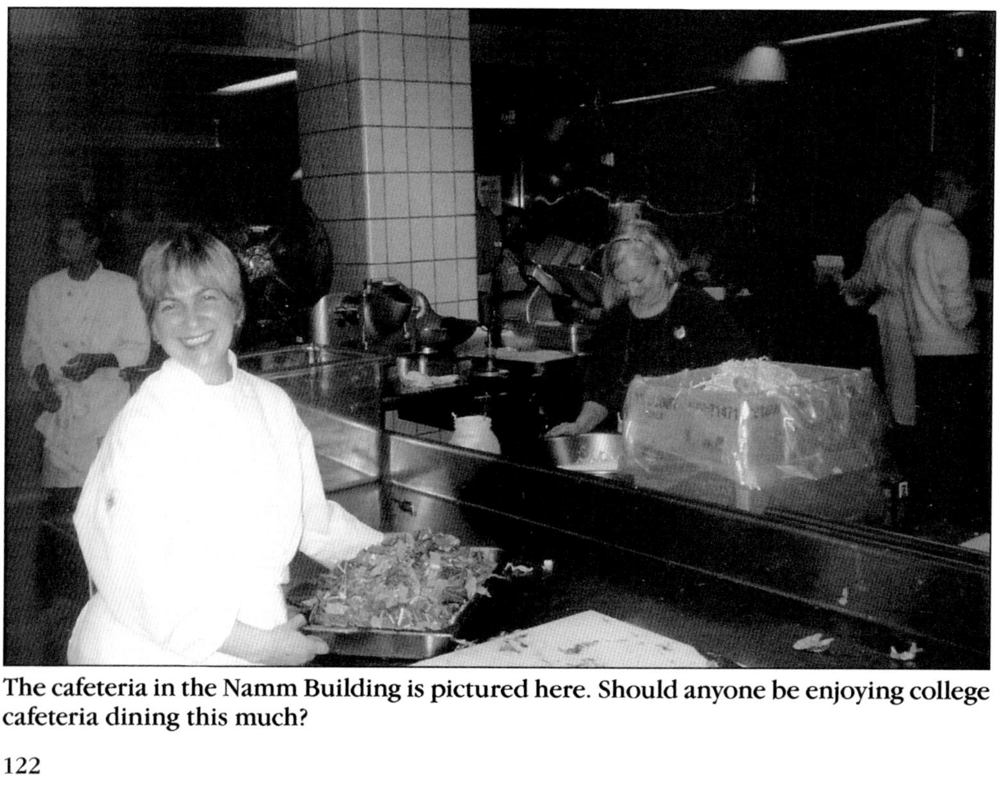

The cafeteria in the Namm Building is pictured here. Should anyone be enjoying college cafeteria dining this much?

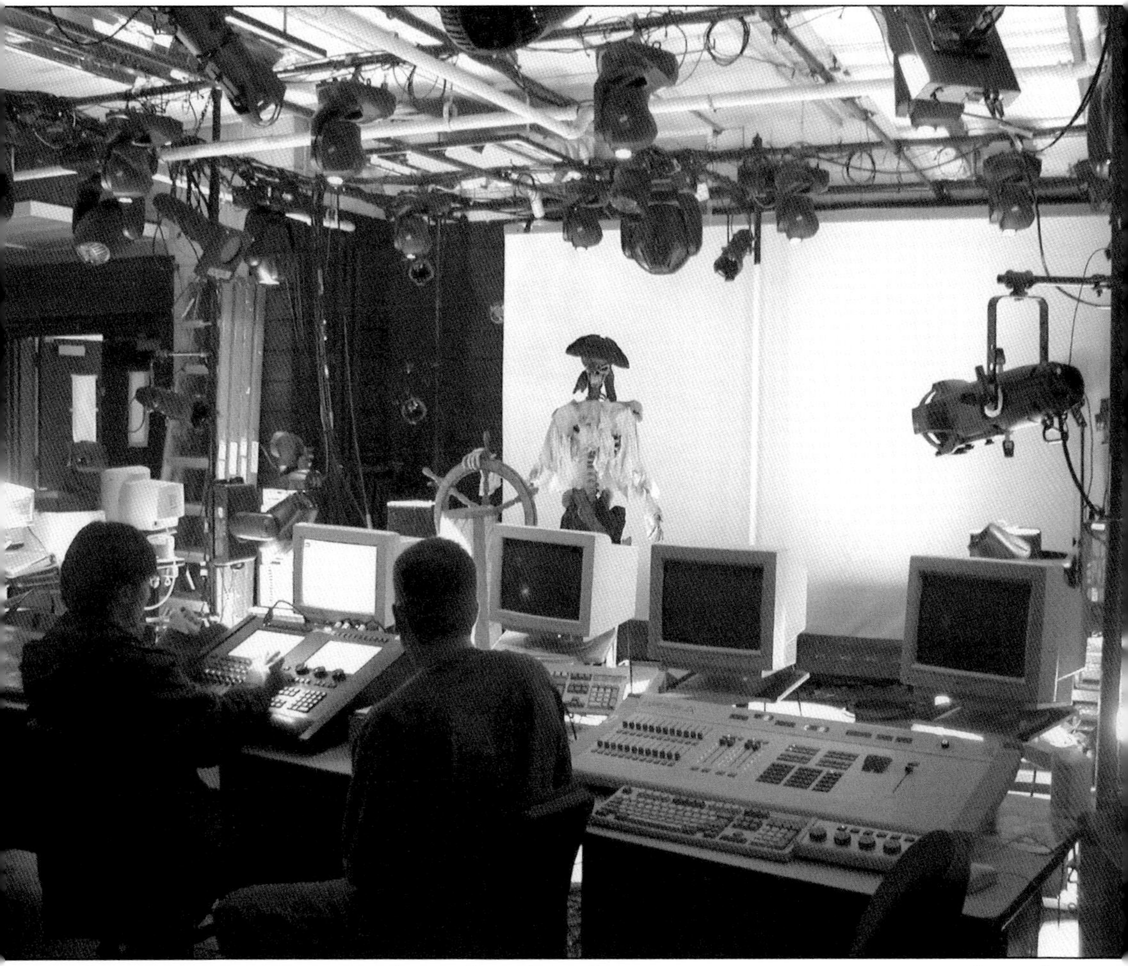

This animatronic pirate, similar to the robotic figures one sees in amusement parks and other entertainment venues, was designed and executed by the New York City College of Technology students in Entertainment Technology Department.

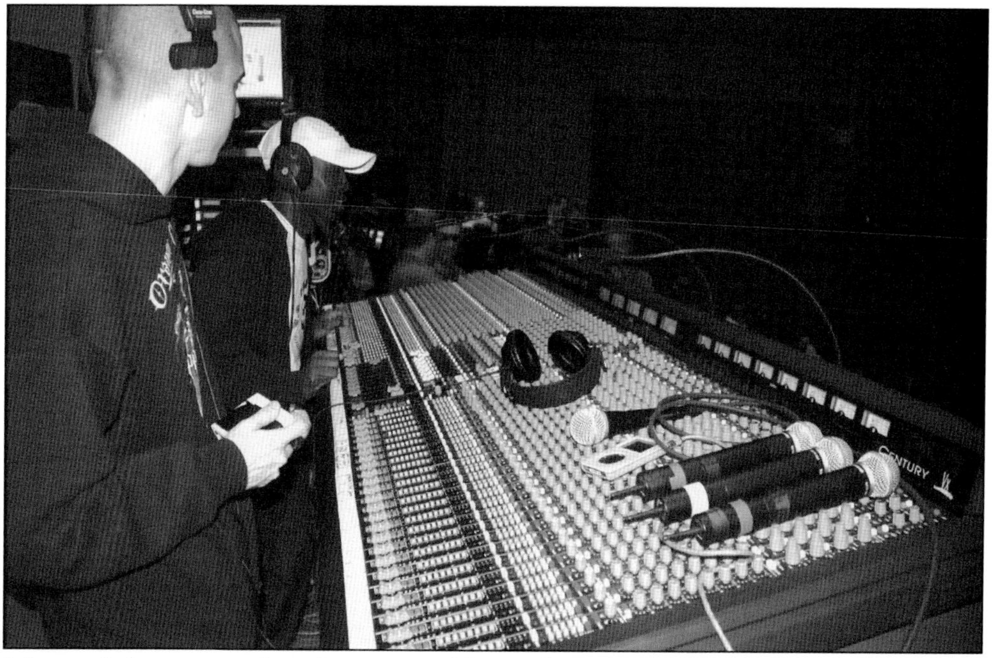

Advanced show control equipment used by students in the Entertainment Technology Department are seen here. This baccalaureate program, the only one of its kind east of the Rockies, is a unique blend of advanced technologies and the other skills needed to support the enormous portion of the economy it serves.

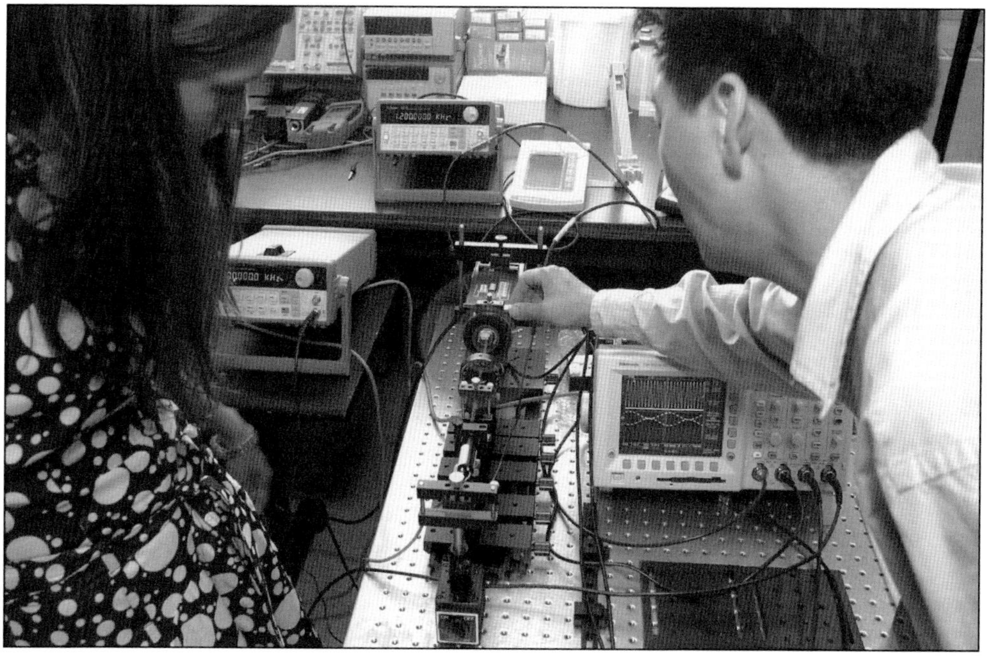

In a new laboratory created by Electrical Engineering Technology professor Xiang Dong Li, using National Science Foundation funding, laser light refracted through liquids can be measured to determine the sucrose content of the liquid. The research that will be conducted in this laboratory has enormous potential for biomedical applications.

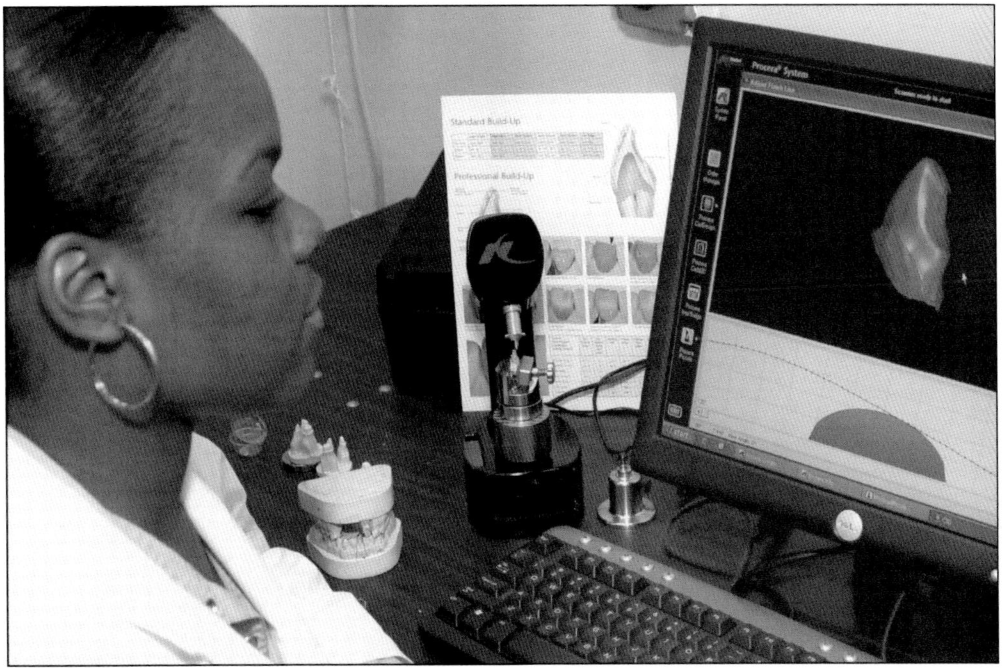

This Dental Laboratory Technology student is using cutting edge technology that combines scanning and computer modeling to produce a dental replacement that is then constructed in a fully robotized facility. The strong connection of the department with graduates who are leaders in restorative dentistry allows the college to acquire such equipment, available nowhere else in the United States in an associate degree program.

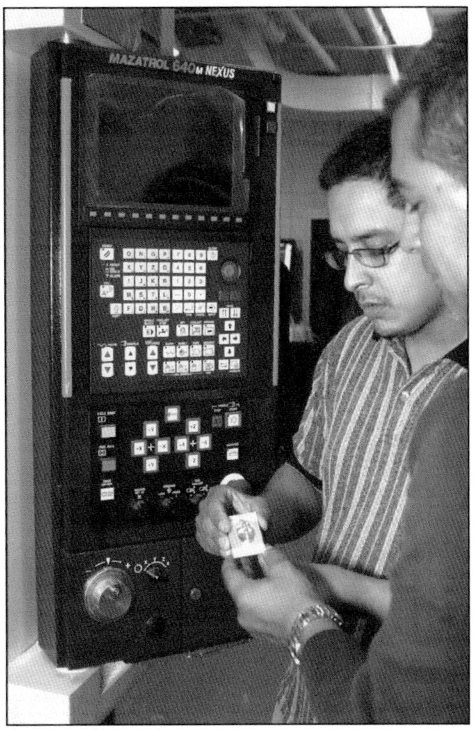

Students in Mechanical Engineering Technology use an advanced instrument for computer-controlled tool building. This 64-bit RISC CPU "fuses" the power of the most advanced computer numerical control (CNC) system with the communications capabilities of a PC. Students who leave the college with a background in cutting-edge technologies are well prepared for the challenges of the workplace.

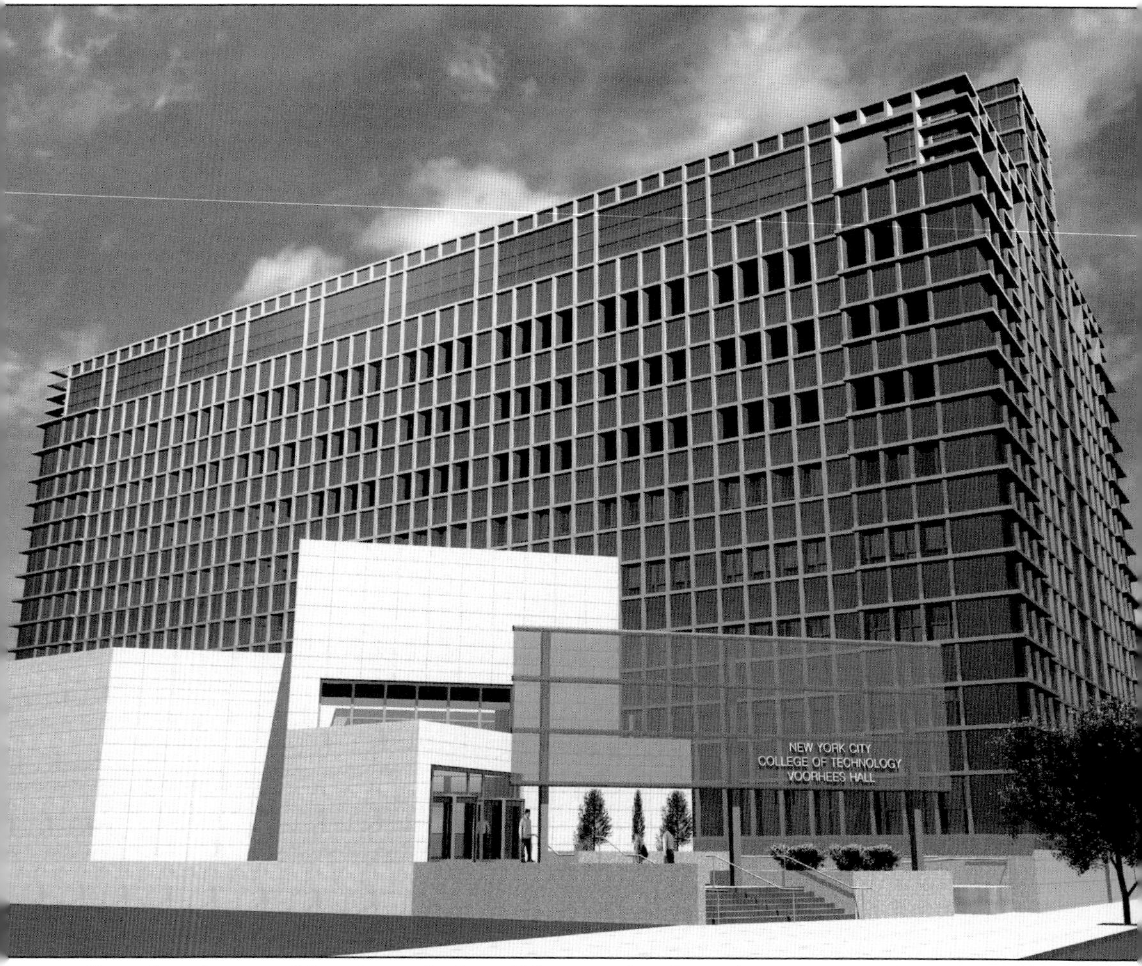

Seen here is an architect's rendering of the new facade and entrance under construction for the Voorhees Building, home to the large majority of the college's programs in engineering technologies. The new look of the building will better represent the advanced work that takes place within.

REFERENCES

Harvey Frommer. *City Tech: The First 40 Years*. Brooklyn: Technical College Press Inc., 1986.

Herbert G. Gutman. *Work, Culture and Society in Industrializing America*. New York: Knopf, 1976.

Pete Hamill. "Introduction" in *The Brooklyn Reader*. Edited by Andrea Wyatt Sexton and Alice Leccese Powers. New York: Crown Trade Paperbacks, 1994.

James Traub. *City on a Hill: Testing the American Dream at City College*. Reading Addison Wesley: Publishing Company, 1994.